# The Actor
# at
# Work

### Fifth Edition

### ROBERT BENEDETTI

PRENTICE HALL,   Englewood Cliffs, New Jersey 07632

*Library of Congress Cataloging-in-Publication Data*

Benedetti, Robert L.
    The actor at work / Robert Benedetti ; foreword by Ted Danson.—
5th ed.

        p.   cm.
        Bibliography: p.
        Includes index.
        ISBN—0-13-004508-X
        1. Acting.   I. Title.
    PN2061.B39 1990
    792'.028—dc20
            89-33564
                CIP

Sub. Head

LCC#

LCCN

Editorial/production supervision: *Edith Riker/DebraAnn Thompson*
Cover design: *Wanda Lubelska Design*
Manufacturing buyer: *Carol Bystrom*

ISBN    0-13-004508-X

Prentice-Hall International (UK) Limited, *London*
Prentice-Hall of Australia Pty. Limited, *Sydney*
Prentice-Hall Canada Inc., *Toronto*
Prentice-Hall Hispanoamericana, S.A., *Mexico*
Prentice-Hall of India Private Limited, *New Delhi*
Prentice-Hall of Japan, Inc., *Tokyo*
Simon & Schuster Asia Pte. Ltd., *Singapore*
Editora Prentice-Hall do Brasil, Ltda., *Rio de Janeiro*

# Contents

# List of Exercises

# Foreword

## Ted Danson

I met Bob Benedetti (or "Beny," as he likes to be called) nineteen years ago, when I was in his second-year acting class at Carnegie Tech. As long as I have known him, he has been exploring, discovering, and sharing what it means to act.

His classes filled me with the kind of excitement athletes must feel when they are in full stride. He taught me how to get acting out of my mind, out of theory, and into my body, into action; he gave me a point of concentration, so that my mind would not be censoring every impulse that came up.

He was also fun to be around, and he planted in me the thought that acting, and performing could be joyous. I will cherish him always for that, because as far as I'm concerned, acting, if it is nothing else, had best be joyous, both in the childlike spirit of play and as a profound celebration of life. For me, acting is a wonderful excuse to live life as fully as possible.

My mother had a prayer that has always stayed with me: "Dear Lord," she would say, "please help me to become fully human." The job of all of us in life is to experience the human condition and our own humanity fully; your job as an actor is to reflect what you have experienced in a way that clarifies and enhances people's life.

As an actor, you are a *pleader of causes.* The characters you play have a cause, a purpose, and it is up to you to plead it with utmost integrity and commitment, as if a life depended on it—for in fact, it does.

To be able to do this, you must master the techniques of acting. You stretch your body, your voice, your thoughts and feelings so as to encompass as much of the human condition as possible; you must develop the capacity to reflect it all, not just that small portion with which you feel comfortable.

You must also live the same way: You must push past the comfortable, easy answers and explore the scary side of life and of yourself, for finally you have nothing to offer but yourself, your insights, your truth, your slice of the human condition. As you grow and expand, remember that at any moment in your personal journey as an actor, you have only yourself to offer: who you are at that moment is enough.

As you work to master technique, then, keep your attention focused outward. Don't worry about yourself, think about everybody else; don't worry about being interesting, just be interested in everybody else, in life itself. All the technique in the world will be meaningless unless you have something worth sharing through it; technique is the tool you will use to communicate whatever you have to say, through the characters you choose to play, about the human condition.

To me, acting has itself become a life process. Whatever is next in my development as a human being will happen either through my everyday life or through my acting; they are completely intertwined. This blending of acting and living is never more obvious to me than when I am working on a film (or a play or any other creative group effort); when everyone is aligned toward the common purpose, then there are no more "accidents;" everything that happens at home, on my way to work, in front of the camera, all contributes to our creative purpose.

Only when you hold your acting separate from your life do they interfere with one another; when they are aligned, they feed each other. You can become a better actor by becoming a more complete human being, and you can become a more complete human being by becoming a better actor.

Back to technique!

# Preface

## HOW TO USE THIS BOOK

In most situations, each of the four Parts of this book provides a full semester or quarter of study. For advanced high school students and beginning college students this book presents a two-year acting course.

If you are working within a program in which voice, speech, and movement are taught in separate classes, this book can be used as an acting studio text by skipping some of Part One and proceeding to the concept of action in Part Two. Depending on prior experience of the students, you may wish to begin with Lessons Seven and Eight which contain excellent introductory exercises to induce a playful and unselfconscious frame of mind. Intermediate students could begin directly with Part Two.

If either of these strategies is followed, I recommend that you read Part One carefully, as it contains basic principles important to the later work.

For an introductory class when no outside classes in technique are available, you might consider working on Parts One and Two simultaneously, using the development of physical and vocal skills as an ongoing parallel development within the acting class.

I would like to thank the following people for their assistance in reviewing *The Actor at Work* 5/E. Marc Powers, The Ohio State University; Michael J. Hood, University of Alaska, Anchorage; and John Cooke, George Mason University.

# Introduction

# The Actor in You

You are already an actor. You "play a role" every time you adjust your behavior in order to achieve some desired goal: to get someone to do something, to persuade someone of something, to win love or respect. In various circumstances, in various relationships, you pursue your needs by behaving in certain ways, doing things to other people and reacting to the things they do to you. It is this interaction with your world, this give and take of doing things to others and having things done to you, that shapes and expresses your personality, your *character*, in everyday life.

In fact, you play *several* roles everyday—student, son or daughter, friend, employee—each with its own appropriate behavior, speech, thought and feelings; your own little repertory company!

To this extent, you already know how to act, because the art of acting is based upon these same life principles. As an art, however, acting requires that these everyday abilities and processes must be heightened and purified. As Brian Bates of the Royal Academy of Dramatic Art says in his book, *The Way of the Actor,*

> Almost everything that actors do can be identified with things we do in less dramatic form, in everyday life. But in order to express the concentrated truths which are the life-stuff of drama, and to project convincing performances before large audiences, and the piercing eye of the film and television camera,

the actor must develop depths of self-knowledge and powers of expression far beyond those with which most of us are familiar.[1]

It is the development of your everyday acting skills and capacities into the greater power of artistic technique that is the aim of this book.

## ACTING AND YOUR PERSONAL GROWTH

The development of these "depths of self-knowledge and powers of expression" is a long-term goal that for serious actors becomes an unending process of personal as well as artistic growth; in fact, it is exactly this opportunity for ongoing personal growth which attracts many to the profession of acting.

Even if you do not commit to a lifelong involvement with acting, your study of the acting process can enrich you in many ways. Brian Bates, who is both an acting teacher and a psychologist, lists some of the ways in which the study of acting can contribute to your personal growth:

> Finding our inner identity. Changing ourselves. Realizing and integrating our life experience. Seeing life freshly and with insight into others. Becoming aware of the powers of our mind. Risking and commitment. Learning how to concentrate our lives into the present, and the secrets of presence and charisma. Extending our sense of who we are, and achieving liberation from restricted concepts of what a person is.[2]

The study of acting, then, is not only a technical and artistic process, it can also be a means for tremendous personal development. In fact, my experience is that the best *artistic* results are achieved when it also functions in this way, both because actors receive an extra measure of motivation and inspiration when they are growing through their art, and because audiences enjoy and benefit from such work. Witnessing the growth of the actor through his or her art reminds the audience of their own potential to grow and to celebrate life.

Buddhists have an attractive way of describing the process of personal growth called the "threefold way" of *the ground, the path,* and *the fruition.* You begin by preparing the ground, in the way a gardener might cultivate the soil to make it more fertile. You next open a path (a way of doing), as the gardener plants the seed and tends the young plant. The fruition then follows naturally, and the gardener helps to perfect the plant by pruning and tending, though always with respect for its own nature.

We will use this idea of the three-fold way in the organization of our study of acting. The first part of this book will help you to prepare yourself, especially your body, voice, and speech, as the "ground," the instrument, of your work as an actor.

The second part opens the "path," which for the actor is the idea of *action*, the experience of real needs within the circumstances of the character, and the things the character does to try and meet those needs.

The third part of the book treats in detail the techniques of textual analysis; every play presents its own problems and demands its own solutions, and every play contains the seeds that generate those solutions if the actor knows how to find them.

The fourth part deals with the "fruition," the principles involved in putting your skills and insights to work in the process of creation.

These four parts are called "The Actor's Tools," "Action," "The Actor's Blueprint," and finally "The Actor at Work." My aim is to help you understand what your job is, what skills you need to do it, and what methods of work you may adopt in relation to a given role.

Your task will be to recognize, focus, and strengthen the natural actor you already are. Only you can do it, but this book can assist. What I can supply here are physical, intellectual, and spiritual techniques that can help you to realize yourself within the demands of the theatrical art, not just for your sake but also for the sake of the contribution that you may someday make through the theatre. That is why I have written this book: to provide experiences and insights that may help you to fulfill that promise so that you, the theatre, and the world may benefit.

## THE EXERCISES AND READINGS

The exercises that accompany each lesson are meant to serve as a program of self-discovery and self-development. They are arranged roughly according to a "natural" acquisition of skills and insights. The experiences they provide are essential to a true understanding (in the muscles as well as in the mind) of this book's point of view, so please be sure to read each exercise, even if you do not do it. At the least, there can be some benefit from imagining yourself doing them.

These exercises have no "right" outcome, so try not to premeditate the results. Just follow the instructions and enjoy the experiences that follow. The results of many of the exercises can be properly measured only by their cumulative, long-range effect; do not be in too much of a hurry.

In addition to the exercises, the examples and sample analyses taken from plays will be important to your understanding of the work. I have drawn my examples from a few plays of representative types, and if you will take time to read them at the outset you will benefit much more from the examples themselves. There are nine of them: Shakespeares's *King Lear, Measure for Measure,* and *Romeo and Juliet,* Brecht's *Mother Courage,* Miller's *Death of a Salesman,* Williams' *The Glass Menagerie* and

*A Streetcar Named Desire*, Albee's *The Zoo Story*, and Beckett's *Waiting for Godot*.

A good journey to you!

*Part One: The Actor's Tools*

# Introduction to Part One: The Preparation of Self

"Mister Duffy lived at a little distance from his body." This description of one of James Joyce's characters applies to many of us in our everyday lives; we go through life largely unconscious of our physical existence.

On the other hand, some of us may be distanced from parts of our intellectual and emotional selves; there are certain feelings and thoughts which we block out, certain kinds of events to which we will not respond, and certain forms of expression which we do not permit ourselves to use.

As an actor you can no more maintain this distance from any aspect of yourself than could a violinist refuse contact with his violin. Your job requires that you put such inhibitions aside and make your whole self—body, voice, thoughts and feelings, available and controllable. They are the tools of your trade!

Moreover, you must *integrate* these aspects of yourself. As you study acting, you will sometimes work separately on your body, voice, or on your emotional and conceptual skills, but when you act, you must see, hear, think, move, speak and feel as one action of your whole self, not as a collection of disintegrated parts or skills.

The most common disintegration from which people in our culture suffer is the disassociation of "mind" and "body." Partly because of the impact of television, we have become a nation of "talking heads," and it is one of the missions of the live theatre to restore to our culture the full dimensions of integrated human expressiveness.

You did not start out in life divided between a physical and an intellectual self, and now your work as an actor requires that you rediscover your original natural wholeness. You will do this not so much through effort as through relaxation: in other words, you don't need to *do* anything to reintegrate yourself, you need only to *stop* doing whatever it is that you are doing to disintegrate yourself.

As you begin to regain your natural integration, you will see how this wholeness of yourself provides the wholeness of your work as an actor: it is the thread that connects the words printed on the page of your script with all aspects of your eventual performance.

In this first Part you will prepare yourself as the "ground" of your work. You will begin the process of reintegration while developing technical control of your physical and vocal capacities. Your aim is to make yourself available to your work; as one psychologist has so exactly put it, you must "invade your own privacy." This will be the business of the next six lessons.

# Lesson
# One

# Relaxing and Breathing

The first step in contacting yourself is relaxation. When we speak of relaxation for the actor, we do not mean it in the ordinary sense of reduced energy or slackness; rather we mean that all unnecessary tensions have been removed, the remaining energy has been purposefully focused, and awareness is acute. The kind of relaxation you want could be defined as a state in which you are *most ready to react*. All tensions which would inhibit movement are lifted, and you are in a state of balance in which you are free to move or react in any way required.

The best description of the relaxed actor's state is what meditators call "restful alertness." You are already capable of restful alertness; you don't need to do anything to achieve it, you only need to become still enough to experience it. You can do this right now, as you sit here reading this exercise developed by Roger and Alexandra Pierce at their studio, The Center of Balance.

**Exercise 1:**
**Just Breathing**

Sit comfortably and in good alignment, with back erect but not rigid.

Before reading beyond the end of this paragraph, take a few moments to close your eyes and feel the movement of your body as it breathes. Don't control your breathing, just feel it; avoid self-criticism. This initial experience will give you a "before" to compare with what follows.

(pause)

Now, let your awareness focus on your expiration. Follow it to the very end, and find the moment of rest between the end of your expiration and the beginning of your inspiration.

Don't control. If you know how you "should" breathe, let it go for now, and just be attentive to what happens.

(pause)

Keep awareness particularly on the resting moment; notice that you can deepen your awareness breath by breath, as if you were using that moment of peace as a pathway to journey deeper and deeper within. Each step inward is a release of tension, and each release registers as a change in your breathing pattern.

(Pause 20 or 30 seconds)

You might imagine that your inspiration is a flow of fresh, new energy that comes from deep within your body. Picture this energy as flowing through your flesh, penetrating into every cell, creating a gentle expansion everywhere.

(pause)

Now tune your awareness to the movement of your breath in your lower ribs; the ribs are gently moving outward on inspiration and inward on expiration. (This is not an invitation to push your ribs, or in any way to take voluntary control; let your conscious mind remain observant and receptive, without manipulating.)

(pause)

Now let your awareness move from your ribs to your mid-back, while still sensing movement. Imagine that the pit of your stomach is gently falling into your back with each expiration and is being penetrated and softened with each inspiration.

(pause)

Now take your awareness to your head. Feel (or imagine that you feel) the flow of your breath through the inside of your head, still as if it were arising from deep within you.

(pause)

Now take your awareness deep inside your pelvis, and feel the movement of your breathing. Sense the floor of your pelvis to be a sheet of muscle very much like the diaphragm; feel it moving in harmony with the diaphragm.

(pause)

Feel the gentle action of your lower back, as if it were the line of communication between diaphragm and pelvis.

(pause)

Now tune in on your body breathing as a whole, as if there were no part that were not participating.

(pause)

Before you finish, recall your "before" experience of breathing, and compare.

(pause)

Lastly, slowly and easily stand up; sense any change in the balance and flexibility of your body. When you drop tension by releasing your breathing, the way you support your own weight in the field of gravity will tend to shift to a more balanced and centered carriage. Enjoy it.

(stand for a time, then move around a bit)

If a favorable change has happened, invite yourself to find future occasions for this sequence of experiences. Repetition will tend to deepen self-awareness and to create a more open, released breathing pattern that will become habitual. Some suggested times are when you are going to sleep (you may find you rest better); when you are waking up; when you get upset; and when you are tired or in pain. This need not be a lengthy ritual. Following a single breath through its full cycle (particularly down into that pause after expiration) can drop your tension level significantly.

(NOTE: You may want to read the directions for this exercise into a tape recorder so that you can play them back to yourself, or have someone else read them to you. Read slowly, with pauses as indicated.)

Now that you have begun to experience restful alertness, the next step in achieving relaxation is to identify, localize, and rid yourself of any chronic muscular tensions, some of which may have become so familiar that you have lost consciousness of them. Take time to inspect the tensions within your body.

### Exercise 2:
### Playing Cat

Lie on the floor comfortably in a surrounding that is not too distracting. Stretch yourself out face up, hands at your sides. Put yourself at rest by yawning and stretching.

To see yawning and stretching at their luxurious best, watch a cat just awakening from a siesta. It arches its back, extends to the utmost legs, feet, and toes, drops its jaw, and all the while balloons itself up with air. Once it has swelled until it occupies its very maximum of space, it permits itself slowly to collapse—and then is ready for new business.[1]

Act like a cat. Stretch, arch your back, extend all your limbs to their utmost, drop your jaw, wiggle your arms and hands, and breathe deeply (not once, but many times); each time taking in more and more air. When a real yawn comes, encourage it; let the full natural sound of the yawn pour out. Then settle back with your knees raised enough to make the small of your back lie completely flat against the floor. Place your toes, heels, hip joints, and shoulders on two imaginary parallel lines (see Figure 1). We will call this our *floor alignment.*

Using your cat stretching as a preparation, you will now take systematic inventory of your body, looking for any residual bundles of tension. The following exercise was developed by a pioneer in the field of relaxation,

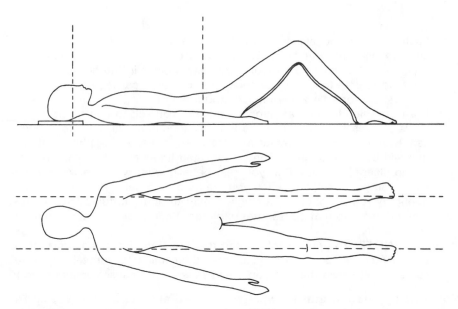

**FIGURE 1.** Floor alignment. The head is level (a small pad may be placed under it); the waistline is also level. *The knees are raised to avoid any strain on the lower back.*

Dr. Edmund Jacobson. The exercise works best if it is repeated over a long period of time, in the course of which chronic tensions will surface and be dissolved by the natural wisdom of the body.

Remember that you are dealing with habits and structures that have formed over a lifetime; have the patience and discipline to adopt a long-term program of correction and maintenance; Jacobson's Phasic Relaxation Exercise can be the foundation of such a program.

### Exercise 3:
### Phasic Relaxation

Begin in floor alignment. Breath is again the focus of your awareness: Imagine that each inhalation is a warm, fresh, energy-filled fluid flowing into your body. Each exhalation carries away with it tension and inhibition, like a refreshing wave. Breathe deeply and easily in a slow, natural, regular rhythm; don't "act" your breathing or artificially exaggerate it.

Each successive breath will be sent into a different part of the body, awakening that area. As the breath flows into a new area, let its energy cause the muscles there to contract as much as they can; then, as the breath flows out, the muscles release and the breath carries all the tension away with it, leaving the area refreshed and at ease. *Exhaling is letting go.*

The sequence of breaths will move from the top of the body downward, and the regular rhythm of your breathing should make the muscular contractions and relaxations flow smoothly down the body like a slow wave. Allow only one area at a time to be involved.

Your total awareness follows the breath into each of the following areas:

*The forehead and scalp,* furling the brow, then releasing it; The eyes at rest, closed and turned slightly downward;

*The jaw,* clenching, then falling easily downward until the teeth are about one-half inch apart;

*The tongue,* extending, then lying easily in the mouth;

*The front of the neck,* with the chin extending down to touch the chest, stretching the back of the neck—then rolling the head easily back down;

*The back of the neck* with the top of the head rolling under to touch the floor, stretching the front of the neck—then rolling the head slowly down and lengthening the neck;

*The upper chest,* swelling outward in all directions so that the shoulders are widened—then easily subsiding, feeling the shoulder blades spread and melt into the floor, wider than before;

*The arms and hands,* becoming stiff and straight like steel rods; the hands clenching into fists, then easily uncurling and melting into the floor, uncurling;

*The pit of the stomach,* clenching, becoming a small, hard ball—then, with a sigh, releasing;

*The buttocks,* clenching, then releasing and widening so that the pelvis is wider than before;

*The knees,* stiffening as the legs straighten, the feet being pushed downward by this action—then releasing the legs and feeling them melt into the floor;

*The toes,* reaching up to touch the eyes (but the heels remain on the floor)—then releasing and falling into a natural position;

*The heels and the shoulder blades,* simultaneously pushing downward into the floor so that the whole body lifts in a long arch—then, with a sigh, you slowly fall, the body lengthening as it relaxes, melting deep into the floor.

*Now take ten deep, slow, regular breaths,* and with each breath move more deeply into relaxation, remaining alert and refreshed. The flow of breath is a continuous cycle of energy that is stored comfortably in the lower body; with each breath this store of energy is increased. Whenever a yawn comes to you, enjoy it fully; vocalize the exhalation, letting the sound of the yawn freely pour out.

Again, a tape recording of the exercise with the necessary pauses would be useful. As you repeat this exercise on successive days, you can begin to give yourself the instructions silently, reminding yourself of the specific activities in each phase. Keep a steady rhythm that follows the tempo of deep, relaxed breathing. Gradually the action of the exercise will become natural, and you will no longer need to think of the instructions, giving your full awareness to the flow of contractions and relaxations that follow the breath as it travels down the body like a wave, awakening, refreshing, and relaxing it, making you ready for work. You can use this exercise as an easy, quick preparation for all future work.

## THE HERE AND NOW

Relaxation in the sense of being "ready to react" requires that you immerse yourself in the present instant, because it is only now that you exist. In everyday life we rarely achieve complete contact with the present: we prefer to create a sense of comfortable continuity by blurring the lines that separate the present from the past and future. The past, in memory, and the future, in expectation, can both be controlled by your consciousness; but the present can be met only on its own terms. Although you can never specifically isolate it, you can put yourself in touch with the unending flow of the present. As the psychologist Fritz Perls put it,

> The wish to seize the present and pin it down—to mount it, as it were, like a butterfly in a case—is doomed to failure. Actuality forever changes. In healthy persons, the feeling of actuality is steady and continuous but, like the view from a train window, the scenery is always different.[2]

### Exercise 4:
### Here and Now

As you sit here reading this, put yourself at rest and focus your awareness on your breath for a time.
(pause)
Begin to say to yourself sentences describing your immediate awareness; for example "Right now I am doing an exercise, I am making up sentences, what will I think of first, my right hand is a little cold," and so on. Do this as long as you can.
(pause)
How far did you go? Why did you stop where you did? Was there anything you ignored or avoided? Begin again and go farther.
(pause)
Where did your awareness take you? How hard was it for you to stay completely in the present? Did you wander backward into memory, or into the future? What did you avoid?

For most of us, the full awareness of immediate reality is a very special experience. As Fritz Perls put it,

> To reacquire the full feeling of actuality is an experience of tremendous impact, moving to the core. In the clinical situation, patients have cried out, "Suddenly I feel like jumping into the air!" And, "I'm walking, really walking!" And, "I feel so peculiar—the world is there, really there!" And, "I have eyes, real eyes!" But there is a long road . . . to such a full experience.[3]

The immediate purpose of this exercise has been more or less fulfilled when the temptation to wander into the past or the future has been overcome, and you can remain comfortably and effortlessly in the present. As you repeat this exercise on successive days, allow the sentences describing the endless present to fade gradually away, leaving only a restful alertness; your mind will be like a pool of still water, ready to reflect anything, as if the lightest touch of a falling leaf would send ripples into the farthest corners of your consciousness.

## THE BREATH AND THE WORLD

The breath is life. The word psychology means "study of the soul," and the word for soul, psyche, originally meant "vital breath." A common superstition is that the expiring breath of a dying person is the soul leaving the body.

Our breath constantly reflects our relationship to our world. It is through the breath that we literally bring the outside world into our bodies and then expel it again, and the way we feel about that outside world will be expressed by the way we breathe it in and breathe it out.

Take for example, a sudden and unexpected danger. It would seem that the need to deal with whatever is threatening us would make us breathe rapidly in order to oxygenate our muscles. But our initial reaction is just the opposite: we gasp and hold our breath. It is as if we are saying to the outside world, "You threaten me; you can't come in; I'm closing the door to you." We are "playing dead inside our skins," and this can go to the extreme of fainting!

If we do not faint, our fearful breathing resumes in quick, shallow panting, again refusing to allow any more of the threatening world to enter us than is absolutely necessary, even though our muscles need to be oxygenated in the face of danger. When the danger is past, our sigh of relief helps to expel our tension and fear, and as we breath deeply we "re-enter" the world and allow the world to "re-enter" us: yawning, laughter, or sobbing often erupt during such a release of tension.

It is this involvement of the breath in life experience that led the Gestalt psychologists to define anxiety as "difficulty in breathing while having a blocked (unresolved) experience." We often yawn, for instance, as a way of preparing for a threatening situation; you can see sobbing, laughing, gasping, sighing, and all the other forms of breathing as tangible reflections of our relationship with our world.

### Exercise 5:
### Breath and Awareness

Place yourself at rest as you sit reading this. Be aware of your breath: its frequency, its rhythm, its depth.
(pause)
Begin to gently manipulate your breath as if you were improvising on a musical instrument; play with the sounds and feel of the breath.
(pause)

You will become aware of thoughts and feelings shifting across your consciousness as a result of your changing breath pattern; perhaps memories of past experiences, or fantasies of the future, will arise. When you become aware of them, simply acknowledge them, return your awareness to your breath, and explore a new pattern.

## MINIMIZING EFFORT

Acting, both in rehearsal and performance, arouses anxiety, both pleasurable (in the quest for creative discovery) and unpleasurable (in the fear of exposure and ridicule). As we mentioned above, anxiety tends to disrupt our breathing, and to generally raise the level of our bodily tension. Such tension interferes with our readiness to react; it "freezes" us and literally reduces our creativity.

When we find ourselves in such a state of tension, we often attempt to compensate by "trying harder," putting more effort into the work and trying to "muscle" our way past our own tension. Unfortunately, this is exactly the wrong thing to do. It is counterproductive in that it only *increases* our tension and further reduces our freedom of creative response. It is common to see students in beginning acting classes who make the mistake of "trying harder," and the harder they try, the worse they get.

Excessive effort destroys the acting process in another way: it makes us so *self-aware* that the give-and-take required in acting becomes impossible. When you use excessive effort, you literally obscure your own experience of what you are doing. Movement therapist Moshe Feldenkrais uses the example of trying to open a sticking drawer: If you tug indiscriminately at it, chances are that it will let loose all at once and go flying back, spilling the contents. Because you were using excessive force, you failed to perceive the exact moment when the drawer loosened; you had ceased to experience the drawer and were experiencing *only your own effort!*

The ability to experience exactly what is happening is obviously crucial to you as an actor; it is the only way you can be truly in touch with the here and now and become engrossed in your action. Unfortunately, many actors are driven to excessive effort; in their desire to deliver an acceptable performance, they do too much. Their assumption seems to be that they are unworthy of the audience's attention unless they *do* something to earn it; the option of doing nothing, of simply allowing themselves to "be there," is terrifying. They feel naked, exposed, and become desperate to do something—anything! As a result, they have difficulty experiencing the scene and instead experience only their own effort.

See if you can let go of this need so that your stage choices will no longer be compensations for your sense of unworthiness.

## Exercise 6:
## Being There

Take turns standing in front of the group. Place yourself in restful alertness and simply "be there." Let go of your need to do something until you are quite still.

Fully experience stillness both as actor and as audience; support one another with quiet attention. See how interesting the simple, unadorned presence of a human being can be!

# Lesson
# Two

# Limbering and Aligning

Movement therapists like Moshe Feldenkrais say that *there is no new thought where there is no new movement*; that is, our capacity to "see the world" in a new way is reflected in our capacity to move within that world in a new way. In fact, when we are infants we explore the world mainly through movement, and our "self" begins to develop during this movement-oriented exploration; research has found, for instance, that bound infants (like those of some tribal cultures) have greatly reduced personality development during the period of their confinement.

Your ability to move is therefore critical to you as an actor, not only because you will eventually express your character through movement, but because your ability to move is a necessary part of the process by which you will discover and develop the character itself!

So, having begun to remove unwanted tensions from the body through the techniques of relaxation, you will now proceed to loosen the body and make it more limber, more free in its capacity for movement, and more *ready to respond.*

You begin limbering with an expanding of the joints. Like any mechanism your skeletal structure produces friction and requires a certain degree of looseness and lubrication which permits the skeletal structure to slide easily against one another. Your muscles are housed in sheaths of smooth tissue that permit them to slide easily; your joints have spaces filled with viscous fluids in them that lubricate. Distorted posture or muscular habit may compress the joints or hold them rigid, or cause the sheaths of interstitial tissue to shrink into permanent misalignment. When this happens, your capacity and readiness to move is reduced and you become less responsive, both physically and mentally; the voice may also be profoundly affected by such bodily tensions.

Sometimes such bodily distortions or areas of rigidity may be so severe as to require forceful intervention through massage techniques as Rolfing, or, more moderately, Shiatsu; more gradual and gentle, though also powerful, is the Alexander Technique (which is of special interest to us since it was developed by an actor). In all such cases, of course, only the most qualified professionals should provide treatment.

For most of us, however, it is sufficient to direct the energies of our own bodies toward the release of misalignments, or to engage in a gentle, pleasurable massage by a caring and careful partner. In this way, the following exercises will begin to lengthen and widen your torso, expanding your joints, and opening your body to maximum size.

### Exercise 7:
### Massage for Size

Have your partner assume floor alignment while you gently and steadily lengthen and widen his or her torso according to the following instructions. During the exercise, the partner on the floor gives full awareness to your actions by sending their breath into your hands.

1. The head is cupped gently in the hands from above, and is rolled and rocked while being gently pulled directly upward along the axis

**FIGURE 2.**  Stretching the Neck.

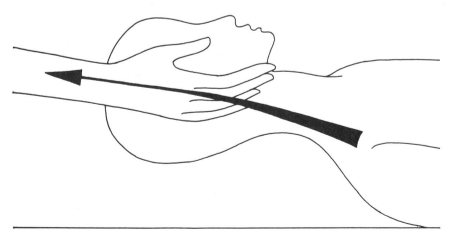

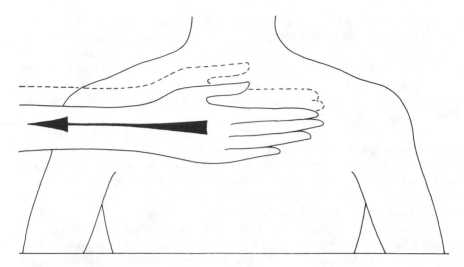

**FIGURE 3.** Opening the Shoulders.

of the spine; do not pull the head in such a way that the chin lifts (see Figure 2).

2.  Placing one hand palm up under the center of your partner's back and the other palm down just below the base of the neck, massage and pull gradually outward toward the side. You will see the shoulder visibly widen and flatten. Repeat with the other side (see Figure 3).

3.  Massaging the whole arm, beginning in the armpit, draw the arm steadily downward, continuing through the hand and into the fingers. Repeat with the other arm.

4.  Repeat this same action with each leg.

5.  Trade roles and repeat the exercise.

When you and your partner have done this exercise a few times, you may recall the experience for yourself by taking floor alignment and remembering the actions of your partner's hands, cuing yourself to "lengthen" and "widen" on your own; in this way, your body can be taught to massage itself! The following exercise does not require a partner.

### Exercise 8:
### Lengthening and Widening

1.  In floor alignment, slowly rock your pelvis upward; feel the thrust as a downward, curving motion as indicated by the arrow in Figure 4. The motion is a flowing undulation; one after another, each vertebra is lifted until the back is raised as far as the midback (dotted line); then it is rolled back down vertebra by vertebra in a steady motion; the back is longer when it comes down than when it went up.

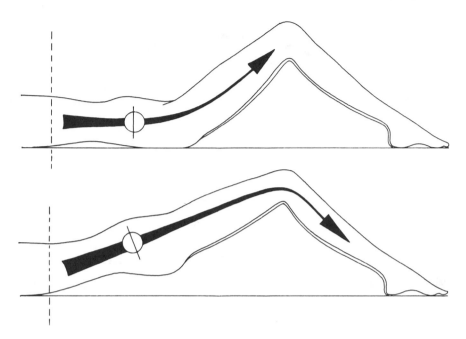

**FIGURE 4.**  Lengthening the Back.

Breathe in on the way down and out on the way up, counting aloud seven counts up and silently seven counts down. Release completely between each series; begin with four repetitions.

2. Begin again but extend the upward motion until you are lifted well up onto your shoulders; the thrust is still downward, and your raised position should feel like a long arch from heels to shoulder. Do not thrust the stomach upward, causing the small of the back to bend sharply (see Figure 5). After reaching the top of the arch, lower the back, vertebra by vertebra, with a smooth slow motion. Leave the arms relaxed and the head free to roll from side to side. The breath and counting pattern is the same; repeat four times. **DO NOT DO THIS EXERCISE IF YOU SUFFER FROM LOWER BACK PAIN OR IF YOU ENCOUNTER PAIN DURING THE EXERCISE!**

3. Stretch in all directions at once, again playing cat, and then fall easily back into the floor alignment position. Let the noise of your stretches be full and natural. Again, encourage any yawn that occurs spontaneously, letting the sound freely pour out. The yawn is a good friend to us in our work.

Eventually, try all of the exercises so far as a single uninterrupted experience; let your liberated consciousness explore its new freedom within the body.

As you begin to experience your own physical being fully, you experience also the natural wholeness of your organism and the innate integra-

**Right**

**Wrong**

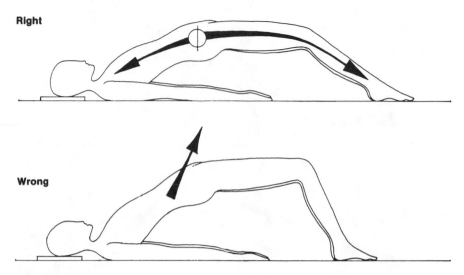

**FIGURE 5.** Lifting the Back.

tion of body and consciousness. The actor strives to maintain this sense of wholeness because the stage demands total responsiveness simultaneously from all the aspects of the self; only an integrated organism can supply such responses.

We will now continue to limber and align the body in a standing position.

## STANDING ALIGNMENT

As you stand, focus your awareness on your skeleton. In the course of man's evolution, the skeleton has begun (and is still) adapting itself to an erect posture, so that we can stand against the force of gravity with a minimum of muscular strain. Imagine the bones as building blocks; if each is set properly above the one below, they can almost stand erect by themselves.

This sense of bringing each part of your body into the proper position to permit its weight to flow directly downward through the body into the ground will not only give you stability, it will also place you in the most responsive alignment from which movement or sound in any direction is free and easy.

The following sequence of exercises will give you a direct experience of this alignment and centeredness. We will begin by examining the structure of the body as it relates to movement.

**Exercise 9:**
**Finding the Joints**

A. With a partner, stand and face each other. Help each other to find the two joints in the spinal column; one is high in the head, inside the valley that runs up the back of the neck, underneath the bony ridge that can be felt at the top of this valley. The joint itself is inside the head roughly level with the eyes. The other joint is at the base of the spine, roughly on a level with the hip joints. Find the hip joints by lifting each leg and feeling for them; they are higher than you may suppose, roughly level with your center.

It is common to think of the spine as having many "joints," but in fact only these two, at top and bottom, are true joints. The rest of the spine is capable of considerable flexibility, of course, but too often we try to make small areas of the spine do the work of joints; for instance, we commonly behave as if the back were jointed at points A and B in Figure 6, while it is actually jointed only at points X and Y.

This widespread misuse of the spine produces the back and neck problems so common in our culture. For the actor, however, the bad effects of this misuse are even more severe; you can see immediately how bending the back at point B causes the abdomen to be constricted, severely limiting the action of the diaphragm and thus limiting breath support. Likewise, bending the neck at point A causes you to crush the voice box, disturbing the natural production of vocal tone. You can experience this for yourself by sounding and moving the head from the real joint, and then from the false joint. Try it.

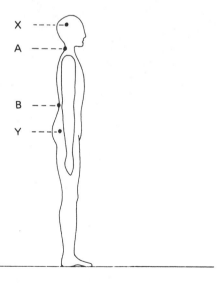

**FIGURE 6.** The Spine.

In the next section of the exercise, try to loosen and expand the true joints in your spine and feel yourself moving more fluidly. Notice also how your sound can remain full and free when you move in this way.

B. Again facing each other, one partner reaches out and cups the other's head in his hands, as in Figure 7. Gently, lift the head slightly upward along the central axis of your partner's body. The partner being lifted hangs loosely, like a medical student's skeleton on a spring. As your partner slowly moves the head in many directions, the hanging partner allows their body to respond easily and makes sound, experiencing their voice through a variety of motions.

C. Change roles and repeat. After you have experienced these exercises with a partner, you may repeat them alone by remembering the feeling of your partner's lift; the remainder of the exercise does not require a partner.

D. Moving on your own with the memory of your partner's lift, explore the balance of your body when it moves as a single system hinged at the real joints.

**Exercise 10:**
**Sitting and Standing**

A. Using a plain, straight backed chair, sit comfortably. Have your partner from the previous exercise gently cup your head and lift up and forward. Feel your weight shift forward, then up as you stand,

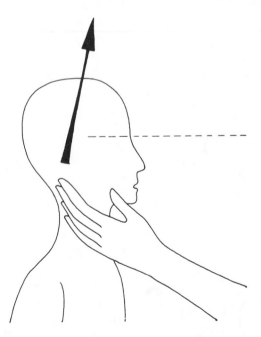

**FIGURE 7.** Lifting the Head. *Be sure that the head remains level as it is lifted.*

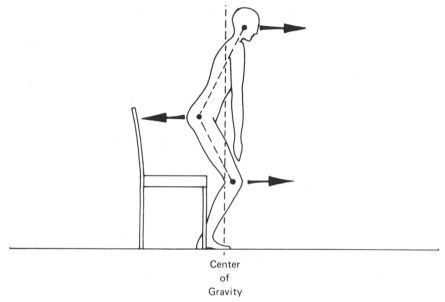

Center
of
Gravity

**FIGURE 8.**  Sitting and Standing.

maintaining continuous balance between the system formed by your ankles, knees, hips, and head. (See Figure 8) Notice that the back needn't bend, and that your effort can be greatly reduced when you maintain the balance (or *poise*) of your system.

B.  Repeat the experience on your own, remembering the touch of your partner's hands. Let your energy originate deep in the center of your body and flow effortlessly up the spine and out the top and front of your head as if a partner were still lifting you.

In this exercise, energy flows upward through your spine and out of the top of your head. Become aware of the point at which your spine would protrude from the scalp if it were extended upward; for most of us it is also the center of the whirlpool-like swirl in our hair. You and your partner can help each other to determine this point. When you are lifted upward from this point, your head remains perfectly level, with your chin, neither lifting it toward the ceiling nor dropping toward your chest.

In the next exercise, we translate this upward lift along the central axis of your body into an "unfolding" motion that produces good standing alignment.

### Exercise 11:
### Hanging Yourself Up

Stand, then bend at the hip joint and let the entire top half of your body fall forward and downward so that you are folded like a rag doll hanging from a string tied to the base of its spine. Don't strain; simply hang as limply as you can with knees locked (but not tense). If necessary your partner may hold you at first.

Imagine now that the string has been moved up one vertebra, and you are now hanging from a point a few inches farther up your back. Steadily, the "string" moves up your back, vertebra by vertebra; your head and arms hang loosely as you straighten up until the head at last floats upward as the "string" reaches the last of the small vertebrae in your neck and comes out the top of your head.

The overall movement is of an undulation or wave motion as you "uncurl" into standing alignment (see Figure 9). You will feel taller and lighter, you will have a sense of openness, and the distance from your ears to your shoulders will be greater. Avoid "pushing" up from below; try to feel yourself being "pulled" up from above.

Feel how little effort is required to move from this properly aligned position.

These exercises may have revealed tensions and distortions in your body of which you were not previously aware. Everyone has some habitual, unconscious way of holding the tensions of everyday life in their muscles; over a long period of time the tendons and connective tissue within the

**FIGURE 9.** Standing Alignment. The feet are spread to shoulder width, the knees pointing out directly over the toes.

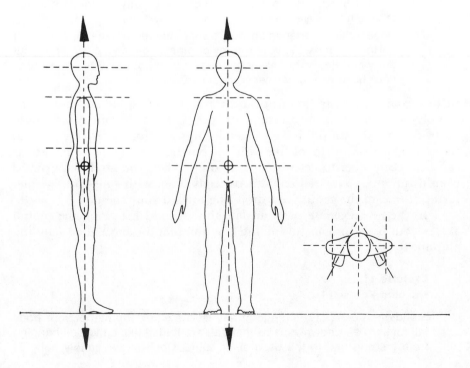

body may become distorted under the influence of these habits, resulting in a semipermanent misalignment or actual change in the shape of the body. Part of the way we read "body language" in real life is through our unconscious recognition of these patterns, and this is an important aspect of the expression of dramatic character in the theatre; we will explore this subject more in a later lesson.

For now, be aware that distorted alignment may create impediments in your work as an actor, making it harder to move freely and may even prejudice you to certain kinds of emotional moods, psychological qualities, or certain kinds of attitudes toward other people. Use these exercises to help your body remember its natural, "undistorted" condition; you will find that over a period of time your body will automatically begin to restore itself to good natural alignment without effort on your part. Again, what is needed is not that you *do* anything, but rather that you *stop doing* whatever it is that is distorting your natural condition!

### Exercise 12:
### Lets Get Big!

As a continuation of the preceding exercises, stand easily in good alignment with the eyes closed:

A. Let your conscious awareness roam at random throughout the body.

B. Mentally measure the distances within the body from point to point; are you as big as you can be in a relaxed way?

C. Become aware of all kinds of paired relationships within the body; explore the connections between various sensations and parts of the body. What does the stomach do when you breathe, what does your tongue do when you clench your buttocks, and so forth?

D. Finally, breathing very easily and feeling the warm energy of the breath flowing into and out of the body, make a neutral sound without effort or change in the breath stream; simply "let" a sound be there for a moment. What bodily activities support the sound? Do you see that a tiny change is required to produce sound? Did you truly experience sound as an aspect of the breath, and the breath as an aspect of the wholeness of your mind and body?

For all its dynamism and seeming complexity, the body is at any moment a single, totally unique, harmonious entity. So all of the activities of which you are capable, even your very consciousness, express this same wholeness and spring from the same source.

This sense of a common source, or center, from which all your life energy springs, can help you to experience wholeness. When your center becomes felt and fully energized, you will begin to move, sound, and even think in a more integrated way, with greater continuity and effectiveness. The next lesson will help you to enjoy your center as you begin to move and produce sound.

# Lesson
# Three

# Centering, Grounding, and Moving

Incarnation: bodying forth. Is this not our whole concern? The bodying forth of our sense of life? . . . We body forth our ideals in personal acts, either alone or with others in society. We body forth felt experience in a poem's image and sound. We body forth our inner residence in the architecture of our homes and common buildings. We body forth our struggles and our revelations in the space of theatre. That is what form is: the bodying forth. . .[1]

This thought is from a book called *Centering* by Mary Caroline Richards, a poet and potter. As a potter she knows how the centering of the clay upon the wheel is essential to creation in pottery, for only from perfectly centered clay can the motion of the wheel and the potter's hands bring the pot's shape freely and naturally toward its ultimate form. As a poet she also knows how the experiences of one's life must touch a personal center before they can, in turn, flow outward and be embodied in the form of a poem. As an actor you must also center yourself so that your energy, like the clay, will flow outward into the new form of yourself demanded by your role.

This idea of a personal center is not just a metaphor; it has a tangible physical dimension. Finding and activating your bodily center is a necessary first step in laying a foundation for good stage movement and voice; the sense of center can integrate your responses and give you strength by involving your total organism in your actions.

Developing your physical center is also a way of developing a psychological and spiritual centeredness as well, because at this deep level your energy exists simultaneously in physical and psychological forms; movement, feeling, thought, and the beginnings of sound, all intermingle here. This deep *psychophysical* energy is the raw material of the acting process; like the potter's clay, you must gather it, make it responsive, and center it so that it can be shaped easily into new forms.

As you work on a role, this psychophysical energy flows outward into new forms of behavior demanded by your character's actions and the style of the play. As this happens, you begin to experience yourself anew. As you come to experience this new form of yourself more fully, you begin to enter into a new state of being, which in turn summons new energies from you; this is the creative cycle of the acting process.

Having begun the unending task of developing relaxation and limbering your body, then, you will now explore the experience of centering. In this lesson you will explore the physical dimension of centering; later you will see how its psychological dimension can be a primary tool of characterization.

Here is an exercise to help you localize a specific sense of your physical center.

### Exercise 13:
### Finding Center

Place yourself in standing alignment, clear your mind, and witness your body as it performs the following activities:

A.  Move either foot out to the side about two feet; rock from foot to foot, feeling your center of gravity moving from side to side. Quickly make your rocking smaller and smaller, like a bowling pin that almost falls down; come to rest on center.

B.  Move either foot forward about two feet; find your center with front-to-back motions as described above.

C.  Move your center around rotationally, exploring the limits of various stances. Feel the weight of your body flowing into the ground and out of your center through the legs;

D.  Point into your body at the spot which you feel is your center; don't be concerned about where it "ought" to be; sense where it really is.

E.  Explore how your center is involved in moving and speaking.

As you become aware of your center over a period of days, you will notice that it moves within the body as your mood changes; frequently, your center will rise upward when you are in an excited or fearful state or downward in states of well-being or determination. You will notice, too, that different people have different characteristic centers and that the locations of their centers are very appropriate to their personalities. Such diversity can be found in people who have a "lot of guts," who "follow their nose," "lead with their chins," are "all heart," "drag their feet," "have their heads in the clouds," and so on.

This sense of centeredness is, for the actor, rooted in a literal, specific recognition of a physical center from which all impulses to move or make sound flow outwardly and into the external world.

## THE PURE CENTER
## AND THE VOICE

In the martial arts a "pure" sense of center is taught which is the natural biomechanical center of an undistorted body. This "ideal" center is deep within the body, in an area roughly three finger-widths below your navel. It is here that the breath (and therefore the voice) originates, as well as all large motions of the body. This area is the literal center of gravity of your body, as shown by Leonardo Da Vinci's famous drawing (see Figure 10).

You will want to develop a sense of your pure center, for it is from this center that your deepest impulses spring. If you are operating instead from some higher center (such as the chest, or even the neck) you will inevitably look and sound "stiff" and "superficial"; the movements and sounds you will produce will not be deeply motivated or complete because they will not be originating from the true center of your being, and your voice in particular will not have the fullness and expressiveness required for good stage speech.

The committed worker is often the noisy one; humming, singing, laughing, or grunting; all action usually flows into the world through sound as well as motion. The student of karate learns this—the outward flow of energy from our deepest center naturally carries the breath, and hence the voice, with it. Unfortunately, we sometimes inhibit this natural flow of sound out of fear or because our upbringing has taught us to restrain our natural impulse to move, breathe, and sound.

The following exercise will give you an experience of the breath flowing from your center, carrying sound and motion with it.

### Exercise 14:
### Moving and Sounding
### from Center

A. Align and center yourself as in the previous exercises.
   1. Breathe easily and slowly, feeling the breath as an expansion and a release of the center. As you breathe in, the center becomes larger and you feel yourself expanding in all directions; as you breathe out, the center is effortlessly released, and it draws to itself the energy of the breath you have just taken. Feel each breath as a gathering of energy into your center.

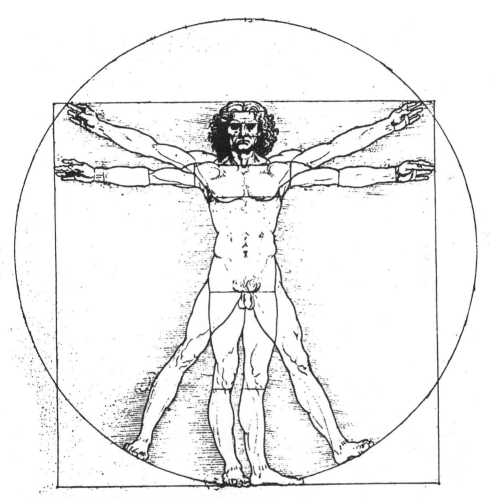

**FIGURE 10.**   The Bodily Center According to Leonardo.

2. Become aware of the breath rising and falling in the body from the center.

3. As the breath travels outward, make sound lightly; do not disturb the breath, just allow it to vibrate. This is your voice: your vibrating breath carrying energy from your center into the outside world.

4. Reach effortlessly with your vibrating breath into the world around you.

B. Put yourself, at random, into a new position; sit, bend over, or lean to one side. Repeat the above exercise in this new position and experience the breath flowing through this newly shaped pathway. What changes are there in the voice? Explore a variety of positions, but avoid strain; simply let the breath vibrate as it flows out of the center in each new bodily composition.

C. Begin moving from your center, allowing the breath to vibrate so that the energy of each motion is the same energy that produces your vibrating breath. Your sound should become an audible symptom of your motion, so that it flows as easily as the motion flows, and it takes on all the changing qualities of the motion and breath.

D. Come gradually to stillness and let each breath vibrate. As you continue to produce sound, feel the vibrations of that sound spreading into every part of your body: out of the neck into the head and chest, into the back, the stomach, the buttocks, into the arms and hands, into the legs and feet, and into the scalp. As each area of the body opens to the vibration, let the easy energy of the sound lift you and open you so that you rise first to your knees, then to a standing position. Feel the sound radiating from every part of your body!

E. Remain standing and vibrate; with a light fingertip touch, check every surface of your body. Are there "dead spots" that are not participating in the sound?

Examine your experience during sounding: Were there parts of your body that did not join in the vibration? Did you have a new sense of the capacity of your entire body to join in the act of sounding? Did you feel more in touch with yourself, and with the space around you, as if your sound were literally reaching outside yourself in a tangible way? Are you now more alert, refreshed, and relaxed?

Those areas of your body that are not available for sounding will relate in some way to the distortions and chronic tensions that you identified during your phasic relaxation work; examine each and find the relationship. A disused abdomen will cause a shallow, unsupported tone because the breath is not flowing freely from the center. A rigid or pinched chest and shoulders will withhold the chest from sound, robbing the voice of the deep resonances that give it richness; a tense neck and jaw may pinch the tone and force it into a narrow channel, causing a strident or sharp quality.

Whatever your findings, you see that vocal and physical qualities are integral with one another, because the breath, body, and voice are all integral with one another. As you begin to gain freedom and ease in one, you will enhance the other; enhancing, too, a quality of mind important to your work, for your consciousness is itself a partner in this same wholeness.

## THE ACTOR'S USE OF CENTER

Just as we experienced relaxation as a readiness to react, so our aim in aligning and centering the body is to put ourselves in the most responsive physiovocal condition. The "pure" center is an undistorted condition from which we begin our work so that we may develop in any direction required by the role without the impediment or bias of our personal distortions.

While we *begin* from a pure center, however, we certainly do not *end* there. We are not interested in "correct" posture or voice for performance, for there is no "correct" voice or posture for the actor until they are determined by the demands of the role. Though you will work to develop your "pure" center as the basis from which you will begin the creative process, be aware that each character you play will have his or her own center which functions as the source of that character's breathing, motion, and sound. You must learn to support this character center from your own ideal acting center.

Any dramatic characterization is, in a sense, a set of distortions created to express the particular nature and artistic purpose of the role. Dramatic characters are almost never whole and healthy people, for such people tend (on stage at least) to be dull; rather the characters of plays are caught in difficult situations, driven by neurotic needs, or in other ways bent out of "normal" shape. It will be a major aspect of your work to discover the particular "abnormalities" which comprise the unique nature of each role you play.

In order to do this, you begin from as undistorted or "neutral" a base as you can, exploring and testing the particular qualities useful in creating the role. In truth, of course, you will never eradicate *all* your personal idiosyncracies, nor should you; they give your work special and individual qualities which enable you, when at your best, to bring special insights and qualities to the roles you play. But those personal misalignments, inhibitions, and unconscious mannerisms—like regional dialects, unnatural postural or breathing habits, repetitive gestures—must be brought within the control of your conscious artistic discipline or they may forever limit the roles and qualities you can play.

And note that we wish not to *eliminate* these habits and qualities, but rather to bring them within our control. We actors shouldn't throw anything away; any quality, mannerism, way of speaking, or experience might be needed someday! But we must hold all these in such a way that *we are controlling them instead of them controlling us.*

In these lessons we are working to achieve a neutral but energized condition where you are ready to move in any way necessary to fulfill your dramatic task.

## THE CYCLE OF ENERGY

You are preparing yourself as the "ground" of your work. Your relaxed and aligned body is ready to move and your energy is ready to flow spontaneously from your deepest center. This energy, flowing into the outside world, may take a variety of external forms: Its visible aspects are movements, its audible aspects are sounds and words, its psychological aspects are emotions. All of these are only different modes of the same energy; any impulse may flow into any of these forms or into all of them simultaneously. All of these forms—movement, sound, and feeling—are as integral to one another as you are to yourself. To whatever degree your movement, sound, and feelings are not integral with one another, you are less whole and less accessible to yourself in your work—your work will inevitably exhibit this same fragmentation.

We turn next to consider the *cycle* of energy that flows from our center outward toward the world *and back again*. Whenever we try to do something, to achieve some objective—in short, whenever we *act*—we send energy flowing out from our center into forms of sound, speech, or gesture in the outer world. We then receive a *reaction* to our action, and this energy flows into us and touches our center, in turn eliciting a further reaction from us, and so on. As this cycle flows out, then in, then out again, we see that there is no truly unilateral action; we do not *do* unless we have been *done to*, and vice versa. In the theatre, we like to say that *acting is reacting*!

This sense of a cycle of energy is central to the Oriental martial arts, such as T'ai Chi Ch'uan, and study in these arts can be of great benefit to the actor. Developing this sense of the cycle of energy can also help to open and free the passageway through which our voice naturally flows.

### Exercise 15:
### The Cycle of Energy

Sit up, directly on the bony points you can feel just below the surface of each buttock; spread your legs as wide as is comfortable, with the knees slightly raised (see Figure 11). Feel lifted from your center out of the top of your head so that your back and neck are long and wide. The head is level, eyes ahead, and the waist is level as well. You should do this exercise as a continuous flow, not as a series of positions; the tempo and flow of the exercise are determined by slow, deep breathing, and each cycle uses one complete breath.

  A.  Breathing out, reach forward and down, keeping your back and neck long and shoulders wide. Imagine that you are bowing to someone sitting at the back of a theatre.

  B.  As you begin to breathe in, draw the breath into the lower part of your body by drawing the small of your back to the rear and scooping "energy" into the funnel formed by your legs with your hands.

  C.  As the breath begins to fill you, feel its warmth and power flowing up within you. Follow its upward movement with your hands.

  D.  As the breath rises in your body, it lifts you, straightening and lengthening the upper torso and neck, lifting the head, widening the shoulders and the throat as it flows upward like a wave moving you in a slow undulation. You unfurl like a fern opening.

  E.  The breath then flows into the outer world, with the feelings and sound of a yawn; you are giving this sound to that person sitting

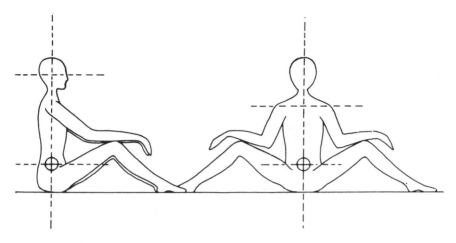

**FIGURE 11.** Sitting in Balance.

at the back of the theatre, and you accompany it with an unfolding gesture of the arms toward him. Your eyes are alive; you "see" the person.

F.  As the power of the breath begins to diminish, you easily close your mouth so that the "ah" sound of the yawn becomes an "m," and you experience a tingling sensation in your mouth and nose areas. The smooth flow of the sound produces a trisyllable word, "ah-oh-m" or *om*.

G.  As the breath and sound begin to die away, your body again bows forward and down, your back is still long and wide, and your arms are reaching forward to scoop in a new quantity of breath energy.

H.  As the breath and sound are completely used up, your body has sunk low in its bow, and the cycle begins again. At no time do you strain or pinch the voice, for the breath always lifts the head, widens and relaxes the throat, and pours easily out with the feeling of a yawn.

I.  Repeat the entire cycle: As the breath enters and leaves your body, feel the continuity of inward and outward breaths as two aspects of one cycle; change over easily from one to the other so that the entire exercise becomes one unbroken, flowing experience with no "sharp corners," only smoothly curving patterns of time, energy, motion, and sound.

J.  When you have completed enough cycles of this exercise to feel the full integration of breath, motion, and sound in an unbroken pattern, hold in the erect position and begin to produce a continuous tone, pausing easily for breath. (If you are in a group, the entire group should produce one continuous, harmonious sound, and each member of the group should feel part of the group sound and the group sound a part of them.)

## BEING GROUNDED: YOUR RELATIONSHIP TO GRAVITY

As our species evolved, we became gradually more and more erect, standing within the field of gravity (though this adaptation is far from complete; some feel that our common lower back problems may be partly due to an incomplete adaptation to being erect). Your relationship to gravity is continuous; even when lying down, you are making constant adjustments within the field of gravity.

The way in which you experience gravity is a fundamental expression of your relationship to your world. Some days, it seems that we wake up pounds heavier, with "the weight of the world" on our shoulders. At such times, we speak of feeling "down," and at the saddest times we say we have a "heavy heart." On the other hand, sometimes we feel "light as a feather," "floating on cloud nine," and the most "light-hearted" moments are often expressed by a physical action which ignores gravity, skipping. Try to imagine a sad tap dance!

A person's attitude toward gravity can be seen in their posture. When Arthur Miller opens *A Death of a Salesman* with Willy Loman crossing the stage, back bent under the weight of his sample case, his sense of defeat and hopelessness are directly expressed in the way he is losing his fight with gravity.

We also seem to receive strength from gravity when we feel at one with it; at such times we speak of "knowing where we stand," or "holding our ground." One of the qualities of some Classical heroes like Oedipus or Electra, for example, is their oneness with the earth and the way the power of nature flows up through the earth and into them. Perhaps for this reason, I have noticed that it is impossible to play a strong character if the feet are kept too close together. Not only does such a character need a wide, stable base, but they also need to be open to receive the flow of energy that is coming upward from the earth.

As you begin to sense your physical center more acutely, also begin to feel the way your energy interacts with gravity. Your energy flows downward into the ground as well as upward, and there is also energy coming into your center from the earth. We can speak, therefore, not only of being "centered," but also of being "grounded."

There is great power in being grounded, and several contemporary theatre makers have placed special emphasis on developing this quality, most notably the Japanese director Tadashi Suzuki, whose actor training system is based on a series of walks, many of which attack the earth as if to penetrate it. At the same time, some types of characters can be best expressed by a *lack* of grounding, by a floating or even flying quality.

Here is an exercise to help you experience the various ways in which we can experience gravity.

### Exercise 16:
### Roots

Imagine yourself standing on a mirror. Below you is your other self with its own center; imagine a bond between your center and that in your mirror image. This imaginary bond of energy is like a root, giving you stability, strength, and nourishment.

As your energy flows into your root, it also flows upward, so that your rootedness permits you to stand taller, to be stronger. As you move, your rootedness moves with you; you "detach" your rooted center, and at your destination you "plant" or ground yourself again.

A.   Select a destination; lift your rooted center, move to the destination, and *plant* yourself there.

B.   Now move to a destination without lifting the root; *plow* yourself there. Don't act this out; simply experience moving with this image and feel what it is like to *plow*. Extend this feeling so that you are pushing your way through the air itself, as if you are *molding* space as you move through it.

C.   Now lift your root and leave it dangling all the time, whether moving or still: *float*. Again, give yourself time to experience *floating*.

D.   Now imagine the root being drawn upward, still attached at your center, but now lifting your center upward and out of the top of your head. Move with the sense that you have to reach down to touch the floor: you are *flying*!

There is a distinct difference between the experiences of *molding, floating,* and *flying,* though each state offers numerous possibilities: molding, for instance, can feel like dejection or defeat, but it might also feel like determination or commitment; floating can feel like joy or enthusiasm, but it might also feel like confusion or vulnerability. The particular emotional quality of any one of these states can be determined only by *context,* and our bodily expression cannot be understood according to any sort of fixed or abstract system (though in the past, particularly in the Nineteenth Century, there were attempts to construct such systems and a few, notably the Delsarte system in which various body centers were related to emotions and qualities of thought, were temporarily popular).

The states we have named "molding, floating, and flying" are different bodily *dynamics,* and are adapted from the analysis of "effort shape" made by Rudolf Laban, who developed the system used for notating dance choreography. Beside the dynamic quality of physical energy, he spoke also of two other qualities: *flow,* which was either "direct" or "indirect," and *charge,* which was either "weak" or "strong." Let's extend this exercise to explore these other qualities of our "effort shape."

**Exercise 17:**
**Effort Shape**

Begin by relaxing and aligning yourself: be aware again of your center.

A. As you move, be aware of the quality of energy flowing from your center into that movement: is it *weak* or *strong*? Experiment with each.

B. As your energy leaves your body and enters the outside world, how does it contact others: is it *direct* or *indirect*? Experiment with each.

C. Now randomly select qualities from the chart below and experience various effort shapes: for instance, try molding with a strong charge and a direct flow, and then try floating with a weak charge and an indirect flow, and so on.

Virtually any quality of movement can be created by using these variables. On stage, your performance is partly a dance which, without appearing to be dance-like, is nevertheless composed, intensified, and purified through repeated testing and rehearsal (even if this process is rarely a conscious one). Your aim here is *not* to become self-consciously controlling of your movements, but rather to begin to experience the almost limitless range of movement qualities of which we are capable: this is one of the "palettes" from which you will "paint" as an actor, and you want to be sure that you have a wide choice of colors available to you!

**FIGURE 12.**   Effort Shape.

| Motion Factors | *Effort Elements* | | *Measurable Aspects (objective function)* |
|---|---|---|---|
| | *(fighting)* | *(yielding)* | |
| Weight | firm | gentle | Resistance<br>  strong (or lesser degrees to weak) |
| Time | sudden | sustained | Speed<br>  quick (or lesser degrees to slow) |
| Space | direct | flexible | Direction<br>  straight (or lesser degrees to wavy) |
| Flow | bound | free | Control<br>  stopping (or lesser degrees to releasing) |

## ARTICULATING MOVEMENT

During the exercise called "Roots," you began to move through space by "lifting" your rooted center, and moving, then "planting" your rooted center again at your destination. Review this experience; did it give you a heightened sense of clarity and purposefulness in your movements?

An actor moving from one point to another on stage goes through much the same process as the musician playing a note on an instrument. The actor chooses a destination, just as the musician selects a pitch. Then, deep within the body where the largest muscle systems intersect, the first energy of the movement is initiated, just as the musician's muscles produce the breath that causes the reed of the instrument to vibrate. Finally, the movement, like the sound of the instrument, erupts into the outside world in all its fullness. When the destination has been reached, the energy that initiated the entire process is expended and the movement ceases, just as the musician's note dies away when the breath stops.

Like the musician's music, and like your speech on stage, your stage movement needs to be well *phrased* and *articulated*, with a clear beginning, middle, and end to each phrase.

### Exercise 18:
### Articulating Movement

As in Exercise 15, begin by creating the experience of your own rooted center in relationship to your mirror image beneath the floor. Now make a movement by following each of these steps:

A. Select your destination: locate a specific spot with your eyes and let your face turn toward it so that your movement "follows your nose;"

B. Begin to move by *lifting* the root; exaggerate this motion at first;

C. Carry your root to your destination and "land" there;

D. As you land, "spear" your root into the floor to complete your movement.

E. Repeat this action several times, paying special attention to the sense of beginning, middle, and end to each movement phrase.

F. Now begin to play with this cycle. For instance, exaggerate it so that your lift is large and *away* from your destination, then *throw* your root toward your destination and *fly* there, landing with a large jump. This is the kind of movement we associate with styles like *Commedia dell'Arte*.

# Lesson Four

## Gesture

The word *express* means "to move outward." When you have a feeling or idea, it is natural to externalize it, to "move it outward." This process goes on even when you are alone, and although your expressive behavior communicates your feelings and ideas to others, it is also an organic and automatic part of your thought process itself, so gestural behavior goes on all the time. Watch people driving on the freeway, for instance; you will see some amazingly animated conversations going on even though people are alone in their cars!

Just as some movement therapists say that "there is no new idea where there is no new movement," we can say also that there is no thought or feeling which is not reflected in muscular activity, even though it may be only an invisible change in our inner dynamic.

When you have an impulse, feeling, or idea, then, it arouses an energy at your deep center that then naturally flows outward, reaching the outer world in many forms: words, sounds, motions, or postures. Broadly speaking, any such external sign of a feeling or thought may be called a *gesture*.

We will, for purposes of examining them systematically, break the wide range of gestures down into two main types: *bodily* and *vocal*. These terms refer to gestures that can be seen and those that can be heard, respectively. This lesson treats bodily gestures; the next lesson will examine vocal gestures and will divide these further into two subtypes, verbal (the speaking of words) and nonverbal (the many sounds we make other than words).

When performing scripted material, the playwright will have provided your verbal gestures in the words of the text. Your creative contribution as an actor will therefore consist mainly of the nonverbal aspect of your performance—the physical gestures, postures, vocal inflections, facial expressions, and so on. As you will see in Part Three of this book, the verbal language of the text is rich in implications about nonverbal gesture, so that a good playwright uses not only the vocabulary of words, but also that of the gestures *implied* by the text. You will learn to recognize and expand on these gestural implications of the text.

## GESTURE AS COMMUNICATION

Our culture has a large shared vocabulary of gestures that we use to augment and often to substitute for verbal communication. Some gestures have fairly consistent meanings when they appear in similar situations, hence the phrase "body language." While our verbal language provides a system for the communication of fairly precise meanings, our gestural language provides information about feelings and actions with greater expressiveness than words alone. Simply put, words can best say *what we mean* and gestures can best tell *how we feel* about it.

Psychologists have for years been interested in body language, and this area of study has been given the name "Kinesics" by Professor Raymond Birdwhistle. He defines it as "the study of body motion as related to the nonverbal aspects of interpersonal communication." Several of his basic premises are of interest to the actor: first, body motion patterns are socially learned; second, no gesture carries meaning by itself, so that all gestures must be interpreted in context; third, it is the physiological similarity of our bodies and the generally similar influences of our environment that cause many gestures to develop roughly standardized meanings within our culture.

Here is a brief example of nonverbal expression at work as observed by Professor Birdwhistle. He recorded this scene from real life and describes the nonverbal action just as a playwright would give "stage directions."

> *(The situation is that a guest of honor at a party arrives forty-five minutes late. Three couples besides the host and hostess have been waiting. The doorbell rings.)*

HOSTESS:   Oh! We were afraid you weren't coming; but good. *(As the hostess opened the door to admit her guest, she smiled a closed-toothed smile.*

> *As she began speaking she drew her hands, drawn into loose fists, up between her breasts. Opening her eyes very wide, she then closed them slowly and held them closed for several words. As she began to speak, she dropped her head to one side and then moved it toward the guest in a slow sweep. She then pursed her lips momentarily before continuing to speak, nodded, shut her eyes again, and spread her arms, indicating that he should enter.)*

GUEST:  I'm very sorry; got held up you know, calls and all that. *(He looked at her fixedly; shook his head, and spread his arms with his hands held open. He then began to shuffle his feet and raise one hand, turning it slightly outward. He nodded, raised his other hand, and turned it palm-side up as he continued his vocalization. Then he dropped both hands and held them palms forward, to the side and away from his thighs. He continued his shuffling.)*

HOSTESS:  Put your wraps here. People are dying to meet you. I've told them all about you. *(She smiled at him, lips pulled back from clenched teeth, then, as she indicated where he should put his coat, she dropped her face momentarily into an expressionless pose. She smiled toothily again, clucked and slowly shut, opened, and shut her eyes again as she pointed to the guests with her lips. She then swept her head from one side to the other. As she said the word "all" she moved her head in a sweep up and down from one side to the other, shut her eyes slowly again, pursed her lips, and grasped the guest's lapel.)*

GUEST:  You have! Well, I don't know. . . . Yes. . . . No. . . . I'd love to meet them. *(The guest hunched his shoulders, which pulled his lapel out of the hostess' grasp. He held his coat with both hands, frowned, and then blinked rapidly as he slipped the coat off. He continued to hold tightly to his coat.)*[1]

As you reconstruct this scene in your mind's eye, it is obvious that the nonverbal behavior is very eloquent; moreover, it tends to express feelings that run counter to the surface meaning of the words being spoken. This is an extremely important aspect of nonverbal expression: it often "counter-points" or even contradicts our verbal expression and "safely" expresses feelings that the situation may force us to suppress. In acting terms, nonverbal expression often conveys the *subtext*, the feelings running beneath the surface of the dialogue.

We can deduce a great deal of specific information from the gestures recorded in the scene above. The "logic of the body" has, within our culture, provided some gestures with conventionalized meanings that are apparent within this scene. The clenching of the teeth beneath the smile, the making of fists, the shuffling of feet, all tend to have similar meanings when they appear in similar situations.

Professor Birdwhistle is not the first to engage in the observation and "decoding" of nonverbal behavior. Here is the famous detective Sherlock Holmes in action, from "A Case of Identity" by Sir Arthur Conan Doyle:

He had risen from his chair and was standing between the parted blinds, gazing down into the dull neutral-tinted London street. . . . On the pavement opposite there stood a large woman with a heavy fur boa around her neck, and a large curling red feather in a broad-brimmed hat which was tilted in a coquettish Duchess of Devonshire fashion over her ear. From under this great panoply she peeped up in a nervous, hesitating fashion at our window, while her body oscillated backward and forward, and her fingers fidgeted with her glove buttons. Suddenly, with a plunge as of the swimmer who leaves the bank, she hurled across the road and we heard the sharp clang of the bell. "I have seen these symptoms before," said Holmes, throwing his cigarette into the fire. "Oscillation upon the pavement always means an affair de coeur. She would like advice, but is not sure that the matter is not too delicate for communication. And yet even here we may discriminate. When a woman has been seriously wronged by a man she no longer oscillates, and the usual symptom is a broken bell wire. Here we may take it that there is a love matter, but that the maiden is not so much angered as perplexed, or grieved. But here she comes in person to resolve our doubts."[2]

In his book *The Silent Language,* Edward Hall comments on this passage by saying that Holmes "made explicit a highly complex process which many of us go through without knowing that we are involved. Those of us who keep our eyes open can read volumes into what we see going on around us."[3] The actor has special need to engage in this kind of acute observation. As Brian Bates reports in his book, *The Way of the Actor:*

Liv Ullmann regards observing other people as an essential path to 'becoming other people' more fully and truthfully. . . . Actors have been observers for centuries, for without this keen attention to others, performances are limited to the prison of one's own personal life.[4]

**Exercise 19:**
**The Science of Deduction**

Have each person in your group examine the hostess/guest scene recorded by Professor Birdwhistle as if they were Sherlock Holmes. Each of you should recreate as completely as you can the reasons for the behavior of both characters and create a personality profile for each.

Then, as a group, compare your accounts to see what similar deductions you have made. What areas were the most commonly agreed upon, and what evidence was the most persuasive? Be specific: Why did you draw the conclusions you reached from each bit of evidence?

While the scientific study of body language is fairly new, our interest in it is very old. One of the first studies of the "silent language" (which may have been influential on the style of acting of its time) was John Bulwer's *Chirologia and Chironomia,* written in 1644. The book calls itself a study of "the Speaking Motions, and Discoursing Gestures, the patheticalle motions of the minde." The book discussed and illustrated an enormous number of feelings as expressed by nonverbal gestures (see Fig. 13). Similar attempts

**FIGURE 13.** From *Chirologia and Chironomia*, 1644.

to categorize physical gestures for the performer were made throughout the seventeenth, eighteenth, and nineteenth centuries. Even a few modern systems of acting use, in a very modified form, a formalized approach to the physical expression of emotion by locating "emotional centers" in the body, an idea borrowed from Oriental acting and medicine.

## THE ORIGINS OF GESTURE

While the actor is very often interested in the unique behavior of individual people, he is also profoundly concerned with the typical aspects of behavior that are common within the culture. As we have seen, some of our body language has a common meaning within similar situations, so that it forms a sort of gestural sub-vocabulary. This is made possible by the fact that some gestures have a common origin.

Some of these gestures derive their meaning from the structure of the body itself. For example, a man hitching up his pants is usually asserting his masculinity, since this action refers attention to his genitals. Likewise, a woman covering her cheeks with her hands is probably expressing embarassment, and her gesture is a substitute blush as the hands rise to the face in the same way that the blood would have rushed to the cheeks in a real blush.

Other gestures derive their meaning by representing actions that we would have performed at an earlier, more primitive stage of our evolution as a species. Although our present state of cultural development has changed the purpose of much of our physical behavior, we still feel the impulse for older, practical actions. The way in which vestiges of physical behavior can live on as symbolic activity, even after the action has ceased to be practical, was explained by Charles Darwin as part of his Theory of Evolution in *The Expression of Emotion in Man and Animal*. Darwin's ideas are expanded on here by Robert S. Breen:

> Consider the expressive value of behavior that was once in our human history adaptive, but is no longer so except in a vestigial sense—for example, the baring of teeth in the preparation for attack or defense. In primitive experience, the use of the teeth for tearing and rending an enemy was common enough, and a very effective means of adapting to an environmental necessity. Today, the use of teeth in this primitive fashion is rare, but the baring of the teeth is still very much with us. In an attitude of pugnacity, men will frequently clench their teeth and draw back their lips to expose their teeth. This action is a reinstatement of the primitive pattern of biting, though there is no real intention of using the teeth in such a fashion. The "tough guy" talks through his teeth because he is habituated to an attitude of aggressiveness. When he bares his teeth, it is a warning to all who see him that he is prepared to attack or to defend himself. His speech is characterized by a nasality because his

oral cavity is closed, and his breath escapes primarily through his nose. Lip action in speech is curtailed because the jaw is held so close to the upper jaw that there is little room between the lips for even their normal activity. Restriction of the lip action results in the tough guy's talking out of the corner of his mouth.

When we see a person bare his clenched teeth, curl his lip, narrow his eyes, deepen his breathing, etc., we conclude that he is angry. These are the signs of attack in our ancestors which have become for us *social symbols expressive of an emotional state* known as *anger*.[5]

### Exercise 20:
### Animal Gestures

A.  Select a strongly physical action directed toward another, such as intimidation, seduction, rejection, or approval. Adopt the characteristics of an ape or prehistoric man performing the same function. When you have begun to experience the activity on a purely physical, "animalistic" level, begin gradually to "civilize" the behavior. Do not premeditate; let the activity itself lead you as it gradually becomes less and less practical and more and more "symbolic."

B.  Using the hostess/guest scene quoted above, work with a partner to develop this scene as it might have happened between two animals.

You will probably notice that the "animalized" version of even the most genteel behavior involves more overt participation of the lower body than its civilized offspring, though the modern, symbolic version still springs from the same deep center and covertly carries the same quality of action.

It is useful for the actor to reawaken a sense of the origins of expressive behavior. Even as you perform the "polite" contemporary behavior, your memory of its animal origins can serve as a source of power and deep involvement in it. This does not mean that your performance appears animal-like, but only that you have established within yourself a link with the deepest origins of human behavior.

## FUNCTIONS OF GESTURE

We can divide the language of gestures into four broad functional categories:

1.  Illustrative, or imitative;
2.  Indicative;
3.  Emphatic;
4.  Autistic.

Illustrative gestures are "pantomimic" in communicating specific information ("the box was about this high and this wide").

The indicative gesture points ("it's right over there").

The emphatic gesture provides subjective rather than objective information, relating how we *felt* about something (as we say "Now listen here!" we pound our fist on the table or jab our finger into our opponent's face).

The autistic gesture (meaning literally "to the self") is not intended for social communication but is rather a way in which we communicate privately to ourselves. Suppose that as I listen to you I have hostile feelings, which for some reason I must conceal from you. With my arms crossed over my chest, I am viciously clutching the flesh under one of my armpits. In this secret manner, I am having a symbolic satisfaction in strangling you, the flesh of my armpit substituting for your neck. While such gestures are usually hidden, they are often "unconsciously" perceived and recognized by the people around us, so that you may become dimly aware of my hostile feelings despite my efforts to conceal them.

Obviously, these four categories of gesture are not actually separate in practice and are for the convenience of our study only. Almost every gesture we make serves a combination of two or three of these functions simultaneously.

### Exercise 21:
### Physical Gesture Scene

Select a simple and highly physical action. Perform it four times, each time utilizing a different kind of gesture. For example, if your action is to lift a heavy box and move it across the room, you would

1. Illustrate lifting it, as if you were telling us about how you would lift it without actually doing it. In this case, you may use words together with physical gestures.
2. Indicate lifting it. ("I'll pick it up from over there and carry it over here.")
3. Use emphatic gestures that are symbolic (rather than illustrative) as you show and tell us how it felt to lift the heavy box. Notice how your voice is affected.
4. Finally, perform the action symbolically and secretly using autistic gestures (for example, hitching up your belt as a substitute for lifting the box).

Compare your experiences of each category. Do you see why indirect and symbolic gesture is often more effective and interesting than obvious pantomime or indication?

### Exercise 22:
### Implied Gestures
### in the Text

A. The verbal language of a play's script often makes nonverbal demands on us. The following speech from *King Lear* suggests gestures of all four types; read it and feel the strong, specific impulses to gesture it gives you. Try performing it four times, each time emphasizing a different category of gesture:

When I do stare, see how the subject quakes. I pardon that man's life. What was thy cause? Adultery? Thou shalt not die. Die for adultery? The wren goes to't, and the small gilded fly does lecher in my sight. Let copulation thrive, for Gloucester's bastard son was kinder to his father than my daughter's got 'tween the lawful sheets. To't luxury, pell-mell! for I lack soldiers. Behold yond simpering dame, whose face between her forks presages snow, that minces virtue, and does shake the head to hear of pleasure's name: The fitchew nor the soiled horse goes to't with a more riotous appetite. Down from the waist they are centaurs, though women all above. But to the girdle do the gods inherit, beneath is all the fiend's. There's hell, there's darkness, there is the sulfurous pit: burning, scalding, stench, consumption. Fie, fie, fie! pah, pah! Give me an ounce of civet, good apothecary, to sweeten my imagination. There's money for thee.

B.  Now perform an "animalization" of the speech; see how far you can go, allowing the impulses for gesture to return to their deepest animal origins in biting, hitting, spitting, vomiting, embracing, and so on. Allow the words themselves to "regress" into the sounds of these activities.

## THE ELEMENTS OF GESTURE

As a way of helping you to expand your gestural range, we will break gesture into its fundamental elements. Since gestures are the observable symptoms of energy which has begun flowing from the character's center, they will be consistent with the qualities of energy we have already explored in our use of "effort shape:"

*Charge:* The character's gestures will be consistent with the charge of their center, and may be typically strong or weak.

*Dynamic:* The gestures will generally have the quality of molding, floating, or flying, or of some mix appropriate to the character's feeling and action.

*Flow:* The character's gestural energy will contact the world either directly or indirectly.

To these three we can add two more and our list will be sufficient to describe almost any quality of gesture:

*Tempo:* The character's gestures may be typically fast or slow.

*Integration:* The person's energy flow may be continuous or sporadic, and the body may be integrated or broken into disassociated parts. (Such disassociation of the body parts is typical of schizoid characters.)

These categories actually work in combination to produce the quality of the person's gesture. Each quality is relative to situation, of course; a person whose basic tempo is slow may, in a specific situation, gesture or move very quickly, but it will be a different quickness than that exhibited in the same situation by a character whose dominant tempo is fast to begin with.

Notice how these qualities of gesture are the automatic reflections of the total character structure from which the gestures come.

### Exercise 23:
### Your Gestural Range

Using the list of five qualities above, examine your own gestural range. What is your dominant altitude? Are your gestures typically weak or strong? Slow or fast? And so on. Remember that you are not always one way or another; in each category find the range within which you tend to function.

Do you need to expand your range in any of these ways for stage purposes? For example, an actor who tends to make strong, direct, and fast gestural choices in real life may need to devote special attention to a character whose gestures need to be more in the soft, indirect, and slow range.

# Lesson
# Five

# Voice

Speech is more than sound: it is at once verbal and nonverbal. Speech may be viewed as primarily expressive movement, "gestured meaning," or in the most limited sense, mouth gesture. . . . When speech is expressing ideas, we are content to accept it as symbolic, but when speech is understood as an expression of the whole personality, we must recognize the importance of the mimetic features that are essentially nonverbal.[1]

As Robert Breen and Wallace Bacon here point out in their book, *Literature as Experience*, all of us use nonverbal means of conveying ideas and feelings as an accompaniment to, and sometimes a substitute for, words. The great emphasis our culture places on words as a way of imparting information sometimes makes us forget that the voice, apart from the speaking of words, is a major part of our expressive mechanism. While articulated speech is probably a socially learned ability, vocal expressiveness is instinctive; in fact, the beginnings of speech have been observed in two-month-old infants, so it is possible that speech itself is more instinctive than we have previously thought.

In any case, we tend in everyday life to be much more consciously aware of formal speech than of natural nonverbal noises. Actors suffer from this dictatorship of words and are usually reticent to embellish their speaking of the dialogue with even a fraction of the expressive nonverbal sound we use in daily life. This is unfortunate, since vocal sounds are an important type of gesture, highly expressive of personality and universal in appeal. As Margaret Schlauch puts it in *The Gift of Language:*

> A cry, a tonal inflection, a gesture, are means of communication far more universal than language as we understand it. They are, in fact, universal enough to be conveyed to animals as well as other human beings.[2]

In the next lesson we will discuss the articulation of words as a special category of "gestured meaning": in this lesson, however, you will begin to explore the wide range of vocal behavior that surrounds and supports the speaking of words. Some theorists believe that these nonverbal sounds are, in fact, the source from which our spoken language evolved: in any case, they are still used to express those deep feelings that are "beyond speaking of."

## THE VOICE
## AS AN ORGANIC FUNCTION

When we examine the physical process which produces sound, a rather surprising fact comes to light. As linguist Edward Sapir points out, "There are properly speaking no organs of speech. There are only organs that are incidentally useful in the production of speech sounds."[3]

Speech is called an "overlaid function," a sort of double duty performed by organs and muscles that evolved originally for breathing, eating, or both: The diaphragm and lungs evolved for breathing, the larynx for swallowing, the tongue, the teeth, and the lips for chewing, the palate and tongue for tasting. Speech, then, by its physiological genesis, is integrally connected with these most basic functions.

The network of muscles and overlaid functions that produce the voice are so complex and far reaching that the production of speech ultimately involves the participation of the entire body. Radio actors in the great days of radio drama knew this; though their audiences could not see them, they did not decrease the extent of their physical activity while performing; in fact, they did quite the opposite. Since the audience was depending solely on the sound of their voices to create in the mind's eye a visual picture of what was happening, these actors would often exaggerate the movement of their bodies while performing so that their voices would carry the effect of their physical involvement.

### Exercise 24:
### Radio Shows

A. Select a physical activity such as lifting a heavy box or swatting a fly; while the rest of the class have their eyes shut, use vocal noise (not words) to communicate your activity to them. Use only the sound of your voice and other sound effects that you can produce. As they listen, they should try to mimic your action.

B. Form a group of three or four persons and select some simple dramatic situation that requires no dialogue (like someone being mugged in the park). Prepare a "radio show" for the rest of the class who, of course, keep their eyes shut as they listen.

## THE VOICE
## AND YOUR INNER DYNAMIC

We said in the last lesson that your natural impulse is to externalize your ideas and feelings and that these externalizations are, in fact, an integral part of emotion. According to linguist Edward Sapir:

> The sound of pain or the sound of joy does not, as such, indicate the emotion, it does not stand aloof, as it were, and announce that such and such an emotion is being felt. What it does is to serve as a more or less automatic overflow of the emotional energy: in a sense, it is part and parcel of the emotion itself.[4]

There are two important ideas here: first, that the voice in emotion results in an "overflow," a sort of safety-valve action when our inner dynamic becomes so high that we can no longer contain ourselves; second, that such vocalizations of our inner feelings are an automatic and integral part of the feelings themselves.

### Exercise 25:
### Vocal Overflow

This is an exercise in experiencing the "overflow" of vocal and physical gesture. Try reading the speech by *King Lear* in Exercise 22 aloud, but remain perfectly expressionless and still, suppressing all impulses for vocal and physical gesture. Do this several times until you feel the demand for physical and vocal gesture growing so strong that you are finally forced to move.

There is an old story about a highly mannered, flamboyant actress who gestured so indiscriminately that her movements ceased to have any organic relationship to the scene she was performing. Her director tied her hands together with a string. "When your impulse to move is so strong that you must break the string," he said, "then you may move."

The director was forcing her, through the string, to hold her responses in (to suppress them); a psychologist would say he was "raising her threshold of response" so that only the strongest (and therefore the most dramatically important) responses would flow over her threshold, and the less important would be filtered out.

By raising her threshold of response, he was also intensifying those impulses which persisted. There is a short film that shows the great cinema director, Jean Renoir, working with an actress in preparation for a highly emotional close-up. Instead of tying her hands with string, he sits her before the camera with the script and instructs her to read the words of her speech without emotion. She goes over the speech several times, and each time her natural responses to the highly-charged material prompted her to start reacting; at the slightest sign of emotion, however, Renoir sternly says, "no, no, just the words!" You can literally see the emotional pressure rising in her as the suppressed responses struggle harder and harder to break free. Finally, when she is about to explode, Renoir calls "action!" and the camera captures a splendid performance.

The repeated suppression of the impulses tended not only to filter out the weaker, less impactful ones, but it also strengthened those which remained by building their "inner pressure," or *inner dynamic*. This is why we often say that "less is more," and why Stanislavski encouraged actors over the course of a rehearsal process to "cut 80%."

Here is an exercise that will enable you to experience this inner dynamic and to hear its profound effect on the voice.

### Exercise 26:
### Running on the Inside

You are to stand and run in place, counting every other step aloud from 1 to 50, but when you reach 30, stop running "outside" but continue to run "inside;" hear the effect this has on your voice.

Inner dynamic is essential to the sense of drama, because it arouses suspense. A person with a lot of energy "inside" but without much being released "outside" commands our attention because we wonder "what is he or she going to do?" This produces, for instance, the quality of "danger" which some actors have.

This fact is of special importance to the voice, since the voice automatically carries so much of this "hidden" energy out into the world, even when we are trying to suppress it! For instance, it is extremely moving to hear newscasters reporting a great tragedy, like the assassination of President John F. Kennedy, because they are trying to remain "objective," yet despite their disciplined efforts, the emotion is forcing itself through. Such a performance is doubly moving because of the feelings connected to the situation *plus* the effort of the speaker to suppress them.

This is why what you *don't* do on stage is often much more important than what you *do*. While you wish to respond freely and fully to your role, you must always do so with a sense of necessity, economy, and discrimination. Remember that what happens *inside* enriches your performance without any conscious effort to *show* it, and that the voice in its journey from your deepest center out toward the world literally turns you "inside out."

## THE VOICE AND SUBTEXT

The words we speak carry the information we wish to impart, while our attitude about that information is usually carried by our tone of voice. The most obvious example is sarcasm. If, during an argument, I say to you, "Well, you certainly are an expert on the subject," it is my tone of voice that lets you know that I really mean "You don't know what you're talking about!"

There are also *unconscious* ways in which the voice communicates attitude. We sometimes find ourselves in situations where we cannot say what we really mean or feel; at such time we will—consciously or not—express ourselves indirectly, saying or doing one thing when we really mean another. In acting terminology, such "hidden" meanings are called *subtext*.

If, for example, I am attempting to convince you that I feel strongly about what I am saying, I may increase the volume of my voice, elevate my pitch slightly, and enunciate sharply by hitting the hard consonants as a sort of vocal "pounding-on-the table"; but when I interrupt my speech to take a breath, the breath turns out to be a sigh that is very close to a yawn. I have unwittingly revealed that I am actually bored with what I am saying (and probably with you as well).

In such instances, it will be the quality of my voice which will communicate my true meaning and, as with physical gestures, it is because these sounds have their source in the common construction of our bodies and in our evolutionary background that they are so powerfully communicative. You will remember Charles Darwin's explanation of physical gesture as a vestige of animal behavior in the last lesson; he also believed that many vocal gestures were symbolic of general bodily functions, as explained here by Robert Breen:

> Darwin pointed to the primitive practice of children who expressed their dislike for someone or something by sticking out their tongues and making a sound something like a bleating sheep. Sticking out the tongue was for Darwin a primitive reflex of vomiting or rejecting something distasteful; so, too, was the sound, which got its peculiar vocal quality from the extremely open throat through which it came. The open throat was, of course, a feature of the regurgitation, or vomiting, reflex. It is interesting that the civilized adult will show his contempt or distaste in much the same fashion, though much repressed. We are all familiar with the tone of voice which we recognize as "superior" or "contemptuous" because it has that "open throat" quality.[5]

So the "hidden" attitudes we call "subtext" are automatically revealed *without conscious effort* by the body's memory and automatic involvement of fundamental actions like regurgitating or biting. Think back to the hostess/guest scene in the previous lesson; as the Hostess greeted the overdue guest, she *"smiled a close-toothed smile."* The quality of voice that would go with this gesture has the sound of biting, and although she is saying "Oh, we were afraid you weren't coming. But good," her gesture and tone of voice is expressing the subtext, "I'm furious with you for being late!"

## FINDING AND USING YOUR OWN VOICE

We see in all this that the voice is a tremendously personal thing. In fact, the words *personal* or *personality* themselves come from the root *per sona*, meaning "through sound," and specifically the sound of the voice. As we said above, the voice travels from your deepest center on its way toward the outer world and it carries with it the qualities of your "inner world." For this reason, we said that the act of speaking literally *turns you inside out.*

This is true when the voice is allowed to function in its normal, undistorted way. But when we distort our voices in some way, for example, when we try to sound older, or more sophisticated, or sexier, or to present any desired image of ourselves that is not entirely truthful, our voice is no longer authentically personal. In a very real sense we can say that *because our own voice is not there*, we *are not there!*

This fact is of special importance to you as an actor. Your whole aim is to put yourself into the place of the character, and you make that journey first and most actively by saying what your character says. If you do not say it with your own voice—if *you are not there*—you will be cut off from this initial, fundamental point of entry into the character.

I often hear actors make this mistake, even at the very first readings of plays, because they choose to adopt an artificialized voice for the sake of "creating a character," or "playing age," or—especially with Shakespeare—"being poetic." While it is true that your voice may undergo some degree of transformation in the course of working on a role or on a particular kind of play, this transformation is *the result* of your working process and not a *cause* of it.

No matter how different from yourself the character may be, or how different the character's way of speaking may be from your own, your performance must be based on reality, and the voice is one of your deepest personal realities. No matter how much you may work on your voice in order to make it a richer, more flexible instrument, you will always do so with an aim to perfecting its own natural qualities.

**Exercise 27:**
**Using Your Own Voice**

Select a speech from a play by a character who is quite "different" from you, or whose way of speaking is quite different from your own.

Standing before the group, read this speech in your own voice; become aware of any urge to alter your voice in order to "perform" and simply release any such impulse. Don't try to do anything, simply *allow* yourself to speak the character's words in your own voice.

Of course, most of us need to improve the quality of our own voices to expand the range and responsiveness of our vocal instrument. We do this not by falsifying the quality of our voice but by becoming aware of good vocal technique and relearning any bad habits we have developed. It is a slow and gentle process which, for the working actor, is unending. This book can only hint at some simple beginnings, but the serious acting student will find ways to continue their study with a qualified teacher.

Singing lessons, by the way, though valuable for the working actor, do not adequately treat the problems of the speaking voice for stage purposes, and some old-fashioned "bel canto" singing techniques can actually produce an artificialized delivery which is undesirable for the actor.

Film and television work requires no specialized vocal technique (in fact, any overt manipulation of the voice sounds false to the penetrating ear of the film/TV microphone). For camera acting, one works to develop the natural voice but avoids any hint of performance. In Michael Redgrave's biography, for example, he relates the story of his first day in front of a film camera. After the first take, he asked the director (who was standing behind the camera) how it was: "Fine," the director replied, "except for one thing. I could hear you!"

Just as your body work began with your breath, you will begin developing your personal voice by experiencing how it begins with your breath.

## THE BREATH

Out of the vast range of sounds produced by our bodies, only a limited number are utilized for speech. For one thing, all the sounds of our language are "expiratory," produced by outgoing breath. "Inspiratory" sounds are entirely in the realm of nonverbal vocal gestures (though some of the world's other languages do use them for speech, along with clicking, whistling, and so on). Your speech, then, is produced by outgoing breath, and it is with the breath that you begin to study it.

You have already experienced moving and sounding from center, and you know the integral connection between your activity, emotion, breath, and the voice which is "vibrating breath." The aim of your breath study

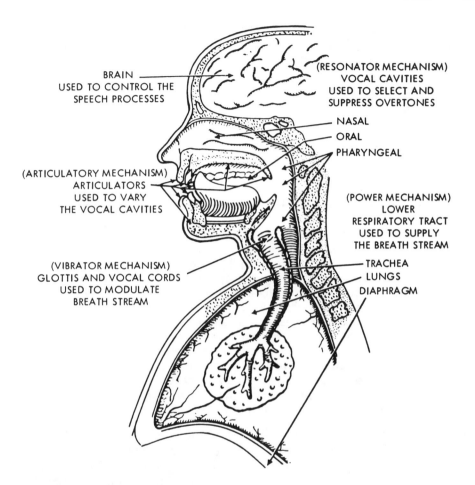

BRAIN
USED TO CONTROL THE
SPEECH PROCESSES

(RESONATOR MECHANISM)
VOCAL CAVITIES
USED TO SELECT AND
SUPPRESS OVERTONES

NASAL
ORAL
PHARYNGEAL

(ARTICULATORY MECHANISM)
ARTICULATORS
USED TO VARY
THE VOCAL CAVITIES

(POWER MECHANISM)
LOWER
RESPIRATORY TRACT
USED TO SUPPLY
THE BREATH STREAM

(VIBRATOR MECHANISM)
GLOTTIS AND VOCAL CORDS
USED TO MODULATE
BREATH STREAM

TRACHEA
LUNGS
DIAPHRAGM

**FIGURE 14.** The Vocal Apparatus.

is to enhance this organic unity of action, emotion, breath, and voice by extending, strengthening, and making more responsive the massive deep muscle system which supports your breath.

As you see in Figure 14, the system of diaphragm, lungs, and bronchial tubes acts as a "bellows" and supports vocal production as well as accent, stress, changes in volume, and resonance. The actor must develop and enhance this system of breath supply. You rarely utilize, in real life, even half of your potential reservoir of air, nor do the demands of everyday speech cause you to develop the muscles that activate this bellows system to anything like their full potential.

This "bellows" operates simply: as the ribs expand and the diaphragm pulls downward, the chest cavity enlarges, creating a slight vacuum, causing air to be drawn into the lungs. As the diaphragm releases, the stored air naturally and effortlessly flows back out through the bronchial tubes and trachea, then through the pharynx and into the throat, mouth, and nasal chambers. This sort of *breathing by relaxation* requires no effort and is the way we wish to breathe on stage. Feel this process in yourself with this simple exercise.

### Exercise 28:
### Breath and Sound

In a standing position, place yourself at rest and in alignment. Easily produce a vocalized tone and explore the endless variations of which that tone is capable.

Place your hand on your stomach (just below your sternum and above your waist) and feel the movement there. Are you tense here, or is your abdomen soft? Tension here can cause the voice to be strained and erratic. Release any tension that you find.

Check also with your hands the areas at the sides of the lower back; are you breathing and responding 360 degrees around your abdomen? Do you feel the lower (floating) ribs spreading easily as you draw air in?

Now place your hand on your upper chest, as if you were saluting the flag. As you breath, does your chest rise and fall more or less than your abdomen? Some of us are "chest breathers" and have an exaggerated motion here; chest movement should be very slight.

Check also for tension here, which can rob the voice of chest resonance. Women who have had extensive ballet training when they were young, and men who attempted to adopt "macho" stance in adolescence may find their chests tight. If so, simply become aware of it and gradually, over a long period, allow yourself to release it.

A regular program of exercise such as the limbering and alignment series, and especially Exercises 14 and 15, *Moving and Sounding from Center* and *The Cycle of Energy* will help you to develop the volume of your breath reservoir; also concentrate on developing the stamina and flexibility of the muscles that control that reservoir of air.

The breath supply is utilized by the body just as it would be by any wind instrument. The outpouring column of air causes vibration as it passes through an aperture (the vocal cords) and the vibration sets the column of air in motion. The tone is then amplified, resonated, and changed in quality by the resonating capacity of the structure of the chest, neck, and head, so that the condition of these structures is automatically reflected in the nature of the voice. This occurs naturally unless you resist or block it in some way.

In the next Lesson, you will trace the breath stream from the vocal cords on as you begin to shape (that is, *articulate*) the breath into that special gesture we call *speech*.

# Lesson
# Six

# Speech

Humankind was once described as "the animal who talks." Nowadays we are examining the possibility that other animals such as whales, dolphins, and chimpanzees, are also capable of using sounds to symbolize things and ideas. Speech is an amazing capacity: it is based on the ability to *symbolize* and to agree with others that a certain sound has a certain meaning even in the absence of any tangible thing to which the sound refers.

Philosopher Ernst Cassirer, when theorizing about how the capacity for speech develops in us, observed that at first the sounds we make are part of feelings like hunger, pain, or joy, not in the sense that we are trying to express these feelings to others, but rather that the sounds are part of the feelings themselves:

> When we seek to follow language back to its earliest beginnings, it seems to be not merely a representative sign for ideas, but also an emotional sign for sensuous drives and stimuli. The ancients knew this derivation of language from emotion from the pathos of sensation, pleasure, and pain . . . it is to this final source which is common to man and beast and hence truly "natural" that we must return, in order to understand the origin of language.[1]

Speech, then, begins with our most fundamental experience of pleasure and pain, though at this stage it is only nonverbal sound, a kind of vocal gesture. In this earliest stage of development, the baby explores the world by grabbing it and literally "taking it in," usually into its mouth. Later, the baby notices that making a certain sound makes Mommy appear, or causes food to be given. It is at this point that the baby notices that "the voice can reach further than the hand," and it is at this moment we notice that we can effect the world by producing certain sounds, and speech is born.

Viewed in this way, speech is *a special kind of doing*; it is the most specific way in which we send our energies into the world in our effort to satisfy our needs.

This is a particularly useful view of speech for the actor. In creating a play, the writer develops the vision of a dramatic action involving a total human situation, then channels the full force of this vision into the relatively few words of the dialogue. Unlike the more descriptive and narrative functions of most prose, the primary function of good dramatic language is *to transmit action*; more intensely than in life or other forms of literature, then, dramatic speech is *a form of doing*.

## THE PROCESS OF VERBALIZATION

In our everyday life, speech has become primarily a means for the communication of information. But for the actor, speech must retain the feelingful and active qualities described above. For us, it is best seen as *a physical process whereby feelings, needs, and thoughts find their expression in the muscular activity that produces articulated sound*. As such, speech is a special type of active gesture directed toward some external objective.

This highly physical aspect of speech is especially important to the actor, since the written language of the playscript is only a representation of the spoken, active language envisioned by the playwright.

As we form our thoughts into the physical activity called speech, we perforce make a great many choices that are expressive of our feelings, needs, values, background and personality, so that the process of verbalization expresses the kind of person we are (character) and the way in which we try to cope with our world (action).

This active nature of the process of verbalization is of prime importance to you as an actor. Your character's speech begins in some felt need or reaction; as the words are chosen and are shaped into phrases and sentences, the character is constantly making conscious and—more often—unconscious choices about emphasis, word choice, and so on. These choices reveal what is really important to them and how they feel about it; it is this living quality of speech *coming to be for the first time* that you must relive in order to enter fully into the character. If you deliver your lines merely as memorized words, you deprive your audience of the living process by which those words came to be, and you deprive yourself of the transformational power of participating actively in your character's thought processes!

Note that this does not require halting speech; slow tempo, long pauses, or muttering and mumbling are too often used as easy substitutes for an honest participation in the character's thought processes. The style of the play will also suggest a characteristic verbal process. The ornate witticisms of Restoration comedy, for example, are formed by a quick, graceful process, a sort of verbal fencing match; some modern plays, on the other hand, tear chunks of speech out of experience in a clumsy, painful manner (as Harold Pinter puts it, "The more acute the experience the less articulate its expression."[2])

Your primary responsibility toward speech on the stage is to recreate the living process of verbalization in a way consistent with the nature of your character and the style of the play. The script is both your starting point and your final judge; it is a finished verbal product which you take apart in rehearsal in order to rediscover the process of its creation; then, by embodying this process in your performance, you arrive once again at a living expression of the text.

### Exercise 29:
### The Process of Verbalization

Choose a short speech (perhaps only a few lines) and, after memorizing it thoroughly, go through it so as to experience the process of verbalization.

A. Begin with movement and sound rooted in the needs and feelings which lie beneath the words, but without the words themselves.

B. Next, allow the words of the speech to evolve gradually out of your movement, like a picture coming into focus. Do this with each phrase or sentence working from the germinal thought, letting the words come from the need to communicate the idea.

Does a sense of character begin to emerge as you understand the choices that are being made during the process of verbalization?

The "process of verbalization" that you explored in this exercise is usually described by the term *diction*, which refers to the selection of the specific words that best express our thoughts. As you shall see in Part Three, the playwright's choice of words for each character reflects both the psychology and physiology of that character. Your ability to revitalize the process of word choice is crucial to your understanding and creation of the character. This is why some schools of acting encourage you to "just say the words," since "saying the words" in the most complete sense involves a total expression of the mind and body of the speaker!

First, however, you must examine something more of the whole physical process by which speech is produced.

## TONE PRODUCTION

In the previous Lesson, you followed the breath to the point at which it becomes tone, which happens when it passes through the aperture of the vocal cords, causing them to vibrate. The power of your voice depends on both an adequate breath supply and efficient vocalization. Unnecessary tension in the vocal cords, or failure to fully utilize your amplification and resonating chambers, wastes your breath supply, no matter how fully you may develop it.

When we consider how the vocal cords operate, we see that they are capable of four basic types of movement:

1.  The vocal cords may be drawn fully apart so that the air stream is permitted to pass through them unhindered;
2.  They may be drawn partly together to produce the quality of speech called "voicelessness" or "stage whisper";
3.  When the cords are nearly closed, the air stream passes through them causing them to vibrate like reeds in the wind, producing tone. By increasing or decreasing their tension, we increase or decrease pitch;
4.  By a quick closing, the vocal cords can interrupt the breath stream entirely, resulting in "glottal stop."

Tension in the throat area will adversely influence the operation of the vocal cords and unnecessarily restrict the flow of breath. It will also detract from the performance, since a tight throat is communicated more quickly to an audience than any other kind of undesirable muscular tension. Actors have been known to perform with a painful back ache with no one in the audience being the wiser; but a tense throat on stage results instantly in a wave of "sympathetic" coughing from the audience.

The primary function of the vocal cords in articulation, then, is to either "voice" the breath stream or allow it to pass freely as a "voiceless" sound. For example, *P* is a voiceless sound, while *B* is voiced; in all other respects, these two sounds are articulated in the same manner. Try it!

You may have noticed that it requires slightly more effort to produce the voiceless sound of *P* than voiced *B* since the voiceless sound requires that you draw the vocal cords fully apart rather than allowing them to remain partly together, which is their normal position. (As you relax just before falling asleep, for instance, you sometimes produce a soft sound as the breath flows through the relaxed vocal cords.) Just as you relax to breathe out, you relax to produce a tone; good speech is mostly a matter of relaxation!

### Exercise 30:
### Voiced
### and Voiceless Sounds

Explore the voiced and voiceless sounds by saying the following very slowly:

**Bob** and his **Pop** thought that the **dog's toy** was a very **funny** but **juicy choice**.

Do not move any part of the jaw, tongue, or palate while producing each pair of voiced and unvoiced sounds. Hold a finger over your pharynx (your Adam's apple) and feel it change.

You have now experienced the first way in which you articulate. As the breath stream, whether voiced or not, passes beyond the pharynx, it encounters three further forms of articulation.

First, the soft palate may raise or lower to direct the breath either into the nasal or the oral area; then, if the breath flows into the mouth, it is either impeded, or allowed to pass freely. Finally, if it is impeded, the location of the point at which it is impeded produces a particular sound. Let's examine each point of articulation in turn.

## NASAL SOUNDS

The first point beyond the vocal cords at which the breath stream is articulated is at the soft palate near the rear of the mouth. As the soft palate lowers or rises, it opens and closes the pathway through which the air stream may pass into the nasal cavity, where it is resonated. In English we have only three basic sounds that depend upon nasal resonance: *m, n,* and *ng* (as in si*ng*).

Nasal resonance plays an important part in causing the subtle variations of tone that produce the individual quality of our speech. Some regional dialects, for instance, feature a particular kind of nasal resonance, like the "twang" of some rural speech. As you perform these exercises, you may notice such vocal mannerisms in yourself; if you do, do not attempt to eliminate them, for you may need them for a role someday! Instead, do all you can to develop other, more "standard" ways of speaking so that you will not be limited to the roles which match your habitual way of speaking.

Of course, actual defects of speech should be treated on an individual basis. If you have such a problem, seek out specialized training to help solve it. Few things can be as limiting to an actor as adverse vocal traits that remain uncorrected. (A tape recording of your voice as you perform the exercises in this lesson will help you in assessing your problems and progress.)

### Exercise 31:
### Nasal Sounds

A. Make a continuous open "ah" sound (as in father) and see how much resonance the nasal cavity can contribute *without altering the basic quality of the tone*; check this by snapping the nostrils open and shut between your fingers while you are making the sound.

   Let the tone flow toward the front of the face, producing strong vibrations in the triangular area around the nose and mouth; this area is called the *mask*.

B. Again produce a continual open "ah," but this time open and close the soft palate (turning the sound of *a* into *ng*).

   Concentrate your awareness on the vibrations produced in your mask area; feel how the power of the vibrating breath moves into the mask for the nasal sound and can be easily felt with the fingertips.

C. Explore all three nasal sounds by saying very slowly:

*M*ad *M*ax *n*ever sa*ng* i*n* the ca*ny*on.

## ORAL SOUNDS:
## VOWELS AND DIPHTHONGS

If the soft palate does not direct the breath into the nasal passages, it flows into the mouth. Here the most complex acts of articulation take place. The breath stream, voiced or unvoiced, may be allowed to pass freely, or it may be impeded in some way; if it passes freely, it may be "shaped" by the positioning of the mouth's movable parts (mainly the jaw, tongue, and lips). The sounds produced in this "open" way are the vowels.

The vowel sounds actually used in English far exceed the simple list, *a, e, i, o,* and *u.* There are four categories of vowel sounds: those produced by shaping the mouth at the front (involving mainly the lips), the middle of the mouth (using mainly tongue and lips), those produced at the back (using mainly the rear of the tongue and jaw), and those combined sounds (called diphthongs) which are unbroken glides from one vowel sound to another (see Figure 15).

### Exercise 32:
### Vowels and Diphthongs

A. Place yourself at rest and in alignment, and using the summary table of vowel sounds (Figure 15), slowly make each sound in turn, concentrating on developing the fullest resonance possible and

| FRONT VOWELS | MIDDLE VOWELS | BACK VOWELS | DIPHTHONGS (Glides from one vowel sound to another in a single syllable) |
|---|---|---|---|
| WE | UP | CHARLES | MAY |
| WILL | FURTHER | WANTS | I |
| MAKE | FURTHER | ALL | JOIN |
| THEM | | OLD | YOU |
| MAD | | BOOKS | NOW |
| FAST | | TOO | JOE |

**FIGURE 15.** Summary Table of Vowel Sounds. Arranged from front to back in the mouth as you read down and across. Note that all vowels and diphthongs are voiced. Adapted from Evangeline Machlin, *Speech for the Stage* (Theatre Arts Books, 1966).

on efficiently using the breath supply. Are you getting maximum volume and resonance for minimum expenditure of air?

B. Exaggerate the "shape" of the mouth in producing each sound. Read the lists in order, concentrating on the movement from front to rear in the mouth, and on changes in the size of the space within the mouth.

C. Speak the diphthongs in slow motion for a time to explore the gliding motion from one sound to another. Do you produce a clearly distinguishable sound for each type?

## ORAL SOUNDS: CONSONANTS

When the breath stream is impeded or interrupted in the mouth, the resulting sounds are the consonants. The consonants are necessarily less resonant and more incisive than the vowels. The word consonant originally meant "sounding with," indicating that these sounds alone cannot comprise a syllable; they must be combined with a vowel. While there are subtle exceptions to this rule, the consonants do serve, by virtue of their shorter duration and sharper tonal quality, as punctuation for the beginning or ending of vowel sounds, thus forming syllables.

When we consider the articulation of consonants, there are two principal questions: first, at what position in the mouth is the breath stream altered, and second, to what extent is it altered? In considering the first of these questions, we see that there are four principal positions within the mouth where articulation may occur (see Figure 16). As the point of articulation moves from the back to the front of the mouth, the quality of sound changes.

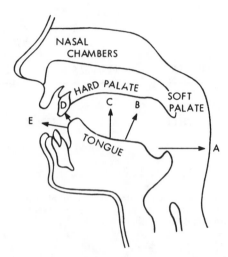

**FIGURE 16.** The Points of Articulation in the Mouth. (A) guttural, (B) rear palatal, (C) middle palatal, (D) dental, (E) labial.

A. Guttural: the rear of the tongue reaches toward the back of the mouth; guttural sounds appear in some languages (like the *ch* in the Yiddish "*Ch*annukah"), but in English purely guttural sounds are used only in nonverbal noises.

B. Rear Palatal: the rear of the tongue may rise up to make contact with the soft palate to make sounds like "**g**un."

C. Middle Palatal: a slightly more forward sound may be produced by the middle of the tongue rising up to contact the roof of the mouth as in "**k**ey."

D. Dental: here the tongue is used in conjunction with either the bony ridge directly behind the upper teeth (as in the sound "*t*ea") or the teeth themselves (as in the sound "*th*ese").

E. Labial: the lips may be involved either by contacting the lower lip with the upper teeth (as in "*f*riend") or by having the lips contact each other (as in "*b*oy").

Notice that in each position different sounds are produced by either voicing or unvoicing the tone without any other alteration.

When we next consider the *extent* to which the breath stream is altered, there are two main questions: is the breath stream entirely interrupted, or is it only impeded? When the breath stream is entirely interrupted, the result is called a *stop* (**b**oy). Stops are also called *plosives*, since they are produced by closing the breath stream off at some point in the mouth and then letting it "explode" suddenly.

On the other hand, when the breath stream is impeded without being stopped altogether, we produce *continuants*, sounds which can be held out over a period of time ("Mmm, good!"). Within the general category of continuants, there are several subcategories:

1. *Nasals, (m, n, ng)* which have already been discussed;
2. *Fricatives*, produced by forcing the breath stream through a narrow passage-

way (*f*riend). Some of these sounds have a hissing quality and are also called *sibilants* (*s*orry);

3. *Blends,* which are combined sounds produced by a plosive palatal sound that blends immediately into a soft fricative or "hushing" sound. Examples are "*ch*oice, *j*oyce";

4. *Glides* are momentary (and relatively slight) constrictions of the breath stream which immediately "glide" into an open vowel sound; these are the "smoothest" of the consonant sounds and share some qualities of the vowels.

   Some of these sounds, like "*l*ovely," are called *laterals* because the breath is blocked in the center of the mouth but allowed to flow around the sides of the tongue, or "laterally."

   Others, like "*r*at," are called *liquids* because there is only a slight constriction of the breath stream involved as it flows easily past, like water.

The summary table of consonant sounds in Figure 17 lists examples of each; notice that nasals and liquids are always voiced, while fricatives and blends are either voiced or unvoiced.

### Exercise 33:
### Consonants

Using the summary table of consonant sounds (Figure 17), explore the relationships between these sounds. Exaggerating the motion or position involved, read each category in slow motion.

   Are you producing a distinctly different sound for each? Are regional peculiarities and bad speech habits affecting any of the sounds? Is the breath supply efficiently used for each? Are you getting maximum resonance from each?

**FIGURE 17.** Summary Table of Consonant Sounds

| POSITION IN THE MOUTH | STOPS | | CONTINUANTS | | | | | |
|---|---|---|---|---|---|---|---|---|
| | *Voiced* | *Unvoiced* | *Nasals* (*Voiced*) | *Fricatives* *Voiced* | *Unvoiced* | *Blends* *Voiced* | *Unvoiced* | *Glides* (*Voiced*) |
| **Labial** | *B*oy | *P*ony | *M*oney | *V*ERY | *F*UNNY | — | — | *WOW* |
| **Dental** | *D*OG | *T*OY | NO*N*E | *TH*ESE *Z*OO | *TH*INK *S*ORRY (SIBILANTS) | — | — | *L*OVEL*Y* |
| Middle Palatal | *G*EEK | *K*EY | CA*NY*ON | PLEA*S*URE | *SH*E | *J*OYCE | *CH*OICE | *R*AT *Y*ES |
| Rear Palatal | *G*UN | *C*UT | SI*NG* | — | *H*OT | — | — | — |

## PROJECTION AND ARTICULATION

The ability to be heard and understood easily and without effort even in a large space is obviously crucial to the stage actor (though as we have mentioned it is not a concern when working before the camera). It is important to realize that adequate projection, even in a large theatre, does *not* require extraordinary volume and bellowing is unnecessary. What *is* required is strong (but not forced) breath support, efficient use of that breath in clean (but not strained) vocalization, and precise (but not self-conscious) articulation.

Many young actors think that being heard is a matter of speaking *loudly*; it is much more a matter of speaking *clearly*. The most common vocal shortcoming in the theatre, in fact, is the actor who can be easily *heard* but not easily *understood*.

Psychotherapists have often noted how vocal projection relates directly to a person's sense of self-esteem and assertiveness. Nothing reduces the effectiveness of the human voice more than a lack of confidence; even if we force ourselves to speak loudly, our insecurity causes our voices to "hide" in unintelligibility. Actors with good basic technique, even if they have only modest voices, can be heard in the largest auditorium *when they fully understand their text and are fully focused on their action*.

One aspect of projection sometimes bothers young actors: how do you make yourself heard when the circumstances of the scene make speaking loudly unrealistic? How, for instance, does one play an intimate love scene in a space as large as most theatres? Does the need to be heard by a spectator perhaps twenty (or even sixty) feet away necessarily falsify the intimacy of the scene?

Of course it doesn't, if the *attitude* and *quality* with which the actor speaks reflects the essential nature of the situation. The audience accepts the need for increased volume as a convention, and requires only that the attitude and quality of intimacy be maintained *without effort*. The actor can do this only if speaking with adequate projection is as effortless for them as intimate speech would be in real life. Development of good breath support, efficient tone production, and most important, clean articulation is more important in this than is sheer volume.

### Exercise 34:
### Projection
### and Articulation

Working with a partner in a large space, speak to one another "in secret" as if you were plotting a crime or exchanging some juicy bit of gossip. Make yourselves understandable to spectators at the back of the room through clarity and precision but not volume. Do not speak *to* them but rather *for* them.

Notice how a strong sense of commitment to what you are saying and to the act of communicating with your partner helps to project the voice without effort.

## ARTICULATION AND CHARACTER

You have probably experienced the shock connected with hearing a recording of your own voice; we rarely think that we "sound like ourselves." This is because we do not hear ourselves accurately "from the inside." Our disembodied voices frighten us because there is a strong sense of personal identity connected with the voice. It is interesting that we generally have much less trouble orienting ourselves to the way we look than to the way we sound. The word *personality*, as we mentioned earlier, comes from two roots: one is the ancient Greek word for *mask*, which in turn came from the older root, *per sona*, "through sound." (This derivation might be explained by the idea that the masks of classical theatre may have served partly as "megaphones" which helped amplify the actors' voices.)

Our study of stage speech focuses not so much on "correctness" as on the ability of the voice to express action, emotion, and character. Along with the development of technical control of articulation, then, you must also develop your "ear," your ability to hear the expressive aspects of articulation.

### Exercise 35:
### Articulation
### and Personality

A. Observe around you the habits of articulation of all sorts of people. How are laziness, timidity, audaciousness, and a host of other personality traits expressed by articulation?
B. What effect do various emotions have upon articulation?
C. What effect does the situation have upon articulation? How do people articulate differently in public and in private, when threatened, when among friends, and so on?
D. Try to recreate articulatory patterns you have observed and examine your feelings when you speak in these various ways.

Situation has an enormous impact on articulation. Since articulation is the muscular action by which you send your voice—your *personality*—into the world, it is extremely expressive of your feelings regarding that world. The emphasizing of hard, biting sounds may indicate an attitude of hostility, while the elongation and softening of open vowel sounds may indicate acceptance. Articulation is a complex muscular act which, like all expressive activity, is rooted in vestiges of earlier practical behavior (remember our discussion of Darwin's idea about this in the last lesson).

The massive muscular actions which produce the voice prior to articulation reflect fundamental states of action and emotion; articulation is the final, subtle, and complex process whereby we specify the intellectual and symbolic functions of speech. Articulation, then, expresses much about the intellectual aspects of character.

As you will see in Lesson 12, the playwright's choice of words to be spoken by a character is determined not only by meaning but also by the way speech reflects personality in both its physical and psychological aspects. As important as it is that you be able to speak "correctly," it is more important that you are able to participate in the consciousness of the character by recreating his or her speech *as if it were your own*. This requires that you extend your everyday vocal capabilities to encompass those of the character and of the style of the play as well.

To sum up, we can say that playwrights write not for the eye but for the human voice; the human voice is deeply involved in the body's musculature; the body's musculature is deeply involved in emotional life and thought. Through this psychophysical network, the playwright's words and implied actions provide a direct route to a fully living, vivid, and appropriate stage experience that will fill your performance with the richness of life.

# Lesson
# Seven

# Working with Others

So far you have been concentrating on yourself, on the world inside of your skin. But drama is concerned primarily with the interaction of people with one another, and your work as an actor is therefore inextricably bound to the work of your partners. During training, your personal skills will properly receive your attention and effort, for a team depends on the individual skill of every member; but you can develop the highest level of individual technique and never participate in the full artistry of the theatre if you remain incapable of working effectively within the creative ensemble.

Your work on your own physical and vocal capacities, then, should enhance your relationship with others by making you more "present," more available, and helping you to experience that you yourself are, by your very nature, an integral part of your world and connected to all who inhabit it.

In fact, your sense of a separate "I" bounded by the physical body is a limited understanding of your actual participation in the whole realm of nature; you are integral with your environment, and it with you. Our ideas of an "inner" and an "outer" world are only different modes of perception, different attitudes toward experience; in actual fact our inner self is part of the outer world, or rather the world is one world, which we merely experience as "inner" and "outer." As Mary Caroline Richards points out in her book, *Centering*:

The innerness of the so-called outer world is nowhere so evident as in the life of our body. The air we breathe one moment will be breathed by someone else the next and has been breathed by someone else before. We exist as respiring, pulsating organisms within a sea of life-serving beings. As we become able to hold this more and more steadily in our consciousness, we experience relatedness at an elemental level. We see that it is not a matter of trying to be related, but rather of living consciously into the actuality of being related. As we yield ourselves to the living presence of this relatedness, we find that life begins to possess an ease and a freedom and a naturalness that fill our hearts with joy.[1]

Take a moment to sit quietly and experience your breath in the way described here.

Just as the breath has been the basis for most of the exercises so far, you will now begin to explore relatedness through your breathing.

### Exercise 36:
### Trading Breath

    A.  Sit down facing your partner, a comfortable distance from each other. One of you begins to breathe in, then out; as they breathe out, the other gently begins to breath in. The breath flows between you like warm water flowing from one vessel into another and back again.

    B.  As you feel energy passing with the breath you are sharing, let the breath vibrate into a tone as you give it, as if the two of you were sawing a log with a saw of sound.

    C.  When you are comfortably sharing the energy of your voices, let your vibrating breath begin to form itself into words. Speak to your partner as you give the energy of your breath. Listen as you receive your partner's breath/words; let a thought pass between you, let it be shared by you both as you share the energy of the breath. Do not be restricted to a regular rhythm; share the rhythm of your communication naturally.

You may have the experience, after some practice with this exercise, of receiving and giving energy to and from your partner on a fundamental level. Even though most dramatic scenes are based on a conflict between the characters, you and your fellow actors remain teammates working together to realize that conflict, and a deep sharing of the energy of the scene produces a more unified and rhythmic result.

In fact, when a dramatic scene is flowing as it should, there will be an unbroken cycle of shared energy passing between the actors through the chain of action and reaction that moves the scene. Sometimes it will be expressed primarily through the words of the dialogue, sometimes as motions and gestures, sometimes as silent looking, but always the energy will flow, being given and being received. When the flow of this give and take, this chain of action and reaction, is broken, the scene and the characters die. As playwright August Strindberg commented a century ago:

> No form of art is as dependent as the actor's. He cannot isolate his particular contribution, show it to someone and say, "This is mine." If he does not get the support of his fellow actors, his performance will lack resonance and depth. He will be held in check and lured into wrong inflections and wrong rhythms. He won't make a good impression no matter how hard he tries. Actors must rely on each other. Occasionally one sees an exceptionally egotistic individual who "upstages" a rival, obliterates him, in order that he and he alone can be seen.
>
> That is why rapport among actors is imperative for the success of a play. I don't care whether you rank yourselves higher or lower than each other, or from side to side, or from inside out—as long as you do it together.[2]

## WEIGHT AND RELATIONSHIP

The sense of your physical center is important to your sense of relationship on stage because we tend to relate to each other from our centers. To see the truth of this, try an experiment: stand so that your pelvis is pointed directly at your partner, then turn your head (without turning your body) so that your face points at someone off to one side. Now, who are you "facing?" That is, with whom do you seem to have the strongest relationship, your partner or the person to one side?

Take the experiment further: turn your face back toward your partner and speak to him; the person at your side interrupts by asking a question, and you turn your head to him and answer; then you turn back to the original partner and continue. Did you feel that your basic relationship with your partner was only suspended while you spoke to the person at your side, so that the side conversation was only a "parenthesis" within the unbroken relationship with your partner?

Again, speak to your partner, but this time when the person at your side interrupts, turn your pelvis toward him as you speak. Do you feel that you have now established a new relationship, that the original relationship with your partner has been broken?

What we do with the actual weight of our bodies, in real life and on the stage, is the most fundamental expression of our relationships with other persons. Since the weight of the body is literally at our center, we tend to read relationships by noticing (usually unconsciously) what people are doing with their centers.

We also tend to express how we feel about someone by the way we dispose our weight either toward or away from them. Imagine yourself in the first stages of an argument that threatens to become a fight; you are confronting your opponent with your hands raised, and you appear to be ready for combat. In this situation, rock your pelvis forward, toward the opponent. Do you feel more truly ready to attack? Now rock your pelvis away from the opponent so that your center of gravity shifts backward. Do you feel on the defensive, perhaps only pretending to fight?

There is no relationship where weight is not given or taken, and there is no way for you to "fake" a relationship if you fail to involve your weight in it. Have you ever seen student actors trying to do a love scene, perhaps even an embrace, while both were holding their weight back? Or actors on a proscenium stage standing so "cheated out" that each is facing the audience more than they are facing each other?

Neither the actors nor the audience can have a truthful sense of the relationship if either partner is falsifying the participation of his bodily center.

### Exercise 37:
### Falling in Love

Your partner stands in a relaxed alignment, and you stand about three feet behind with one foot thrust back for stability (see Figure 18). By mutual agreement and talking to each other the whole time, your partner falls gently backward into your arms, with their body straight but not stiff or tense. You gently raise them back up to their feet.

They fall only a short way at first, and then gradually farther and farther until you are catching them only a few feet above the floor. If your partner becomes frightened and "breaks" their body on the way down, or remains tense as they fall, encourage and reassure them.

Then reverse roles.

**CAUTION: DO NOT ATTEMPT THIS EXERCISE UNLESS YOU ARE CONFIDENT OF BEING ABLE TO CATCH YOUR PARTNER, FOR SERIOUS INJURY COULD RESULT.**

**FIGURE 18.**  Falling.

## TEAMWORK AND COMMITMENT

The greatness of a play lies partly in its unity, and the way in which all of its elements have been synthesized into the meaningful experience of a single dramatic event.

This same kind of unity must exist also in a good stage production, and it can be achieved only when all the many kinds of theatre artists—director, actors, designers, and technicians—have aligned their efforts toward the common goal of embodying the action of the play within the performance.

When the actors, designers and the director have worked as an ensemble in accord with the text, and the audience has likewise given of itself, there occurs one of those rare moments when true theatre lives. All these human energies flow to form one energy that is greater than the sum of its parts; everyone participating in the experience begins to receive more than they have given, and we feel ourselves truly moved beyond ourselves.

This communality is the deepest wonder of the theatre, and it depends entirely on teamwork. Teamwork results from a sense of common purpose and respect. No member of a team needs to sacrifice individuality; rather, each member contributes to the effort of all other members because their work is flowing in the same direction toward the same goal. In this way the ensemble is not a collective, but rather a group of *aligned* individuals, each of whose individual identities is enhanced by membership in the group.

Alignment of effort is achieved within the group when three conditions have been met: first, when each member is genuinely committed to the group effort; second, when each member supports the others in their particular objectives as members of the group; third, when all agree to maintain the possibility of free and open communication so that any difficulties encountered in the work can be thrashed out. Consider each of these points for a moment.

First, *commitment*: It is part of your responsibility as an actor to find a point of personal commitment to each role you play, and each play you perform. Only when you have committed to your work on a deeply personal level will it carry the necessary force to produce a truly powerful performance.

Second, *support for your partners*: We all have different reasons for acting, different reasons for doing particular roles; whatever our reasons, we must support each other's objectives, even if we do not share them. Remember that our *reasons* for being committed don't affect the quality of the work; it only matters that we *are* committed.

Finally, *free and open communication*: Creating theatre is rarely accomplished without some tension arising between members of the ensemble. No matter how friendly and supportive we may be, we are all bound to encounter differences of opinion, conflicting needs, or problems that are simply hard to solve. All of these "problems" can actually be potential opportunities for creativity *as long as we continue to communicate freely about them.* Through sharing, mutual problems can turn into mutual opportunities.

Commitment, support, and communication: these are the cornerstones of teamwork and are equal in importance to all your other acting skills.

## TRANSACTION AND TEAMWORK

So far our sense of ensemble has been based on a general sense of trust, respect, and commitment. Of even greater importance is the specific ability to enter into the teamwork that actually produces a good scene.

As we have said, it is the chain of action and reaction as the characters pursue their objectives that moves the play: this transacted energy flows through all the actors, and at any given moment one or another of them will be "carrying the ball." Each actor, then, must be good at receiving and sending the energy of the scene, since each transaction is a link in the chain that moves the play, and a chain—as we all know—is only as strong as its weakest link. This is why Strindberg said that "actors must rely on each other."

This transfer of energy from actor to actor can be described as a continual process of receiving and sending, leading and following, in which all the actors are both leaders and followers simultaneously. The next sequence of exercises will give you the experience of this simultaneous interdependence of actors and will stress the importance of your sensory responsiveness to your partner in achieving active relatedness.

### Exercise 38:
### Leading and Following

A. BLIND LEADING. You and your partner lightly interlace fingertips up to the first joint. Your partner closes their eyes, and you silently lead them around the room. As you gain confidence and control, begin to move faster and extend the range of your travels. Soon you can run! If your situation permits, you can even take a trip to a destination.

Reverse roles and repeat for the trip back.

B. SOUND LEADING. Begin as above, but when you are well underway, break physical contact and begin to lead your partner by repeating a single word which they follow by sound alone. Again, extend your range and speed. Run!

**CAUTION: BE PREPARED TO GRAB YOUR PARTNER TO PREVENT A COLLISION!**

Check yourself in these exercises: as follower, did you truly commit your weight to your movement, or were you only "pretending" to move while still holding your weight cautiously back? As leader, did you truly help the blind partner to follow?

Watch other partnerships at work: do you see how intense and connected to each other they seem? Our listening and seeing of each other on stage should always have this kind of literal intensity; you will be leading and following each other during a scene just as much as you did in this exercise.

### Exercise 39:
### Cookie Search

All stand together in a clump at the center of your space and close your eyes. Then all spin about a few times until you are disoriented.

Next, move slowly in whatever direction you are facing until you reach a wall or other obstacle. Avoid touching anyone else; feel your way with all of your nonvisual senses.

When all have gone as far as they can (and still have not opened their eyes), begin to search for your partner using only the word "cookie." You must identify every person you touch before moving on, until at last you and your partner find each other.

When you are together, open your eyes and wait in silence for all to finish. Feel the drama of the exercise.

In this exercise you were not led, but had to find your own way toward your partner's sound. Did you feel lonely while searching for your partner and relieved when you found them? Don't be the kind of actor who makes his stage partners feel lonely!

As you have experienced in these exercises, connectedness depends on how well you see, hear, and feel your partner at all times. As simple as this may seem, such significant seeing and hearing are fairly rare on the stage. Some actors are only superficially aware of their teammates; they are aware instead only of what they themselves are doing, and reacting only to their premeditated picture of what they would like their partner to be doing. While such premeditated and false reactions can sometimes fool an audience, the ensemble effort and therefore the play as a whole, will inevitably suffer.

### Exercise 40:
### Mirrors

A.  You and a partner decide who is "A" and who is "B." Stand facing each other; "A" makes slow "underwater" movements that "B" can mirror completely; try to keep the partnership moving in unison. The movements flow organically in a continual changing stream; avoid repeated patterns. Notice that bigger, more complete and more continual movement is easier to follow. Notice also that communication must be a two-way street; "B" can be a better mirror when "A" is also responding to "B".

At a signal from the group leader, the roles are instantly reversed without a break in the action. "B" is now the leader; "A" is the follower. Continue moving from the deep centers of your bodies; feel yourselves beginning to share a common center through your shared movement; with it comes a common breath. Vocalize the breath and continue to share this common sound, which arises organically from your movement.

The roles are reversed a few more times by a signal from the group leader; each time the leadership role changes, the movement and sound continue without interruption.

At last, there is no leader; neither "A" nor "B" leads, but both follow and the partnership continues to move and make sound together. At another signal, both will close their eyes for a few moments while continuing to move, then open them again. How well did you stay together?

B.  Begin again, but this time "A" makes noise (without moving) that makes "B" move; "A" uses sound as a tangible, physical force to control the movement of "B." Again, at a signal from the group leader, the roles are instantly reversed without a break in the action. Gradually, the follower begins to "talk back" to the leader (with sounds but not words). Finally, a "sound scene" begins to pass back and forth between you with a sense of give and take, action and reaction.

Now that you have begun to expand your awareness beyond yourself to your partners, you must also explore the space you inhabit. This will be the business of the next Lesson.

# Lesson
# Eight

# The Performance Environment

In everyday life, we function within our environment and just as we effect it, it effects us. Our environment has physical, psychological, and social aspects which profoundly influence our behavior and experience. We are constantly interacting with our world and are inseparable from it; we can have no meaningful sense of ourselves without a heightened awareness of the world in which we live.

As an actor, you have a special relationship to your workspace. Your job is to allow the "inner" or "private" world of the character to become "public" by finding audible and visible manifestations of that world within the performance space. The audience sees your performance in relationship to that space, and the nature of the space itself colors the experience so powerfully that it literally becomes one of the characters of the piece. You must therefore achieve the same sense of integration and control of your performance space as you have of your own body and voice.

Unfortunately, most of us go through life largely unaware of the space we inhabit, and sometimes even feel isolated from it; this sense of physical isolation inside our "bags of skin" reflects a sense of psychological and spiritual isolation from the world in which we live. Philosopher Alan Watts expressed it this way:

We suffer from a hallucination, from a false and distorted sense of our own existence as living organisms. Most of us have the sensation that "I myself" is a separate center of feeling and action, living inside and bounded by the physical body—a center which "confronts" an "external" world of people and things, making contact through the senses with a universe both alien and strange. Everyday figures of speech reflect this illusion. "I came into this world," "You must face reality," "The conquest of nature." This feeling of being lonely and very temporary visitors in the universe is in flat contradiction to everything known about man (and all other living organisms) in the sciences. We do not "come into" this world; we come out of it, as leaves from a tree. As the ocean "waves," the universe "peoples." Every individual is an expression of the whole realm of nature, a unique action of the total universe.[1]

Your sense of wholeness, then, depends not only on the internal integration you have studied so far, but also on your sense of oneness with both the physical and psychological aspects of your environment. The process of developing an open and responsive relationship to the world outside your skin starts with an exploration of the physical space which you inhabit, and which inhabits you.

### Exercise 41:
### Swimming in Space

After relaxing and placing yourself in standing alignment, begin to move continuously around your space.

A. Moving freely and effortlessly through space, concentrate your whole attention on the fluidity of your movement; become aware of the physical actuality of the space itself as you move through it, of the eddies and currents in space that you are making. Uncover as much of your skin as possible, and feel the resistance of the air as you move, swimming in the ocean of air.

B. Now become aware that every breath you take actually takes in space; you are not only swimming through space, but space is swimming through you.

   The space that you are moving through is a fluid, and there is fluid in every joint and cavity of your body as well. Swim until you feel at one with your space, moving through it, it moving through you, and being carried along by it.

C. As you move, notice that you carry along a certain amount of space; awareness of this will help you to move smoothly, so as not to violate the momentum of your "envelope" of space (unless, of course, such awkward movement is demanded by your role).

D. Now become aware of the total space of the room and all the objects, including yourself, that it contains; see how every movement of your own and every movement of every other person in the space influences the total space.

As you can experience in this exercise, your sense of space is part of your overall awareness of the Here and Now, and your ability to share space with your fellow actors is part of your ability to contact them and help create a sense of ensemble.

Moreover, the stage is a special kind of space: even when empty it has an almost "holy" quality, and we feel the potentiality of the events which are meant to occur upon it. For the next exercise, it is important that you work on a real stage.

### Exercise 42:
### Exploring the Stage

A.  As a group, move at random throughout the stage space; attempt to influence one another's space as you move continually through the stage area. See what effect you have on others by sweeping by them, pushing space at them, and so on; notice also what effect they have on you.

B.  Each of you closes your eyes and, keeping them closed, each moves very slowly throughout the stage space, trying not to touch any physical object or person. Search with your skin, hearing, and smelling for open space; crawl, stretch on tiptoe—whatever is necessary to find the most uninhabited space, but keep moving. See how, through practice, you can move with fewer and fewer collisions. Move more and more freely. Any object or person touched must be identified before moving on.

## TYPES OF STAGES

The famine in ancient Thebes, the capture of Joan of Arc, a fight in a waterfront bar, God confronting mankind, mankind confronting nothingness; it all happens on a stage. The actor can make a stage seem like any place and any time; but it is, first of all, a stage. Until you have come to grips with the physical reality of the stage, you have no foundation upon which to build further; the stage is your space, your environment, your world as an actor. You must work in the Here and Now; the stage is the "here."

Most important, being fully in touch with "where you are" on stage provides a point of contact between you and your environment that anchors and focuses your work. What you create is thus made more "real" and tangible by its derivation from your physical actuality on stage.

What exactly is a stage? It is any area in which actors create for their audience the patterned experience called drama. The spatial relationship of stage and audience is what makes the difference between one sort of stage and another. While your immediate concern may be the stage proper, that stage is only an artificially separated area within the larger theatre. It is the

**FIGURE 19.**  Exploring the Stage.

total theatrical space that is your true working area, and the stage derives
its meaning only from its relation to this total space.

Stages come in many sizes, shapes, and types. Anyone who has played
"on the road," moving from one theatre to another, has had a vivid experience of the importance of an actor's responsiveness to the theatrical space.
Never before has such a wide variety of stage types, each of which demands
a somewhat different spatial attitude, confronted the actor. The basic four
types are *proscenium, thrust, arena,* and *environmental,* though there are
many variations (see Figure 20). Let's consider each of the basic types.

**Proscenium.** The traditional proscenium stage features an arch
through which the audience sees the action. This "picture frame" evolved as
a way of establishing a point of reference for settings painted in perspective
(hence the word pro-scenium which means in *front of the scene*).

The actor on the proscenium stage must realize that the audience is
limited to one side of the playing area. Standing behind the sofa during a
crucial scene may not be a good idea, nor is moving upstage so that the
other actors have to turn their backs on the audience in order to speak
to you (hence the dreaded charge of "upstaging"). But the possibilities of
good proscenium movement are greater than you might think, and it is

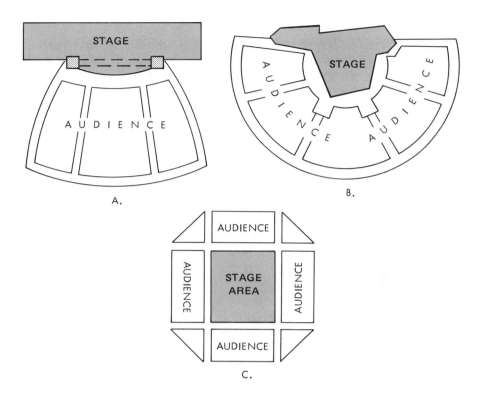

**FIGURE 20.** Types of Stages. (A) traditional proscenium; (B) modern thrust; (C) full-round or "arena":

certainly not necessary to "cheat out" (to turn your body partly out toward the audience). This makes you look as if you are more interested in speaking to the audience than to the person on stage with you. Don't underestimate how much acting you can do with your back; Strindberg said it was beyond his "wildest expectation" that he should ever see an actor's back during an important scene. Thus, while you may make some adjustments because of the audience's location, you must do so without destroying the internal logic of the character's environment.

*Thrust.* In the 1950s the thrust stage (so called because it "thrusts" into the midst of the audience) became very popular. It features the same stage/audience relationship as the Classical and Elizabethan theatres and places the actor into close proximity with the audience, but also limits the use of scenery. For this reason, it is very much an "actor's" theatre and "theatrical pieces," like the classics, sometimes seem more at home here than realistic plays do. Locations on a thrust can be described in the same way as on a proscenium stage, though here you are freer to form three-dimensional patterns. There is some added responsibility to keep *open* to audience view, or at least to distribute your presence equally to all sections of the house, but the increased sense of audience contact inherent in the thrust stage makes such accommodation easy and natural.

*Arena.*   The arena and other types of full-round stages stand at the opposite extreme from proscenium stages. Here the actor enters through the audience area, either down the aisles or from openings cut into the sloped audience area (called "vomitoria"). The actor's problem of keeping open to all sections of the audience is more acute here than on a thrust stage, and you always have your back to someone. The full-round offers a sense of intimacy unlike any other type of stage, and such theatres are usually quite small. For this reason, audiences tend to expect a more detailed and subtle performance here, something closer to what is required for the camera.

*Environmental.*   While most stages are of the three basic types described above, we see increasingly the creation of special environments for specific productions, some of which may abandon entirely the separation of stage and audience. Here, of course, the proximity of the audience demands total commitment and attention to detail, as for film acting. For example, my production of Kafka's *The Trial*, was mounted as an enormous fun house; audience groups of twelve people moved from room to room, each accompanied by an actor performing the role of the hero, Joseph K., and in each of the fifteen rooms a scene from the novel was played out. Conversations between actor and audience arose spontaneously as the groups moved through the environment. A similar environment was created recently for the play *Tamara*, only here the audience was free to move at will throughout a recreated Italian villa in which ten story lines were continuously interwoven.

Whatever kind of stage you are on, your adaptation to the positioning of the audience, the vocal demands of the shape and size of the house, and to the configuration of the stage is essential. Your work is not complete until it has been successfully communicated to your audience.

## DIRECTIONS ON STAGE

Part of being fully at home on a stage involves the ability to find your way around according to the traditional terms used by directors and playscripts. Though there are many different kinds of stages today, we generally use the nomenclature developed for the proscenium.

*Vertical Directions.*   As we mentioned above, the proscenium stage developed as a kind of "picture frame" to establish the forced perspective of the Renaissance stage setting. To enhance this forced perspective, the stage floor was sometimes sloped, or "raked," upward away from the audience. For this reason we still speak of "*down*stage" as being toward the audience and "*up*stage" as being away from the audience, since the stage floor was once actually sloped in this way. To stand "level" with another actor is for both of you to stand perpendicular (in profile) to the audience.

*Lateral directions* are determined by the actor's right or left as they face the audience. Thus *stage right* is the same as the audience's left; *downstage right* means toward the audience and to the actor's right (see Figure 21).

*Turns* are described as being either *in* (toward the center of the stage, whichever side of the stage you are on) or *out* (again, *away* from center).

*Crossing* (that is, moving from one point to another) is usually not in a straight line, but in a slight arc, so that you end the cross facing more profile to the audience than you would if the cross were a straight line. A cross with an exaggerated arc is called a "circle cross" (or sometimes called a "banana").

*Positions as you pivot* relative to the audience are called "one quarter," "half," and "three-quarters" depending on how far you turn from one side to the other. Thus a director may tell you to "cheat out one-quarter," which means to pivot 45 degrees away from center.

This system of directions must become second nature to you. Here is an exercise which will help you to master it.

### Exercise 43:
### Directions On Stage

Have your partner stand in the center of the stage and stand beside them on the stage right side; they will "play director" by giving you the following

**FIGURE 21.**  Traditional Locations on a Proscenium Stage.

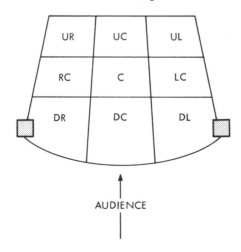

directions. Keep at it until you are able to respond to each term without much conscious thought, then reverse positions.

Go down right. / Turn out and go up right. / Turn and cheat down one-half. / Take a long cross down left, going upstage of me. / Turn in and do a circle cross up, passing on the downstage side of me and ending level with me on the right. / Cheat out one-quarter. / Now turn in one-quarter. / Go straight down and hold center. / Circle up to the right around me and exit left center.

The blocking for film and television is an even more critical matter. Here your movements are expressed not in feet but in inches! Once a shot has been established by the director and cameraman, strips of colored tape are placed on the floor to mark the exact position of each actor's feet; if there are movements within the shot, each interim destination is marked in the same way. As you do the scene, you must "hit your marks" exactly, without looking down! It can even matter which foot your weight is on, since the composition of the shot may require your head to be in a precise location at a precise time.

The nature of film also requires that your eye movements be "blocked;" that is, you must look in precisely the right place at the right time, since the apparent location of the other character must be exactly the right distance away from the lens. If the "eye line" isn't consistent in the various shots of a scene, it can't be edited together. Eye movements are also one of the major factors that determine when an edit will be made, so you may have to provide "a look" to a precise point at a precise time in order to shift focus to another character. Usually, the other actors will stand off camera in the correct locations, but not always.

As difficult as all this sounds, even this kind of critical positioning becomes second nature after a time, and so must your sense of position on stage.

## PATTERNING YOUR
## SPACE ON STAGE

Your movement through space, considered by itself, may have the same kind of abstract beauty as kinetic sculpture or modern dance, but its effectiveness as theatrical movement depends on its ability to express meaningful relationships.

The patterned use of space in a stage performance is called *blocking*. Good stage blocking is much more than the creation of pleasing spatial arrangements; it must also reflect the underlying action of a scene expressed as spatial cause and effect, as well as basic character relationships. Who is dominant at this moment in the scene? What space do they control? Who is on their side? Who is on the attack? Who is retreating? When do they counterattack? These are the kinds of things that determine spatial relationships on the stage.

Though the director is traditionally responsible for blocking, there are a number of ways in which directors approach it. A few preplan the blocking in detail and lay it out for the actors at an early stage of rehearsal (this may be especially necessary in large cast shows or with highly stylized material); most directors prefer the actors to provide the basic movement impulses which generate the blocking, with the director then editing the pattern as needed. Some directors do no blocking at all, waiting for the actors to find the spatial patterns which best express the action of the scene as it unfolds during the rehearsal process.

No matter how the director works, it is the actor's responsiveness to stage movement that makes the blocking truly expressive and not merely "dead" motion, as you will see in the next section. Even without a director's help, you should be able to utilize your stage environment to create spatially logical patterns that express the action of your scene and your relationship to other characters.

Here is an exercise to help you experience the power of stage positioning as an expression of relationship between people.

### Exercise 44:
### Relationship in Space

With a partner, select a simple relationship (for example, mother/son, husband/wife, policeman/criminal, and so on).

Select also a simple message and reply with strong emotional potential (for example, "I'm not mad anymore," and "I still hate your guts").

Begin, without further planning, to move in relationship to each other around the stage. Use no words. Simply move until a spatial relationship emerges that communicates the relationship, message, and reply.

Though this sense of spatial relationship is artistically heightened on the stage, it is based on our sense of blocking in everyday life. Some years ago, I worked at a psychiatric institute helping to analyze the videotapes of family therapy sessions. It was tremendously revealing to notice where people sat in relation to others, who they faced and who they avoided, how patterns of aggression and retreat were expressed by movements, or simply by the shifting of weight when seated. Spend a few days watching the "blocking" of everyday life; notice how attitude, relationship, and action are expressed in the way people place themselves in a room and in relationship to each other.

**FIGURE 22.** Spatial
Relationship Exercises.

## JUSTIFYING THE BLOCKING

Blocking is "dead" movement until it is endowed with meaning by the way you use and experience it as the character.

For example, if the director suggests that you move upstage of the sofa while you say, "I don't want to hear this," that movement may be desirable for spatial or pictorial considerations: the director may, for instance, want you to move there so that focus is thrown to a doorway through which someone is about to enter.

At first, this movement may feel stiff and unnatural, and probably would appear that way to an audience: but as you find ways to *justify* the movement—that is, *to incorporate it as a believable action performed by the character out of a real need*—it no longer seems like a merely compositional movement and has become an expressive part of the whole world of the play. You might, in this example, find that your character needs to protect themself from what the other person is saying at this moment, and so goes to "hide" behind the sofa. By justifying your movement and your spatial relationship to the setting and the other actors, your blocking comes to express a meaning and logic both as good composition *and* as an expression of the dramatic action.

You will also find that the *timing* of lines and crosses makes a critical difference. Deciding whether you should say "I don't want to hear this" before, during, or after the move can change the psychological meaning of the line. These decisions must often be made by trial and error, though this sense of timing is something that will eventually be intuitive: for now, you should sensitize yourself to the differences. Here is an exercise that will give you an opportunity to do this.

### Exercise 45:
### A Blocking Scene

Here again is the blocking pattern you learned in Exercise 44, *Directions On Stage*. This time, we are adding dialogue, so that the blocking appears as stage directions in a playscript (your partner remains at center stage throughout, though they may turn to face you as you move).

> YOU: I've had enough of this. (*Go down right.*)
> PARTNER: I'm really sorry.
> YOU: (*Turn out and go up right*) That's what you said the last time.
> PARTNER: This time I really mean it.
> YOU: (*Turn and cheat down one-half*) I'm not falling for it this time. (*Take a long cross down left, going upstage of partner*) Every time this happens, I end up taking the blame, but not this time. (*Turn in and do a circle cross up, passing on the downstage side of partner and ending level with them on the right*) This time, you are going to have to take your share of the responsibility! (*Cheat out one-quarter*)

And don't look at me like that. (*Turn in one-quarter*) I know you
think I'll probably give in eventually. (*Go straight down and hold
center and speak to audience*) And you know, I probably will. (*Circle
up to the right around partner and stop at left center*) But at least
not for a while! (*exit*)

Justify these movements by entering into the situation: feel what the
relationship might be.

Experiment with timing the crosses to the lines: should a particular
line come before, during, or after the cross?

## THE GROUNDPLAN
## AND THE PSYCHOLOGICAL
## ASPECTS OF THE SET

As we have seen, the performance environment has two main aspects: the
*spatial*, dealing with the size, configuration and other objective properties
of the set, and the *psychological*, dealing with the ways in which the performance environment both expresses and effects the behavior and thought
of the characters.

These two aspects are integral with one another, since the size, shape,
and psychological nature of a space has a profound influence on the action
which occurs within it. The environment in which the play occurs has
been determined by the playwright as part of the given circumstances of
the play (these will be studied in the next few lessons); these environmental
properties are realized physically by your director and the various designers.

The shaping of the stage space and the placement of entrances is a
decision made with particular care by the director and scenic designer; we
call this the creation of the *groundplan*, and it establishes much that influences the blocking and the action itself. When directors and designers
discuss groundplan and setting, for instance, they often pay special attention to "territoriality": to whom does the space belong? Whose taste does
it reflect? Are there areas within it which belong to certain persons (like
Archie Bunker's chair)? Do the entrances and exits reflect status or relationship (for example, strangers use the front door, while family and friends
come in through the kitchen)?

Remember the hostess/guest scene: do you see how the prolonged
encounter at the door, the guest's unwillingness to cross the threshold and
enter the hostess's territory, expressed the situation? Once inside, the guest
refused to surrender his coat as a symbol that he was only a temporary
visitor, that he "didn't belong." How would you imagine him moving in
that room? How would he sit in a chair? How would he eat?

Usually, the scenic design has been completed before rehearsals begin.
As soon as the actors get up on their feet the groundplan will be taped out

on the floor of the rehearsal hall, and a picture or model of the set will be shown to them. It is important that you be able to visualize the space as it will eventually be and begin to work within it early on, so that you are ready to move onto the real set with minimum disruption, and so that the meaningful aspects of the design as selected by the director and designer have a chance to contribute to your creative process.

The other aspects of the physical set and costumes, like the period, decor, color, and so on, will likewise be determined by the director and the costume and lighting designers. Finally, however, *you* must endow the space you inhabit with the subjective properties it requires. No amount of scenery, costuming, and lighting will compensate for the actor's failure to "live" in the character's world, while a skillful actor can create a whole world on an empty stage through the completeness of "being there."

In the next Part you will learn to identify those aspects of the character's world as created by the playwright which are most influential on the action of the play; for now, notice how the psychological implications of an environment may influence the events which occur within it.

### Exercise 46:
### The Psychological Space

Repeat your Blocking Scene from the previous exercise. Place the scene in each of the following situations; experience how each influences the relationship and the action.

A. In your bedroom at 3 a.m.;
B. In your partner's office at 10 a.m.;
C. In a public library on a cold winter day;
D. In a bar on a sweltering and rowdy Saturday night.

## THE SCALE OF PERFORMANCE

The type and size of the performance space requires a fundamental adaptation in the size or scale of the performance. Adjusting the scale of performance is a matter of increasing or decreasing its size without distorting the content, just as you might raise or lower the contrast or color level on a television set without changing the content of the picture.

As we said when discussing vocal projection, an intimate scene can be played in a large theatre by making an overall increase in its size and volume, as long as the behavior and attitudes of the characters continue to conform to the demands of intimacy in all other respects. Your audience accepts the necessity of the adjustment and by convention will reinterpret the scene in their own minds to compensate for it.

In the live theatre, the problem of scale is usually a matter of enlargement; for certain intimate spaces (such as a small full-round stage or an environmental production) you may need to reduce scale so as to focus on the minute details of physical and vocal behavior which might be "washed out" in a larger space. The most extreme instance of small-scale work is acting for the camera. Because of its closeness, the camera lens tends literally *to record your thinking*; it is usually "too much" for the camera if you do anything more than *think* your way through a scene and allow the rest of your behavior to remain as it would be in life; some actors have to actually suppress their real-life behavior for the camera! Many of the actors who act both on stage and for the camera report the importance of learning to "do nothing" for the camera.

Since small details of behavior are usually beyond the bounds of conscious control, the completeness of your inner work and the intensity of your concentration are at a premium before the camera or in intimate theatrical situations. In general, we can say that *as the external scale of a scene decreases, the level of inner dynamic must increase.*

Scale is determined not only by the size and distance of the audience, but also by the style of the material being performed. Broad comedy and especially farce, for instance, depend on a size, energy, and tempo of performance which is heightened beyond the limits of everyday behavior; on the other hand, the comedic naturalism of Chekhov places behavior "under the microscope" of a nearly scientific scrutiny, and great meaning is attached to even the tiniest details, so a more filmic approach is needed here.

Your ability to adjust the scale of your performance to fit the needs of your stage and the style of the play is innate: we regularly adapt the size of our behavior to fit different contexts. This automatic and usually unconscious life process is also the way you will adjust scale in performance, except that the extremes of largeness or smallness are often far greater when acting than in everyday life.

Especially when doing larger forms of performance, it will be important that you do not judge the scale of your performance according to your everyday kinetic sense. I have sometimes videotaped large-scale performances in a wide shot that approximates the way a live audience would see the stage, and when they see themselves the actors invariably say, "I thought I was moving more than that!" Perhaps they had increased the scale of their movement 25% beyond their real-life range, and it felt like a tremendous stretch, but an extension of 50% or more was actually needed!

**Exercise 47:**
**Changing Scale**

Repeat again the Blocking Scene, playing it in each of the following situations, making the adjustment of scale required for each. It will help enormously if you can actually move into physical spaces that are roughly the right size for each.

A. You are being filmed in an extremely close two-shot, so that you move around your partner as required by the blocking pattern with your faces never more than a foot apart;

B. You are in a small full/round theatre at true-to-life size;

C. In a moderately large thrust theatre;

D. In an enormous proscenium theatre.

In each, keep the quality of the scene as unchanged as possible.

## THE AUDIENCE AS ENVIRONMENT

When you perform, you join a community dedicated to experiencing the insights and aliveness offered by the drama. You, your fellow actors, and the audience all work together to achieve this experience, and you each have your own task to perform. Sometimes as actors we forget this, and we think that our sole job is to please our audience, to "play to" them and to show them what our character is feeling and thinking.

This kind of illustrative acting falsifies the character's reality: it says, "look at me! I'll show you what my character is doing, thinking, feeling!" We call this kind of acting *indicating*. Your job is not to *show* us anything, it is simply to *do* it and *become* it. Try to remember, then, that the audience's reaction is *not* the immediate purpose of your performance. Your immediate task as an actor on the stage is always *to do what is necessary at the moment to fulfill your character's dramatic purpose within the play as a whole.*

Your audience's response is certainly important, and you shape your performance with a desire to make the performance accessible to them; but when you are actually performing, your immediate concentration is on what you, as the character, are doing, *not* on the audience's response to it. Your character's task is the foreground of your awareness, and your audience is the background against which you work.

Perhaps it will help to think of the audience's presence as part of your stage environment. To be in touch with your total environment, you must accept the audience's presence just as you accept the presence of your fellow actors. You, your fellow actors, and your audience are all teammates working together to create the drama. You do not "play to" your audience, any more than you "play to" your fellow actors. You play "with" them, and all are working together toward the same goal.

This paradoxical idea of working with complete commitment to your stage reality while simultaneously accepting the audience's presence was summed up by Stanislavski in the term *public solitude*. As a student, Stanislavski suffered from a terrible self-consciousness while on stage; he couldn't forget that he was in front of an audience, and his acting seemed artificial. Then one day, his teacher gave him the simple task of counting the floorboards on the stage floor; it seemed like an odd request, but Stanislavski went ahead while the teacher proceeded with the class. After a time, Stanislavski realized that everyone was watching him, but he had become so engrossed in his task that he had "forgotten" for the first time that he was on a stage! (From this discovery came the idea of playing *objectives*, which we will study in the next Lesson.)

This, then, is the question: Can you work in public "as if" you were in private? Can the content of your performance remain true to the inner world of the character, while it is simultaneously being expressed in a public form worthy of an audience's attention?

This is a form of *dual consciousness* that is required by all acting: to hold the experience of the character (who is "in private") simultaneously with your own awareness as an actor (who is "in public") and fulfilling the demands of both, perhaps even bringing the two into synthesis as a single compound experience!

### Exercise 48:
### Public Solitude

Repeat your Blocking Scene, or simply review your previous performances of it: was your awareness solidly rooted in what your character was doing, or did your awareness of your audience cause you to "indicate?" Ask those who watched your performance to comment on this.

# Summary To Part One

# Discipline

This completes our brief survey of the actor's tools. The material we have covered in these lessons represents the beginnings of a life's work. Advanced training in voice, speech, and movement goes far beyond what has been suggested here, and will continue to challenge and benefit you for the rest of your acting life. Do what you can to seek out such training.

Also seek out opportunities to explore related training in such skills as mime, singing, dancing, clowning, combat, Aikido and other Oriental martial arts, as well as tumbling, and meditation. Each can contribute in its way to your acting skill.

Technique is the means whereby you are able to embody your conception; the word "craft," remember, comes from the German word for "power." As playwright David Mamet put it:

> This is what can and must be passed from one generation to the next. Technique—a knowledge of how to translate inchoate desire into clean action—into action capable of communicating itself to the audience.
>
> This technique, this care, this love of precision, of cleanliness, this love of the theatre, is the best way, for it is love of the *audience*—of that which *unites* the actor and the house; a desire to share something which they know to be true.[1]

Just as most religious disciplines involve physical and vocal activity (chanting, meditating, davening, whirling, dancing) so your work on the techniques of acting will be the mechanism of your total psychophysical and spiritual development.

This is personal discipline in the best sense: your acceptance of the responsibility for your own development through systematic effort, not because you are ordered to do so by someone else or compelled by some external criteria, like a grade or a good review or landing a job, but because you choose to become all that you can be in order to contribute as much as you can to your world through your work.

Discipline is rooted in your respect for yourself, for your fellow workers, as well as for your work, and for the world you serve through that work. Poor discipline is really a way of saying, "I'm not worth it," or "what I do isn't worth it." Discipline will come naturally if you can acknowledge the importance and seriousness of your work. The director Eugenio Barba put it this way in a letter to an undisciplined actor:

> First of all, one gets the impression that your acts are not dictated by that interior conviction or undeniable need which would show itself in the execution of an exercise, or of an improvisation or a scene. . . . You have not proven to yourself the importance of what you want to share with the spectators. How, then, can you hope that the spectator will be captivated by your actions? . . .
>
> The second tendency which I see in you is the fear of considering the complete seriousness of our work: you find the need to laugh, to snigger, to pass humorous remarks upon whatever you and your classmates happen to be performing. It is as if you wanted to flee that responsibility which you sense is joined to our work and which consists of establishing a communication with other men and of facing up to the consequences you discover thereby. . . .
>
> I believe you have never considered that all you are doing, delivering, shaping in your work belongs to the phenomena of life and that as such it deserves consideration and respect.[2]

Discipline also involves regularity. Your work, especially on technical skills, must be a daily affair. Stanislavski, looking back late in his life, had this to say:

> Let someone explain to me why the violinist who plays in an orchestra on the tenth violin must daily perform hour-long exercises or lose his power to play? Why does the dancer work daily over every muscle in his body? Why do the painter, the sculptor, the writer practice their art each day and count that day lost when they do not work? And why may the dramatic artist do nothing, spend his day in coffee houses and hope for the gift [of inspiration] in the evening? Enough. Is this an art when its priests speak like amateurs? There is no art that does not demand virtuosity.[3]

You must have the patience to work each day, to let your techniques and understanding develop slowly. Learning to act is the development of patient, persistent self-discipline.

Patience and a sense of striving together—being able to accept the momentary failure for the sake of the long-range success—are the attitudes that you must nurture. The pressures of our educational system and of the commercial theatre are against these attitudes, as is the normal desire of all of us to be "successful" right now. Resist your desire to be an overnight star and instead explore a variety of approaches and experiences. Most of your explorations will lead up blind alleys, but it is better to suffer momentary disappointments now than to commit yourself to an approach or an attitude that may limit you later. Your discipline is dedicated to the whole of your career. Again, David Mamet:

> Those of you who are called to strive to bring a new theatre, the theatre of your generation, to the stage, are set down for a very exciting life.
>
> You will be pulling against an increasingly strong current, and as you do so, you will reap the great and priceless reward of knowing yourself a truly mature man or woman—if, in the midst of the panic which surrounds you, which calls itself common sense, or commercial viability, you are doing your job simply and well.
>
> If you are going to work in the true theatre, that job is a great job in this time of final decay; that job is to bring to your fellows, through the medium of your understanding and skill, the possibility of communion with what is essential in us all: that we are born to die, that we strive and fail, that we live in ignorance of why we were placed here, and, that, in the midst of this we need to love and be loved, but we are afraid.[4]

# Part Two: Action

# Introduction to Part Two

In Part One you began preparing the ground of your physical, vocal, and psychological skills. These skills will give you power that must be focused within the process of acting itself.

The key that unlocks your power as an actor is the concept of *action*, and this idea and its many aspects will be explored in detail in the next lessons. First, however, we must clear up a common confusion regarding the term "action."

The term was first used in reference to drama over two thousand years ago by the philosopher Aristotle. When describing what happens in a play, he used the word *praxis* (in the same sense of "a doing which accomplishes something" from which we get the word *practical*). For Aristotle, the action of a play is the underlying energy which drives the story. It is not the same thing as the plot, but it causes the events of the plot to occur. For instance, he might have said that the events which occur in Tennessee Williams' *Glass Menagerie* are driven by the underlying struggle between the sense of family duty and the need we all have to find our independent identity. This kind of an action is both "dramatic" and "universal" because it involves a conflict which all children experience as they grow up and leave home.

It is this Aristotelian sense of "dramatic action" which people refer to when they speak of "the action of the play" or "the action in this scene."

Early in this century, however, the term "action" began to be used in a different sense when referring to the acting process. The great Russian director, Constantin Stanislavski, was dissatisfied with the bravura acting style of his time. Too often, he felt, the actor's display of emotion and technique became an end in itself and overshadowed the values of the play. In reaction, he created a new system of acting aimed at economy, greater psychological truthfulness, and above all respect for the ideas of the play.

He based his system on the idea that everything an actor did externally had to be justified by an internal need. As he said:

> There are no physical actions divorced from some desire, some effort in some direction, some objective. . . Everything that happens on the stage has a definite purpose.[1]

It is this Stanislavskian sense of action as *a purposeful doing directed toward a specific objective* that we will use throughout this book.

This having been said, we turn now to the most important single element of your training as an actor, the concept of *action*.

# Lesson
# Nine

# Action and Objective

Imagine a bare light bulb burning in a room; the light it produces doesn't have much effect because it is dispersed in all directions at once. But when we put a reflector behind it and a lens in front of it, we can channel most of its light in one direction, producing a greater effect. We have also made the light more controllable, for the beam of our spotlight can now be colored, shaped, and focused upon a specific objective.

As an actor, your physical and psychic energies are enhanced by the same kind of focus, a single direction or channel through which they may flow toward a single objective. When your energy is focused or concentrated in this way, it becomes, like the spotlight, more potent and controllable.

Such a complete focus of energy has the further value of helping you to synthesize a wide variety of skills, uniting them in a single rhythmic action. The baseball hitter, for instance, rehearses his stance, grip, swing, and breathing; he studies the opposing pitchers and learns their patterns; at the plate, he takes note of the wind, the light, and the position of the fielders: but as he actually begins to swing at a pitch, he ceases to deal with all these matters separately and focuses all of his immediate awareness on the ball. His swing becomes a total, simultaneous action of mind and body into which flow all his rehearsed and intuitive skills which are synthesized into a single, rhythmic gesture of focused energy. Just so, your focus on an objective at the moment of performance can provide you with the same kind of *rhythmic integration.*

Such focus of energy also makes you more *interesting* to an observer. For example, a Canadian mime I once saw began his performances in a striking way: the first spectators to arrive found him sitting alone on the stage, applying his white-face make-up. He worked simply and without the slightest embellishment, but his concentration and involvement were so complete that the spectators quickly became engrossed in watching him. As more and more spectators arrived, they too fell silent and watched in rapt attention. As the hall filled, the intensity of the experience grew, as if the spectators were adding their energy and attention to his, and indeed they were. When at last he finished, many minutes after the theatre was full, there was a tremendous ovation. The bond with the audience which his simple but total action had created was unbreakable for the rest of the evening.

In acting terms, we say that someone with this kind of total focus on a specific objective is "in action."

We often see people in life who are completely in action: an athlete executing a difficult play, people arguing a deeply felt issue, a student studying for a big test, two lovers engrossed in one another. All these people have one thing in common: they are totally focused on what they are doing because they are trying to accomplish something which they consider important; they have a *personally significant objective.* The more important the objective is, the greater and more total is the focus, and the more compelling and powerful, unselfconscious and committed the person becomes.

It is also true that people *reveal* more about themselves when they are in action than at any other time; actions *do* speak louder than words. When someone is in action, we recognize that their energy is totally taken up by what they are doing, and that there is none "left over" for selfaggrandizement or deception; they are so busy *doing* that they have no energy left for *showing* (or, as we call it in acting, *indicating*). As a result, we always judge someone who is fully in action as being authentic and sincere.

All these are powerful reasons why being in action, *having a highly committed focus on a personally significant objective,* is the best state for you as an actor. Through this focus, you may achieve integration of skills, grace, unselfconsciousness, command of your audience's attention, and believability.

## ACTION IN LIFE

You can recall people you have seen who were in action; sporting events, for example, offer abundant opportunities to see people totally focused on personally significant objectives. Watching someone in action is by itself an invigorating and satisfying experience; they seem so "alive" that we feel more alive as we watch them.

The experience of watching someone in action becomes even more exciting when we add conditions that produce suspense, like an unresolved issue with the outcome in doubt, a deadline or some other source of urgency. These, then, are the essential elements of drama: a character with a commitment to a personally significant objective in an urgent situation with an unknown outcome. Situations which combine all these elements are those which we experience as being the most dramatic in life, and on the stage or screen.

For you as an actor, the experiences of being in action which you have had in life can be an important reference for developing the same kind of heightened focus on stage. Think back: In your life you have had experiences during which you were totally "tuned in" to something you were doing, so engrossed in your activity that you became totally unselfconscious, oblivious of passing time or of outside distractions. At these times, you were in what Stanislavski called *public solitude*, and it is this state which enables an athlete to achieve total concentration while making a play in front of millions of spectators. While you were thus "in action," your energy was naturally, unselfconsciously drawn forth; you were integrated with your world in an effortless, rhythmic manifestation of life energy which flowed both into you and out of you.

You can base your work as an actor on these real-life experiences of action, though of course your stage work must be artistically heightened and purified.

### Exercise 49:
### Action in Real Life

A. For the next few days, notice which people attract your attention: What are they doing? How do they feel about it? What makes them interesting?

   Notice especially the people in those situations we think of as highly "dramatic": athletes at crucial moments, people in danger, people in the grip of deeply-held beliefs, etc.

B. Think about those times when *you* have been in action; what enabled you to achieve this level of complete commitment and focus?

C. Keep an actor's journal that records these thoughts and experiences as they occur.

On the stage you will also seek for this same acuteness and completeness of experience. You owe such fullness to your audience, for whatever your play may be saying to them about their world, your performance should be reminding them of their own potential aliveness. Your art is the art of self-definition, of mastery over personal reality, and when you exercise your craft to its fullest potential you awaken in your witnesses a reminder of their own spiritual capability. As David Mamet says,

> Each time we try to subordinate all we do to the necessity of bringing to life simply and completely the intention of the play, we give the audience an experience which enlightens and frees them: the experience of witnessing their fellow human beings saying, "nothing will sway me, nothing will divert me, nothing will dilute my intention of achieving what I have sworn to achieve": in technical terms, "My Objective"; in general terms, my "goal," my "desire," my "responsibility."
>
> If we are true to our ideals we can help to form an ideal society—a society based on an adhering to ethical first principles—not by *preaching* about it, but by *creating* it each night in front of the audience—by showing how it works. In action.[1]

"In action." This is the heart of it, the central concept, the seed that opens the path of growth for you as an actor.

## INNER AND OUTER ACTIONS

What is an action? Simply put, it is something a character does in order to get something they want or need, whether consciously or unconsciously, and the thing they want is called their *objective*. An action, then, is *a doing directed toward an objective.*

It is clear from some of our examples of people in action that action is not the same thing as external motion: the mime applying his make-up moved very little; a jeweler about to split a valuable diamond, hammer raised, beads of sweat dripping from his brow, is not moving at all; yet we recognize the dramatic value of the sense of "doingness" in these people. This is because the sense of dramatic action is felt even before it has manifested itself in external activity; it is present even in the *potential* for doing.

Stanislavski used another way of describing this aspect of action: he spoke of action as operating simultaneously both the internal or *spiritual* and external or *physical* levels:

> The creation of the physical life is half the work on a role because, like us, a role has two natures, physical and spiritual . . . a role (on the stage), more than action in real life, must bring together the two lives—of external and internal action—in mutual effort to achieve a given purpose.[2]

For Stanislavski, then, it was the *integration* of the internal and external actions which produced a truthful stage performance. His system was designed to bring about this integration. Best known are his early psychological techniques (fantasy, emotional recall, etc.) which were designed to work from the internal to the external, but later in the development of his method he also worked from the external toward the internal. As he said,

> The spirit cannot but respond to the actions of the body, provided of course that these are genuine, have a purpose, and are productive. . . (In this way) a part acquires inner content."[3]

During the first half of our century, the British acting tradition stressed the importance of externals in the acting process; our American tradition, on the other hand, stressed the importance of internals. For the past thirty years a real effort has been made on both sides of the Atlantic to synthesize both of these approaches in the training of actors. Both are essential, since each is only a different aspect of the same human phenomenon. As Stanislavski pointed out:

> External action acquires inner meaning and warmth from inner action, while the latter finds its expression in physical terms.[4]

While accepting Stanislavski's principles, we will adjust his description of action: we will not think of "inner" action and "outer" action as in any way separate, but will picture instead a single *flow* of action which moves from a stimulus in the outer world into our inner world, which passes through us, and then flows outward again toward an external objective.

We will examine this flow of action in detail in the next Lesson, but for now we will keep our attention on the objective toward which this flow is directed.

## DEFINING
## PRODUCTIVE OBJECTIVES

Actors are usually taught to form simple verbal descriptions of their objectives, step by step through a scene, as a way of making their focus more intense and specific. Before we discuss this process, let's consider three notes of caution.

First, actions are meant to be *experienced*, not described, and even the most skillful verbal descriptions cannot capture the exact quality of the experience. Second, the ability to describe an objective (which comes from the analytical left side of the brain) is not a guarantee of the ability to surrender to the playing of it (which comes from the intuitive right side of the brain) and the two sometimes tend to get in each other's way. Finally, it is important that you remember that your purpose in defining your objectives is to provide a more specific and compelling focus for *you* in the playing of the scene; it is *not* your intention to show the audience what the objective is.

Fortunately, your sense of playable objectives will eventually become "intuitive" and you will not need to think of them in any formal way; but at first it *may* help you to think of them in simple verbal terms, as long as you remember that the descriptions are valuable *only* insofar as they contribute to the actual playing of the scene.

These reservations having now been expressed, let's go on to consider the ways in which defining objectives help us to act well. First, your awareness while playing a scene, either in rehearsal or performance, is best focused on the objective that drives the action rather than on the external behavior itself. That is, you focus on what you want to achieve rather than on the external things you do in trying to achieve it. In this way, your sense of objective can generate your behavior "as if for the first time" each time you enact it; otherwise you might just "go through the motions" and fail to fill your actions with the inner life that can make them fully alive.

This does *not* mean that your performance is erratic or unstable; during the rehearsal process you gradually *refine* your action so that your "doings" become dependable, consistent, and stageworthy. But your immediate awareness while actually playing the scene is on the objective which triggers and synthesizes these well-rehearsed doings; like the baseball hitter, you must keep your eye on the "ball" of your objective.

Some ways of thinking about objectives are more useful to an actor than others. A well-chosen objective can actually help to produce stageworthy externals which meet the demands of the play and at the same time it compels the actor's total involvement. These are what Stanislavski called "productive" objectives.

You want therefore to find the sense of objective which will best accomplish several goals: first, it must compel your own attention so that your self-awareness is reduced in favor of complete involvement with your stage task. Second, it must be important enough to energize you so that it leads naturally to stageworthy activity. Third, it must connect you to the give-and-take with the other characters which drives the scene forward. An objective which accomplishes all three of these things is called *playable*.

Objectives become more playable when they are directed toward a *single, immediate, and personally important goal. Singular* because you wish to focus your energy on one thing rather than diffuse it by trying to do two things at once; *immediate* because the dramatic event is always occurring in the here and now, and a character's memory of the past or hopes for the future are important only insofar as they effect their present behavior; *personally important* because it is the importance of the objective which energizes you. We will remember these three points as the acronym "SIP."

Besides being "SIP," the most productive objectives must also bring you into meaningful contact with the other characters in the scene, since plays involve people acting upon one another. Now, if a character is motivated to act upon someone else, it is obvious that they wish to *change* something about that other person, to get them to behave or think differently. Therefore, you will find that the most playable objectives are *a desired change in another character.* Defining the objective in this way helps to bring you into meaningful *transaction* with the other character, and this heightened give and take produces a livelier, more dramatic scene.

The transaction will be even stronger if you can translate your sense of objective into a *specific, observable* change you want to bring about in the other character. Ask yourself, "How would I know I was achieving my objective? What change might I see in the other character which would encourage me that my approach is working?" The late director Duncan Ross even encouraged his actors to think of this as "a change in the other character's eyes," a strategy which encouraged maximum give and take between the characters. In the scene between Willy Loman and his new boss, for example, your aim might be "to make the boss look at me with approval." Your full attention is on him, watching to see if your behavior is indeed producing the desired effect, or whether you might have to try a different approach.

## PHRASING PLAYABLE ACTIONS

As we have said, your action is what you do in order to try to win your objective. A playable objective will help produce a strong action, but you should also learn to recognize the most useful ways of thinking about the action itself.

We can suggest three principles for stating playable objectives. The first is to use *a simple verb phrase* in a *transitive* form, that is, a verb which involves a doing directed toward someone else, such as "to persuade him." Avoid forms of the verb "to be," since these are intransitive verbs; they have no external object and their energy turns back upon itself, certainly not a good condition for an actor whose energies must continually flow outward into the scene! You are never interested, for example, in "being angry" or "being a victim." Strive instead for *doing*, a transitive condition in which your energy flows toward an object which, as we have said, is usually a change in another character.

The second principle follows from the first: include the object of the verb, the other character and the thing you want from them, in your definition. Don't think only of the verb, "to persuade," but to think of the specific objective, "to persuade him to give me back my old territory." Here are a few examples from other scenes mentioned in this book; can you identify the characters? *To hide the fact that he is my son from them; to convince him to enter the hovel; to trick him into picking up the knife.* Do you see how each of these conforms to the two principles listed above? One of the best things about understanding action in this way is that it helps you to enter into a more vivid and specific transaction with your stage partners.

Which brings us to the third principle: to include adverbs or adverbial phrases that specify the particular *strategy* employed by the character to achieve the objective. As we will see in the next Lesson, the choice of a course of action always involves a sense of strategy, of selecting the doing that seems to offer the greatest chance for success in the given circumstances. In the examples we listed above, the adverbial qualifiers expressing the strategies might be: to regain my territory *by reminding him of my past service*; to convince him to enter the hovel *by letting him take Mad Tom with us*; to trick him into picking up the knife *by threatening his manhood*; to hide the fact that he is my son *by pretending indifference*.

This sense of strategy is extremely important. A character will usually pursue a strategy until it either succeeds or fails. If it is not working, they will shift to a new strategy; if it works and they achieve their immediate objective, they move on to another objective. Each shift, whether a change in strategy or a change in objective, can be felt as a change in the rhythm of the scene; each creates a new "unit of action," which are usually called *beats*. The moment in which the shift takes place is called a *beat change*.

In the scene from *Death of a Salesman* which we mentioned earlier, Willy Loman tries several ways to regain his territory from his new boss; by flattery, by appealing for justice, by generating guilt, by demanding, by begging. Each strategy is abandoned as it fails and Willy grows more desperate; each shift in strategy is a "beat change" and moves the scene in a new direction.

We will learn to define the beats within a scene in a later lesson. For now, we can summarize all that we have said about playable objectives and actions as follows: the most playable objectives are *a change we want to bring about in another character which is "SIP" (singular, immediate, and personally important)*. This objective is pursued through an action expressed as *a transitive verb phrase including the object and strategy*.

Here is an exercise to explore the sense of playable objectives and actions. It is an exercise which should be done many times until the experience of action becomes familiar to you.

### Exercise 50:
### Simple Action
### Improvisation

A. Invent an objective involving someone in the room: to get them to go out on a date with you, to borrow money from them, to get them to lie for you, etc. Make it a single thing, and make it something possible and specifically related to them. Most of all, make it something important to you.

Now select an initial strategy that seems likely to succeed, such as "to get Sam to take me to my folks' house by promising him dinner there." Remember to phrase your action as a transitive verb including the object and the strategy.

B.  Without explaining any of this to anyone, go for it! Shift strategy if you're not getting anywhere.

(Those who are on the receiving end: accept the reality of whatever your partner brings to you; help generate the drama of the scene by resisting through retreating or counterattacking; make it *difficult but not impossible* for them to earn their objective.)

In this exercise you were acting in your own person, inventing your own objective and actions. When working on a play, one of your early steps in rehearsal will be to discover each of your character's immediate objectives, step-by-step through each scene, as well as the logic of their sequence (which in acting terms is called the *through-line* of the action). By making some working definitions of playable objectives early in the rehearsal process, you can begin to experience the logic and momentum of the scene so that it begins to "play" almost on its own.

These early definitions are, of course, liable to later adjustment or even rejection, but they are designed to help you begin exploring your scene and character *through experience* as quickly as possible, for it is only as you begin to experience the flow of action and reaction with your partners in the scene that you naturally begin to make the most valuable creative discoveries. You are then truly being moved beyond yourself, taking inspiration from the energies of others and from the play itself, participating in a whole that is greater than the sum of its parts. Under the influence of such an experience you can be swept beyond yourself and begin to discover not only what you already are, but also what you may become, as your character, that new version of yourself, grows.

## INDICATING IN LIFE
## AND ON STAGE

In his 1957 book, *The Presentation of Self in Everyday Life*, social psychologist Erving Goffman analyzed social behavior as if it were a stage performance. He found that most of us have a highly developed capacity to play our social roles successfully:

It does take deep skill, long training, and psychological capacity to become a good stage actor. But this fact should not blind us to another one: that almost anyone can quickly learn a script well enough to give a charitable audience some sense of realness in what is being contrived before them. And it seems this is so because ordinary social intercourse is put together as a scene (in a play) is put together, by the exchange of dramatically inflated actions, counteractions, and terminating replies. Scripts even in the hands of unpracticed players can come to life because life itself is a dramatically enacted thing. . . . In short, we all act better than we know how.[5]

While it is true that we all "act" all the time and that acting is a natural and necessary part of everyday life, it is not true that we act *well* all the time: sometimes we fail to achieve our objectives, sometimes we don't make the impression we wish, and sometimes our performance is judged to be "insincere" or "unbelievable."

How do we judge the believability of a performance? Goffman points out that our role-playing behavior always sends two kinds of messages: the information we *give* (the impression we are trying to make) and the information we *give off* (the unconscious things we do that reveal how we really feel). When we observe someone, we read the information "given off" by watching for traces of unconscious behavior such as "body language" and tell-tale qualities of the voice, and we then unconsciously compare this information with the message the performer is purposely giving us; when the two coincide we judge the performance as believable, but when they don't, we feel that the person is being insincere.

For example, if I am trying to convince you that I am extremely interested in what you are saying, but you catch me glancing over your shoulder toward the clock, or tapping my foot, your intuitive "sincerity alarm" goes off. On the stage, I have seen young actors do things like glance at the director or audience looking for approval, or "break" into laughter when the character shouldn't be laughing. These and other behaviors that are *inconsistent with the character's reality* make it impossible to believe in their performance.

In life and on stage, the only way to create a believable illusion is by believing in the illusion completely yourself, at least on one level of your consciousness (there is another level on which artistic choice continues to function). In this way, your unconscious behavior can be consistent with the conscious image you are creating. Every successful salesman learns this; it was also the idea behind Stanislavski's system of acting.

Beside inconsistent behavior, there is another symptom of insincerity which we have all learned to recognize, and that is *over effort*. The seeds of this are laid in childhood, when we try to manipulate mom or dad through displays of feigned emotion and effort. When I ask my daughter to take out the trash, for instance, I am usually treated to a display of nausea and suffering of operatic proportions. I usually persist and she fails in her objective of avoiding the task, but the energy which she expends in the performance would be sufficient not only to take out the trash but to clean the Augean stables as well. My adult mind feebly objects, "why don't you just DO it, for heaven's sake!"

I often have this same response to scenes performed by young acting students. Like my daughter, they tend to do *too much*: in addition to doing "the job," they are also trying to impress me with their acting. In otherwords, they are not so much *doing* something as they are trying to *show* me something about themselves. Their extra effort is saying something like, "Hey, look at how angry I am," or "look at what a victim I am."

In real life we call this "faking" or "grandstanding"; on stage we call it *indicating*. You are indicating *when you are showing us something about your character instead of simply* doing *what the character does.* Actors indicate for various reasons: because it is a way of maintaining control and avoiding surrender to the action; because it is a way of demanding attention; or simply because they think it "feels" like acting.

If you can learn to recognize indicating and avoid it by committing to a playable objective and specific action, you will find that your action will generate and express all the emotion and character needed. The essence of good acting is *to do what the character does completely and with the precise qualities required, but without adding anything superfluous.*

### Exercise 51:
### The Ham in You

Repeat the Simple Action Improvisation exercise; ask your audience to signal by making some sort of noise whenever they feel that you are indicating. Compare their feedback with your own sense of being in action. Are you adding inconsistent or superfluous behavior to your action?

# Lesson
# Ten

# The Process of Action I:
# Motivation and Given
# Circumstances

In the last Lesson you learned three main things:

First, how to think of your character's actions using transitive verbs directed toward objectives that are changes in another character; second, how some ways of defining those objectives are more playable and productive than others; and third, how to commit fully to those objectives so as to avoid "indicating." Now we will take a more detailed look at how these objectives actually operate within a living scene.

At any given moment in a scene your character's objective is actually the result of a *process* of action that has several steps. Although your immediate awareness remains focused on the objective while actually playing the scene, you must live through the entire process which leads to the formation of that objective if your action is to have the necessary momentum.

In order to describe the process of action, let's set up a hypothetical situation. Imagine that you see a notice that I am directing a play. There is a part in this play which you have been dying to play, and you want to approach me about it; even though you fear my possible rejection, your need is strong enough that you come to see me. You begin by "buttering me up" with your admiration for my work; you mention your love for this particular play; then, finally, you ask to read for the particular part, and I agree.

Let's examine what you did in detail. Something happened which aroused you: we will call this your *stimulus*. This arousal had a particular quality depending on what the stimulus meant to you; we will call this your *attitude*. In our example, your stimulus was seeing the notice about the play and your attitude was pleasurable ambition. Having been stimulated in this way, you began to *consider alternative courses of action* through which your aroused need could be satisfied; you might have considered asking someone I knew to approach me on your behalf, or perhaps you thought about merely sending a photo and resume. After surveying your alternatives, you made a *strategic choice* to act in a certain way; you would see me in person, and you would use a flattering approach. Having made your strategic choice, you then engaged in *purposeful activity* directed toward your objective.

This is the whole process of action: *a stimulus arouses an attitude which generates a strategic choice which results in a purposeful activity directed toward an objective.* The steps in this process can be summarized in seven key words:

STIMULUS/ATTITUDE/ALTERNATIVES/CHOICE/
ACTIVITY/OBJECTIVE

This in its most detailed form is the process of dramatic action. You will see this process represented graphically in Figure 23.

In this Figure, the circle represents your skin, the boundary between the "outer" and "inner" worlds. The stimulus sends energy toward you and that energy enters you through your *perception* (seeing, hearing, touching). Once inside you, it arouses a response in you that has a certain quality; it frightens you, or pleases you, or angers you, etc. This is your *attitude* toward it. You may consider *alternative* ways of dealing with it; to do this or that, to react or not, to take a direct or indirect course of action, etc. At the center of the process is the *strategic choice* which creates your *action* and unleashes the *activity* which you hope will win your *objective*.

This process of action moves the scene forward through the transactions it creates between the characters. The energy coming from the scene enters you (through the stimulus), then leaves you (through your action directed toward your objective); your objective then becomes a stimulus for someone else, and the process begins again with action generating reaction, which in turn generates another action which generates another reaction, and so on. Again, *acting is reacting!* We will explore this important sense of *transaction* more in the next Lesson.

Notice that the energy leaving you as action is usually not the same in quality or intensity as the energy which entered you as the stimulus; it has been altered by the nature of your reaction and the choice you made. In a play, your character is required to react in a certain way, moment

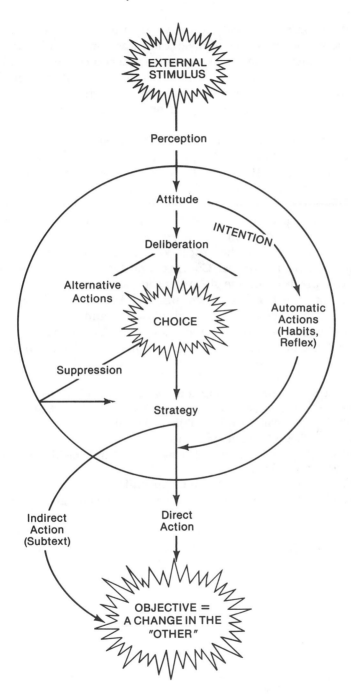

**FIGURE 23.**  The Process of Action.

by moment, in order to move the story forward in the proper direction and with the proper qualities of style and meaning. The playwright has created your character so that these reactions and choices are believable and natural to them. We might say, in fact, that a successful characterization results when the actor discovers the inner process of choice that *justifies* the external activities and manner of expression required by the plot, meaning, and style of the play.

On the stage, as in life, character is both formed and expressed through action. There is an old maxim that the bad playwright will have someone tell you that a man is a villain, while the good playwright simply has him kick a dog. The dynamic nature of theatre requires that you must fulfill your dramatic purpose not through showing or telling, but through *doing*: You cannot simply go on stage and *be* a villain, you must *do* something villainous. This is the difference between narrative literature and drama.

Here is an example of the process of action from a scene in Brecht's *Mother Courage*. Anna (Mother Courage) and her mute daughter Kattrin receive word of the death of one of Anna's sons; Kattrin stares at her mother, whom she blames for her brother's death, and Anna responds by ordering her to polish some spoons. This seemingly cruel and insensitive reaction from the mother can be properly understood only by tracing Anna's inner process. Her "stream of consciousness" or *inner monologue* might sound like this:

1. STIMULUS: "Kattrin is looking at me with blame in her eyes."
2. ATTITUDE: "I feel bad enough already; I don't need her blaming me too. Doesn't she understand that I didn't have any choice?"
3. ALTERNATIVES: "I could ignore her."
4. CHOICE: "I'll take her mind off it by giving her something to do so she won't look at me like that."
5. ACTIVITY: To say aloud, "Polish the spoons!"
6. OBJECTIVE: "To stop her from looking at me by putting her to work."

As we said in the last Lesson, the power of this objective is that it enables the actress playing Mother Courage to focus her energy and awareness "out there" into the scene, onto Kattrin, where the transaction can drive the scene forward.

## THE INSTROKE
## AND THE OUTSTROKE

Notice that the process of action through these six steps has two basic phases, an *inward* phase in which the character is *reacting* to something and an *outward* phase in which they are *acting* toward an external objective. In the "inward" phase, a stimulus coming to us from the outside world arouses us; we are urged toward a choice to act (or perhaps a choice *not* to act); the central choice turns the instroke of reaction into the outstroke of action toward an objective.

Think of this inner process as a "bridge" of invisible energy that connects two outer, visible events: the stimulus is at one end and the objective is at the other. Choice lies at the center of this bridge; it is the point at which the energy flowing into the character from the stimulus is turned around and begins to flow outward toward the objective.

The instroke is called your *motivation*, the outstroke is your *action toward your objective*, or, as Stanislavski sometimes called it, your *aspiration*. In fact, another way to describe the process of action is to say that *motivation leads to aspiration*: motivation is in the past and is driving you forward, and aspiration is in the future and you are striving toward it. Both work together to provide the compelling momentum of a complete dramatic action.

Young actors sometimes fail to experience the instroke of motivation fully; they may *do* something, but they aren't always receiving the stimulus that is *causing* them to do it. As we have said, *acting is reacting*, and the instroke of motivation, from stimulus to choice, is the "reacting" that must generate the "acting."

Acting is not so much *doing* things as it is allowing yourself *to be made to do them*!

We can now simplify the six steps in the process action as we described it above, and think simply of the inward flow coming from the stimulus, the central choice, and the outward flow of action toward the objective defined by the choice.

### STIMULUS/CHOICE/OBJECTIVE

An inner monologue for Mother Courage based on this scheme might sound like this: "Why is she looking at me like that? I'll make her do something. 'Polish the spoons!'"

Let's put this simple sense of the process of action to work in an exercise.

**Exercise 52:**
**The Inner Monologue**

Repeat the previous Simple Action Improvisation, but this time each of you softly speaks aloud the inner stream of thought which connects the external things you do and say. Go slowly and allow yourself to experience each step in the flow from stimulus to choice to objective.

As your partner reacts to what you are doing, you read their reactions and adjust your strategy so as to pursue your objectives. Your inner monologue might sound something like, "Look at that smug smile! He's not buying it at all. Maybe I could appeal to his vanity. . ."

Now that you have experienced the flow of the inner process by which objectives are formed, let us move through the process step by step, examining
each in more detail: you will see that an enormous amount of information
about the character can be gained from a consideration of their actions.

## THE INSTROKE OF MOTIVATION:
## STIMULUS, PERCEPTION, AND ATTITUDE

Though we are sometimes self-stimulating in life, it is extremely rare for
a character in a play to be self-stimulating. It is our purpose to create a
dramatic event in which an audience is able to perceive the cause and effect
of characters acting upon one another, so we must keep the scene *between*
the characters, and not merely within one of them.

For example, there is a scene in *A Streetcar Named Desire* in which
Blanche tells Mitch what happened years ago on the night that her young
fiance killed himself. Too often, actresses play this scene as if the memory
forces itself out of Blanche, and they fall so deeply into it that Mitch fades
into the background; it stops being a scene and becomes a monologue.
Instead, the actress must find the stimulus for the story not in her own
need, but in Mitch. It is his capacity for understanding which triggers and
unleashes her need to share, and her objective throughout the telling of the
story is "to make Mitch understand why I am the way I am so that he will
accept me and take care of me," or, in simple physical terms, "to get him
to hold me," which he finally does.

Remember: your stage stimulus will always be something "out there"
in the scene, something which someone else says or does. Learn to look for
stimuli which are *immediate* and *external*.

When working on a role, it is revealing to notice what sorts of stimuli
your character responds to, or conversely, which stimuli they ignore. Willy
Loman, for instance, responds strongly to the advice of his ghostly brother
Ben, but dismisses the more humane suggestions of his neighbor, Charley.

Next in the process, the immediate and external stimulus must be
perceived (seen, heard, or felt). Too often actors only pretend to perceive
what is really said or done to them, preferring the safety of their own mental
image of what the other character "ought" to be doing, or the generalized
sense of "what we rehearsed." Directors often have to say things like, "you
didn't really hear her say that." You must keep your awareness fresh; receive
each stimulus as it actually happens in the here and now.

Once the stimulus has been received, it must be interpreted; your
character must evaluate it in relationship to their own needs. Is this a
good thing? A threat? A surprise? The evaluation is expressed as an attitude
toward the stimulus. Directors often help actors to be specific about attitude
by asking, "how do you feel about that?" Learn to ask yourself this same
question as a regular part of your acting process.

You may notice that your character has a typical way of reacting to most stimuli; this can express their attitude toward the world in general. Are they optimistic or pessimistic? Does their attitude reveal any feelings that they may have about themselves? Willy Loman, for example, is quick to sense any criticism from others, and it makes him terribly defensive. This almost paranoid sensitivity reveals his fundamental insecurity and low self-esteem.

**Exercise 53:**
**The Instroke of Motivation**

Together with a partner, select a short scene from a play. Each of you identify the significant choices which your character makes within the scene; you will probably find between two and six choices, depending on the nature of the scene, with fewer in classical material and more in modern material; if you find more than six, you are probably including more trivial choices than you should.

Examine each significant choice to see how it is motivated by its stimulus and your character's attitude toward that stimulus:

A.  Identify the external and immediate stimulus for each. Does your character respond more to some stimuli than to others? How do these sensitivities reflect his or her values and needs?

B.  Consider what each stimulus means to your character; how do they feel about each? Does it trigger any needs already within the character? What attitudes of response are typical of your character? What does this say about their attitude toward the world and about themselves?

NOTE: You will use this same scene for several of the exercises to follow, so that eventually you will trace the entire process of action, as we did for Mother Courage in the example above. Work with your partner to select a scene which has some real interest for each of you.

## THE GIVEN CIRCUMSTANCES

Besides the internal factors which influence your character's attitude and choices, there are also external conditions; we call these *the given circumstances*. You must enter into your character's world and do what your character does *as if you were actually in his or her circumstances*. The playwright will have shaped those circumstances to make your character's actions natural within them, so understanding the influence of the circumstances can make your job much easier.

Further, it is often the given circumstances which give an action its particular quality; they also may provide the drive needed for good drama by establishing a sense of deadline or urgency.

The "givens" in any situation fall into four categories: who, where, when, and what.

*Who* refers to the relationship between your character and all the other characters who are important in the scene, whether they are physically present or not. These relationships have two aspects, the *general* relationship (for example, two sisters) and a *specific* relationship (all the special factors which make Blanche and Stella a unique pair of sisters). The general relationship provides a context; in many ways Stella and Blanche are like many other sisters, in that they reminisce about the past, they enjoy going out together for a special occasion, and so on. The specific relationship between Blanche and Stella, however, is fraught with blame and guilt over the past and tension regarding the present situation. The general relationship, then, provides certain basic considerations that make a relationship similar to others of its kind, while the specific relationship reveals what is unique to this particular case.

*Where* the scene happens also has two main aspects, the *physical* and the *social*. The physical environment has a tremendous influence on the action. For example, many of Tennessee Williams's plays must take place in the hot, humid climate of the South; think what an air conditioner would do to *A Streetcar Named Desire*! Shakespeare chose to set another play of great passion, *Othello*, in the similar climate of Cyprus; on the other hand, *Hamlet* requires the cold, isolated, and bleak climate of Denmark. Move Hamlet to the tropical climate of Cyprus and Claudius would be dead by the third act!

Beyond the simple physical influences of climate, the social environment established by the playwright is also of great importance. The society in which Stanley Kowalski moves, for example, is an active part of Stanley's character; we mustn't forget that he was a Marine sergeant, and is still the captain of his bowling team. Think over the plays you have read, and you will see how in each case the influences of the immediate locale and society have been carefully chosen, and are indispensible to the specific quality of the action.

*When* a scene is happening may be equally important, both in terms of the *time of day and year* and also the *historical time*, with all its implications of manners, values, and beliefs. Imagine *The Zoo Story* at night or in the winter, or as an encounter between two Victorians. Or consider the impact of the Elizabethan view of the physical universe on *King Lear*.

Finally, *what* is happening, the specific content and structure of the action which you have already studied in some detail, is the most important element of the scene. Consider here also any *antecedent action*; things that we know have happened in the past which effect the present situation, but the playwright has not bothered to actually show us.

Each of the given circumstances must be evaluated as to its relative importance; you don't want to waste thought and energy on aspects of the character's world which do not contribute to the action. The most important givens, of course, are those which affect the choices of the characters. It is not merely the fact that *Streetcar* and *Othello* are set in hot, humid climates which is important, but the specific way these climates affect the state of mind and therefore the significant choices made by the characters.

### Exercise 54:
### The Givens

Working with your partner, examine your scene; use information drawn from the entire play to identify the given circumstances which most influence the action. Consider each of the following:

1. Who:
   a. General relationship
   b. Specific relationship
2. Where:
   a. Physical environment
   b. Social environment
3. When:
   a. Time of day and year
   b. Historical time
4. What:
   a. The main event of the scene
   b. Any antecedent action that effects this scene

Rehearse your scene to experience the effect of the given circumstances; set up special rehearsal environments or visit actual locations in order to bring the givens fully to life.

I have found that a full experience of the important givens can be one of the most powerful and inspiring experiences an actor can have in rehearsing a scene. Rehearsing in locations that approximate the conditions of the scene can be especially effective; for example, I have several times held rehearsals for Shakespeare's *A Midsummer Night's Dream* at night by lantern light in the woods, and the quality of the experience enriched the stage performance as the actors carried with them the "sense memory" of those experiences.

You can also set conditions that are analogous to the conditions of the scene, as I once did in *King Lear* storm rehearsals in which the actors were exposed to water sprayed from hoses, pelted with empty lemonade cartons, and subjected to other sensations analogous to an actual storm.

Here the idea of *substitution* can be useful: once you have identified the function of a given circumstance in the way it affects your character, you can create rehearsal conditions which will "substitute" for that circumstance by providing an analogous situation. I remember a production of *Oedipus Rex* in which the actor playing Oedipus rehearsed his famous blind entrance by strewing some thumbtacks on the floor, blindfolding himself, and spending a little time each day feeling his way barefoot through them. The sense memory he thus developed especially for this entrance produced an overwhelming effect.

# Lesson Eleven

# The Process of Action II: Alternatives, Choice, and Action

Choice is the essence of drama. Almost all of the most suspenseful moments in plays occur when a character confronts a significant choice. As David Mamet points out, "the only thing we, as audience, care about in the theatre is WHAT HAPPENS NEXT?"[1] From an actor's point of view, this question really should be "What is he or she going to do?" This is called a "turning point" or a moment of *crisis*.

The suspense of a crisis is heightened when the choice is difficult, that is, when the character is choosing between equally compelling (or equally unattractive) alternatives. In tragedy, these choices usually take the form of a "double bind," in which a character must choose, for example, between their sense of truth or duty and their life: *Antigone, A Man for All Seasons, Beckett, An Enemy of the People*, and *The Crucible* all center around such a choice. Critic Jan Kott describes it like this:

> . . .A classic situation of tragedy is the necessity of making a choice between opposing values. . . . The tragedy lies in the very principle of choice by which one of the values must be annihilated. The cruelty of the absolute lies in demanding such a choice and in imposing a situation which excludes the possibility of compromise.[2]

In comedy, the choices are not so serious; we might instead wonder something like, "How is he going to get away with it this time?" But in either case, the essence of suspense resides in the element of choice, and choice requires that there be *alternatives*. Where there are no alternatives, there is no suspenseful choice; when there are alternatives that are nearly equal, suspense is maximized.

There is a scene in the exact center of Shakespeare's *Hamlet*, in which Hamlet finds his enemy, Claudius, praying alone and unarmed. It is a perfect opportunity for revenge, and Hamlet draws his sword and approaches the kneeling figure. At this moment, the actor must convince us that he is indeed going to kill him: as he begins to strike, however, he pauses and realizes that if he kills Claudius now, while he is at prayer, he will die in a state of grace and will be allowed into heaven, whereas the ghost of his father has been forced to suffer in limbo because he died without grace, "With all my imperfections on my head." For a long moment, Hamlet hangs in this agony of choice between the desire for revenge and a sense of justice, and finally chooses to postpone the act until "a fitter time."

It is this inherently dramatic quality of a difficult decision that is the central feature of most plays. Unlike a novelist, who can take you inside a character's mind to show you the process of their thought, a dramatist can only imply it. As an actor, you must recreate it for yourself, and this will be the greatest creative and personal contribution you will make to your performance.

Of course, not every choice is to be given the weight of the significant choices we have been discussing here, but *every* choice which your character makes which effects the progress of the play must be well defined and experienced in each rehearsal or performance.

We can sum up by saying that you must consider not only what your character *does*, but also what he or she *chooses not to do*. When your character is presented with a significant choice (meaning any choice which effects the progress of the play) you must find for yourself the various alternatives they might consider, and decide how they would feel about each. The creation of these alternatives is a powerful way of entering into the character's mind, since they represent an inventory of the way they see the world.

Most important, in rehearsal and performance you must truly live through the choice each time. Unless the alternatives remain real possibilities for you, you will simply be showing us what the character does without *reliving* the actual process whereby he or she chooses to do it. Only by reliving this process of choice can you begin to enter actively into the world and consciousness of the character.

## CHOICE AND CHARACTER

In life, when you are forced to behave a certain way over a period of time, you start to turn into the kind of person who would behave that way. This same natural process, the reliving of your character's choices within their given circumstances *as if they were your own*, is the central process in creating a character for the stage. Stanislavski called this process *the magic if*, and we can state our own version of it: *if you were in the character's circumstance, and if you chose to do what they do, who would it turn you into?*

Choice is the most revealing point in the process of action. In the making of significant choices, your character is responding to needs, to a way of seeing the world, and to relationships, beliefs, and values. If you can experience all the factors influencing your character's significant choices, you will be in touch with everything needed to create the psychological aspect of your characterization.

We have called the choice itself a "strategic" choice because it is based most of all on your character's understanding of his or her situation and of the other characters. Given what they are like, the character chooses the course of action which seems to have the best possibility of success. Learn to ask yourself, "what is it about the other character that makes me choose this particular objective and action?"

Following is a list of all the factors that may influence any particular choice. Carefully examine such influences as a way of understanding your character and the world of the play. These influential factors may be either internal to the character, external in the character's environment, or they may be theatrical conditions of concern to you as an actor.

1.  Internal factors influencing choice:
    a.  Physiology;
    b.  Social background;
    c.  Needs and desires;
    d.  Psychological processes or "way of thinking";
    e.  Ethical values.
2.  External factors influencing choice (the Givens):
    a.  Relationships with, or attitudes toward other characters;
    b.  The social environment;
    c.  The physical environment;
    d.  Specific immediate circumstances.
3.  Theatrical concerns requiring adjustment of choice:
    a.  The style or genre of the play;
    b.  The character's dramatic purpose in the play;
    c.  The visual and auditory demands of the performance space.

While the last three are clearly "actor" concerns rather than "character" concerns, it is part of your job to justify your concerns as a performer as organic aspects of your character's inner world. In this way, the two levels of your "dual consciousness" as actor and character will work together toward the same goal, and may eventually come together as a single experience.

## DOING NOTHING: SUPPRESSION

There is always at least one alternative available to a character in any situation, and that is the choice *not* to act, to suppress or delay action. Though we often think of "doing nothing" as a passive act, it can actually be a form of action. Movement therapist Moshe Feldenkrais says this about the process of delaying or inhibiting impulses:

> The delay between thought process and its translation into action is long enough to make it possible to inhibit it. The possibility of creating the image of an action and then delaying its execution is the basis for imagination and for intellectual judgement. . .
> The possibility of a pause between the creation of a thought pattern for any particular action and the execution of that action is the physical basis for self-awareness. . .
> The possibility of delaying action, prolonging the period between the intention and its execution enables man to know himself.[3]

The decision not to act is made with surprising frequency in drama since it aids in heightening dramatic tension and suspense. As you noticed in Figure 23, when a character chooses to *suppress* an impulse, that unresolved energy is reflected back into them and builds up to become a source of increasing dynamic tension. In fact, if all dramatic characters chose to act upon their impulses, plays would be a great deal shorter and less suspenseful than they are; drama is *not* the shortest distance between two points.

The choice of doing nothing, then, is perfectly serviceable to the actor. Think, for example, of the scene in which Hamlet chooses not to kill the praying Claudius; does this scene lack dramatic tension or playable action merely because "nothing happens?" Quite the contrary, the agony of Hamlet's choice is a source of enormously compelling drama.

Viewed in this way, there are no passive characters on the stage; there are only characters who are aroused but then choose *not* to act, which is itself a positive and playable choice. Even seeming indifference can be described in playable terms such as "to avoid him by reading my book," "to not let her see how upset I am by changing the subject," and so on.

There are characters who are by nature more reactive than active: the most famous example is Hamlet, and others are Peter in *The Zoo Story* and Mitch in *A Streetcar Named Desire*. There are plays in which "nothing happens" in the sense of vigorous external events, such as the plays of Chekhov, Beckett, Pinter, or Shepard. These plays and roles can be difficult for actors if they fail to realize that a "not-doing" is also a "doing" *if* a stimulus provokes an arousal, but the reaction is *suppressed* by a choice *not* to react.

There is a great dramatic value in someone trying to suppress an impulse, even though they may be unsuccessful in doing so. In the scene in which Lear confronts the blinded Gloucester, for example, Lear attempts to suppress the painful recognition of his old friend's condition. At first he tries to make light of what he sees with dark jokes like, "Get thee glass eyes and like a scurvy politician seem to see the things thou dost not." The pain begins to mount, however, as the recognition forces itself toward Lear's consciousness: "Do thy worst, blind Cupid, I'll not love." Finally, as Gloucester begins to weep, Lear can keep the pain away no longer, and begins to weep himself: "If thou wilt weep my fortunes, take my eyes. I know thee well enough, thy name is Gloucester." Such releases of suppressed material are enormously powerful and are called *derepressions*.

Suppressed emotions are bits of "unfinished business" and they continue to influence subsequent behavior. In *A Streetcar Named Desire*, for instance, Blanche carries with her the memory of the night she discovered the boy she loved in a homosexual encounter, whom she rejected and who then killed himself; the sense of betrayal and guilt connected with this experience made her feel unworthy of being loved, and she embarked on a series of casual sexual encounters, depending on "the kindness of strangers" in a desperate attempt to affirm her sense of attractiveness and self-worth. She is finally able to share this memory (to derepress it) with a man who truly loves her, but Mitch is too weak to save her.

Since playwrights cannot take us directly into the minds of their characters, we usually have to deduce or infer that the character is suppressing something. Recreating the through-line of your character's thought (their inner monologue) will help you to discover those moments when he or she chooses to suppress an impulse or feeling. Remember that stage characters, like people in life, may often be feeling and wanting much more than their overt actions indicate. The plays of Chekhov are especially rich as studies of suppression and repression, and prove that the effort to hold an impulse in can be more dramatic than its release.

One way to deal with suppressed material in your preparation of a role is to devote some rehearsal time to allowing the inhibited impulses to be released. By strengthening them in this way, you will be forced to work harder to hold them in when the scene is done in its correct form. It is this effort to inhibit the impulse that turns the "not doing" of suppression into a dramatically suspenseful condition.

**Exercise 55: Choice:**
**The Center of the Bridge**

As in the previous exercise, consider each significant choice made by your character in your scene:

A. Considering your character in the entire play, do you see a pattern of repression or suppression which may be effecting their choices in this scene?

B. Rehearse allowing any suppressed material to be released, then immediately repeat the scene and hold in those same impulses.

C. Beside the possibility of a choice "not" to act, develop at least one other viable alternative which you might consider in each choice.

D. Examine the choice you actually make: What factors influence this choice? Consider each item in the list of factors provided earlier.

E. Rehearse your scene with this awareness; take the time to experience each choice fully.

## THE OUTSTROKE OF ACTION
## TOWARD AN OBJECTIVE

Once the choice to act in a certain way has been made, your outwardly flowing action now becomes a *purposeful activity*, either a doing, a saying, or both, directed toward an objective as you have learned to think of it in the previous lesson. It is this outwardly directed activity which the audience eventually sees and hears, and much of its power and expressiveness derives from the way we can sense the whole human process which lies behind it.

This can happen naturally *if* the actor has truly experienced it, and this fullness of inner experience is what Stanislavski meant by *justifying* an action. To be in action is, in a very real sense, to turn yourself inside out!

An important cautionary note must be made here: the process of action that we have described in detail in no way requires that your performance be ponderously slow. The making of a choice may take only a split-second; in most comedy, for instance, the tempo of the performance requires that this flow occurs quickly (and in truth, comic characters rarely have terribly difficult decisions to make, since the agony of moral choice belongs more to the realm of tragedy).

At the same time, almost every role in every play will offer at least a few crucial decisions that need to be fully experienced and thereby given full dramatic value. The Inner Monologue technique, which can become intuitive with practice, is a good way to insure that you are taking the time to experience such crucial choices. Of course, even the inner monologue will eventually fade away as your technique matures and you are able at last to "just do it."

**Exercise 56:**
**The Outstroke of Action**

  A.  Working in consort with your partner, go through your scene and develop a working definition of each of your actions and objectives according to the principles covered in Lesson Nine: the actions are described by a transitive verb phrase including the object and the strategy, and objectives are SIP and expressed as a desired change in the other character.

  B.  Having now completed your analysis of the entire process of each of your character's actions, rehearse your scene. As soon as possible, learn your lines so that you can freely engage in the Inner Monologue exercise.

## SUBTEXT

Recall the Hostess/Guest scene we discussed in Part One; it showed how people in everyday life often mean one thing while saying or doing another. This is also common in drama, especially in the plays of Chekhov and other naturalistic writers, and we call these hidden intentions *subtext.*

From the actor's point of view, a subtext is really an objective which is pursued *indirectly*; that is, subtext is present whenever a character says or does one thing in order to accomplish something else. This occurs when the character cannot, for some reason, take direct action, and chooses to pursue the objective through some indirect statement or activity. It is represented in Figure 23 by the dotted line of action flowing indirectly from choice to objective.

Indirect action may be a conscious strategy in response to some external obstacle; when a character must circumvent some obstacle through deceit, or when they wish to be perceived in a certain way despite what they are doing. Or, subtext may be unconscious, stemming from an internal barrier; for example, when the character cannot admit the truth about their own behavior to themselves. In either case, there is a clear difference between the surface activity (the text) and the submerged objective (the subtext).

For instance, in *Mother Courage*, Anna's surface activity is to get Kattrin to polish the spoons, while her subtext is to get Kattrin's mind off her brother and what her mother has done; this is a conscious subtext. In *The Glass Menagerie*, on the other hand, Amanda goes to great lengths to prepare Laura for her gentleman caller, but she also puts on her old party dress and hangs colored lights; we realize that Jim is also *her* gentleman caller as she relives her own youth through Laura; this is an unconscious subtext.

In both cases, notice that the author has provided a clear surface activity through which the subtext may be expressed. When a subtext is present, whether it is conscious or unconscious, you must accept the surface activity as your immediate point of attention. It is disastrous to attempt to play the hidden objective overtly; this will bring the subtext to the surface of the text, and will destroy the texture and tension of the scene. Rather, you simply allow the surface activity to be *consistent* with the subtext without letting it show directly.

When actors make the mistake of bringing the subtext to the surface, it makes it impossible for the other characters to respond properly, for they are supposed to see only the surface activity; if the audience can see the subtext, they must wonder why the other characters can't. For example, Iago has a continuous subtextual objective of destroying Othello, but if we see Iago's villainy at any time except when he is alone on stage, then Othello will seem like a fool.

This kind of deceit is an obvious instance of subtext, but there are more subtle uses. For instance, in *The Zoo Story* Jerry attempts to share his feelings about his life with Peter through "The Story of Jerry and the Dog." At the end of the story, he feels that he has failed to communicate and his frustration grows; he begins to attack Peter in a harsher and more physical way by trying to gain control of the bench. His surface activity here is to get Peter off the bench, but his subtext is to set Peter up to participate in his suicide by getting him to fight.

You see from this example that *subtext must be deduced from context.* In a novel, the writer can simply tell you what is really going on inside the character, but in a play only the outward, indirect behaviors springing from the hidden intention are presented. Great discretion and insight are called for in such cases. Your definition of the subtext reflects your interpretation of the inner life of your character and must be continually checked against the demands of the script.

To sum up: subtext occurs when a character must pursue an objective indirectly for internal or external reasons, consciously or unconsciously; the surface activity which results from the subtext should not reveal it but merely be consistent with it.

Trust the text and the audience; they will deduce from the situation what is really going on. Your simple awareness of subtext is enough, and sometimes subtext will work even if you remain unaware of it! Besides, it is part of the fun for the audience to figure these things out for themselves; if you make it obvious, they don't get to play!

### Exercise 57:
### Subtext

Work through your scene with your partner; look for any indirectly expressed or hidden objectives.

1. Is the character conscious or unconscious of them?
2. Why can't they be expressed directly?
3. What surface activity has been provided through which they may be expressed?
4. Rehearse your scene with this awareness: avoid playing the subtext.

## AUTOMATIC ACTIONS

So far we have been describing a process of choice that involves conscious thought. There are obviously a great many things we do in life and on the stage that are not necessarily the result of conscious choice, however. These are called *involuntary* or *automatic actions*.

For example, when riding in a car and presented with sudden danger, you find yourself stepping on the brake, even though you are not driving. Characters on the stage have many responses of a similar kind: when the alarm bell rings, Othello reaches for his sword; when threatened, Laura runs to her menagerie or plays the phonograph. These are habitual actions which serve the needs of these characters on a deep level and they require little or no conscious thought.

It is extremely useful when approaching a part to identify the automatic aspects of your character's behavior as soon as possible, for it is your task to recreate the character's habits in yourself for the purpose of rehearsing and performing the role. It is neither necessary nor desirable that these habits invade your real life; we all have habits that we "turn on and off" to suit the situation, and the habits you develop to play a role will be of this type.

The formation of new habits is accomplished best by regular, spaced drill over a period of time; you cannot count on rehearsals alone to do the job, nor should you waste the group's time on this sort of personal work. You must develop a program of homework that allows the formation of these habits through short daily exercises.

Remember that the aim of this personal work is not to "lose yourself" in your character, but to insure that you don't lose the character in yourself!

When you consider how much of a character's behavior falls into the area of automatic actions, you will see what an important area of concern this is: the voice, the walk, the way clothes are worn, any special skills (like Othello's swordsmanship), these and more must become as natural and habitual to you as they are to your character. It is this kind of thinking that made Lord Laurence Olivier prepare his voice for the role of Othello for a full year; it will also encourage the actress playing Mrs. Malaprop in *The Rivals* to ask for a rehearsal skirt early on, since she knows that the handling of a huge skirt is habitual to her character.

To sum up, follow this general rule: whatever your character doesn't need to think about, you shouldn't need to think about; whatever your character does need to think about, you must think about each and every time you perform that action.

### Exercise 58:
### Automatic Actions

Again, review your scene with your partner; look for any automatic actions required of your character. Examine them to see what they tell you about your character.

What program of homework can you establish to develop these habits in yourself for this role?

# Lesson Twelve

## Beats and Scenes

You have now developed a sense of action as a kind of invisible "bridge" of energy flowing from an external stimulus, through inner choice, to an external objective. You have also understood how your stimulus is usually provided by someone else's action toward you, and that your action will, in turn, become a stimulus for someone else; this will evoke another reaction from them, and so the play will move through the action/reaction/action/reaction chain of energy being passed between the characters. We must next consider how your individual actions fit into this chain of cause and effect, and how the whole effects each of its parts.

Here is an exercise that will explore this question.

### Exercise 59:
### Impulse Circle

Sit in a large circle, in chairs or on the floor, about 18 inches apart. Make the circle perfectly round.

Each person puts his or her left hand out palm up and right hand out palm down, and rests their right hand lightly on the left hand of the person to their right.

The leader will now initiate a light, clean slap with their right hand. The slap is passed on from person to person around the circle and is allowed to flow continuously. Now try the following experiments:

A. Allow your awareness to go to the slap as it moves around the circle. Begin to experience it *as having a life of its own*. Notice any change in its quality as the group begins to experience it as having its own life.
B. Now allow the slap to move as quickly as it can; see what happens when you "get out of its way."
C. Now let it slow down; see how slow it can go *without dying*; bring it right to the brink of extinction. Keep the external slap sharp, and slow it down as it travels internally. See what you need to do to support its life, even while it is not passing directly through you.
D. Drop your hands, and discuss the ways in which this exercise *is like a scene on stage*.

NOTE: Repeat this exercise on subsequent days; it is a good group "warmup."

In your discussion of the exercise, you probably noticed (among other things) that the flow of the impulse was entirely dependent on the ability of every group member to receive and send (react and act) with relaxed concentration. Until people are acting and reacting, there is no chance for a dramatic event to occur; interaction is the essential mechanism of drama.

There are basically three ways in which characters can act upon one another:

1. A unilateral action, in which "A" does something to "B";
2. An interaction, in which "A" does something to "B," then "B" does something back;
3. A transaction in which "A" and "B" are acting upon one another simultaneously.

Plays are always concerned with interaction, and usually with transaction, but never with unilateral action. You must not use your individual sense of objective in a unilateral way, but always remember that "acting is reacting!"

During the exercise you may have also noticed that as you came to believe in the impulse as having a life of its own, your awareness opened and you became more relaxed, less self-conscious, your center lowered, and you stopped judging what you were doing and simply *did* it. You were, in short, *in action*!

You probably also felt that you were part of the whole network through which the impulse flowed all the time, not just when it was "your turn." This is the kind of continuous support and involvement required of every member of a cast, even when they are offstage.

When most of the group was able to relate to the impulse in this way, you noticed that it began to flow more smoothly and powerfully; when you began, it was "chunky," a sequence of individual actions as each of you waited for "my turn," each focused on their part. When everyone focused their awareness on the whole, however, all the individual parts merged into one flowing event.

At that moment, the exercise also became "easier;" you were no longer *making* it happen, it was making *you* happen! You were receiving more energy from it than you were giving to it, and the whole became greater than the sum of its parts.

These are all ways in which the exercise is like an effective scene on stage. Every actor must be connected to the whole, continuously reacting and acting in order to contribute to the specific and independent life of the scene, and receive in turn the energy which the whole brings to them. When this happens, the event begins to evolve under its own power; we simply say that the scene begins "to play."

This is not to say that this exercise is particularly *dramatic*. It is fun to do, and entertaining to watch for a time, but it soon becomes repetitive. The flowing energy of the slap has created a common focus for the group and this has helped everyone to be in action, but the other requirements of drama have not been met: there is no unresolved conflict and very little urgency, so the energy of the slap doesn't have "anywhere to go," whereas a play must have a drive toward its climax. (You could, of course, insert conditions into this exercise which would provide drama, like "Let's get it around fifty times in three minutes!" Your group might enjoy experimenting in this way.)

Now that the flow of energy within the group has established the *potential* for a dramatic event, we must next consider how this flowing energy is endowed with the qualities of drama, which we defined earlier as "a significant issue with the outcome in doubt within a condition of urgency."

## DRAMA AND CONFLICT

Almost all plays derive their suspense and urgency from a *central conflict* which demands to be resolved. In some plays, the central conflict is clearly between two characters (the "protagonist" and the "antagonist"). In its most simple form ("hero" versus "villain") this structure tends toward melodrama and is common in popular entertainment like episodic television. In more complex plays, this two-person conflict can be used to ignite more profound issues: Othello and Iago, Peter and Jerry, Blanche and Stanley are all examples of protagonist-antagonist conflicts, but the issues involved here are far more complex than a mere contest between a "good guy" and a "bad guy."

A central conflict may also reside predominantly within a single character. While there is a conflict between Hamlet and Claudius, for instance, the central conflict of the play really exists within Hamlet himself, between his desire to follow the Ghost's command for vengeance and his moral reticence to commit murder.

A central conflict may also involve a character or characters confronting a difficult situation. In Beckett's *Waiting for Godot*, for example, there is little conflict between the characters: rather, they are in conflict with a situation which forces them to wait for someone (or something) which is unknown and which may or may not come. The main event of the play is that Godot does not come, a "non-event" which expresses Beckett's view of life itself.

We see that all plays are organized around some sort of a central conflict, whether it is within the protagonist, between a protagonist and antagonist, or between the characters and their situation. In all these forms, conflict serves the play as a source of potential energy; because we feel the conflict between opposing forces, we expect that something is about to happen and this provides the essential ingredient of *suspense*.

In fact, suspense, the feeling that something *might* happen, is more important than the event itself. This is how contemporary plays with few "events" in the traditional sense (Beckett's *Waiting for Godot*, Pinter's *The Collection*, Shepard's *Buried Child*, to name a few) can still be dramatically satisfying.

When creating a role you must connect with the central dramatic conflict of the play, whatever its form, and shape your characterization so as to contribute to that central conflict. For example, if you were playing Charlie the next-door neighbor in Miller's *Death of a Salesman*, you would have to see that the central conflict of the play is the choice facing Willy between his Brother Ben's way of life (which is based on struggle and material success) and Charlie's way of life (which is based on acceptance and spiritual success). Your main purpose in creating the role would be to epitomize this alternative which, if Willy could but choose it, would save his life.

## THE SHAPE OF DRAMA

A central conflict and a sense of urgency are not by themselves enough to provide a satisfying dramatic experience. In a great play, the dramatic event is distilled to its essence and shaped to form a satisfying "two hours traffic on the stage," as Shakespeare put it. It is this *shaping* of the play's events in a way that heightens their dramatic impact which we will examine next.

When the conflict has built up and is on the verge of being released, suspense is at its peak. In the previous Lesson you learned that this moment of greatest suspense, when the outcome hangs in the balance, is called a *crisis* (a "turning point"). The function of everything that happens before the crisis is to lead toward it with rising suspense, while everything after the crisis flows naturally from it with a sense of resolution. Therefore, it is on the crisis that we focus our attention. (Remember that the crisis points in a play are most often significant choices made by the characters.)

This, then, is the fundamental shape of all dramatic events: an arousal, a crisis, and a resolution. (See Figure 24.) It is a shape common to all of the performing arts; symphonies and ballets have it. It is the fundamental unit of rhythm, because it is the shape of a muscular contraction and relaxation. It is the fundamental shape of life itself, from birth to death. We can experience it within a single breath!

### Exercise 60:
### A Dramatic Breath

You can experience the shape of a whole play in a single breath. A breath has a period of rising action (inhaling), a crisis (a momentary holding of the breath), and a release (exhaling). Try taking a breath in a way that heightens its dramatic potential: involve the entire body in the rise, crisis, and release pattern; start as "empty" as you can and rise to a high crisis; prolong the crisis, feeling the full strength of the held-back energy; and then release it completely. A single breath can be an exciting event!

In this exercise you have heightened the "drama" of the breath by intensifying it in two ways: You extended its *dynamic range,* or *arc,* by stretching the low and high points of the action farther apart; you also *prolonged the crisis* so as to savor the period of maximum suspense. These same principles will apply to the shaping of a scene and the units of action within that scene.

Continue now to explore how this dramatic shape works in larger patterns.

**FIGURE 24.** The Shape of Drama

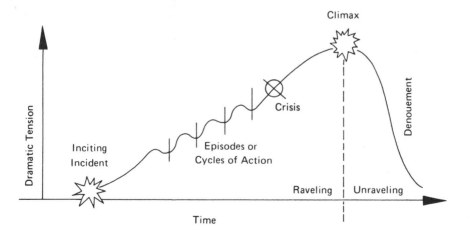

### Exercise 61:
### Shaping Action Phrases

Perform the following sequence of actions, attempting to fully experience the dramatic potential of each. Remember to focus your attention on the crisis in each pattern: treat all that goes before as leading up to the crisis, and all that follows as flowing from it.

1. A single step. Where is the crisis of a step? To intensify the experience, involve your breath by inhaling during the rising action, holding the breath during the crisis, and exhaling during the release.
2. Three steps experienced as one phrase, with the crisis in the third step. The first two steps still have mini-crises of their own, but now they lead up to the main crisis of the phrase in the third step.
3. Three steps with the crisis in the first step, so that the mini-crises of the second and third steps will "follow-through" from the first.
4. Now try a pattern composed of three units of three steps each, with the crisis of the whole pattern in the third step of the second unit.

In this exercise you experienced how a number of small units of action (like breaths or steps) could be connected into one larger phrase having a shape of its own; likewise, these larger phrases could be connected into a still larger pattern which could be experienced as having a shape of its own, and on all these levels the fundamental shape of rise, crisis, and release is the same. (See Figure 25.)

This is how the parts of a play go together to compose the whole play. We begin with the "smallest" units, the individual transactions between characters, which we call *moments*. Moments work together to form larger units called *beats*, and the beats work together to form *scenes*; the scenes

**FIGURE 25.**  Compound Events

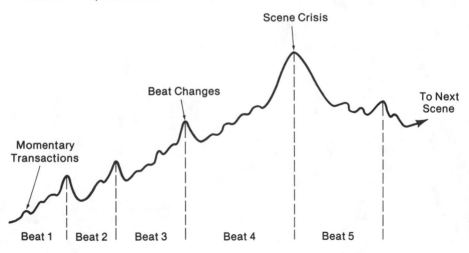

work together to form *acts* or sections of the play, and the acts flow toward the *main event* of the play as a whole.

Compare this idea to the structure of this book: the sentences are arranged to form paragraphs, just as individual transactions make up beats; paragraphs work together to form chapters, just as beats work together to form scenes; the chapters flow together to develop the subject of each part, just as scenes work together to form acts or sections of a play; finally the parts work in sequence to develop the main idea of the book, just as the acts flow toward the main event of the play.

On every level, each of the elements has a central unifying focus. Just as a sentence expresses one idea, one *transaction* contains one action and reaction over a particular issue; just as a paragraph has a main idea, so a *beat* has one main issue; as a chapter has a main topic, so a *scene* contains one major development which furthers the plot of the play. If the play is divided into *acts* or sections, each has its own development and crisis. Finally, as we have seen, the play has a shape of its own which is created by the funding of the parts to focus on one main event.

Each of these levels has the same basic shape of rise and fall, and each has its own mini-crisis, but they all fit together to form the single *compound rhythm* of the whole.

This may at first seem to be a complicated way of looking at the shape of drama, but it actually makes your job easier! It means that you can concentrate on mastering the simplest and most immediate action-pattern, the linking of moments to produce a beat. In rehearsal, you develop each beat so that it will link to achieve the shape of the scene, and you develop each scene in order to achieve the shape of the plot. In this way, you can keep your focus on a simple level of action in the here and now, and still be fulfilling the requirements of the whole!

Therefore, we will begin by learning to define beats, since this is the level on which you will best focus your awareness during rehearsal and performance.

## DEFINING BEATS

Some believe that the word "beat" was a misunderstanding of someone with a Russian accent saying "bits," meaning particles of action. As we have said, a beat is comprised of several transactions between characters. A beat is the smallest unit of action that has its own complete shape, with a central conflict and mini-crisis. Stanislavski sometimes referred to beats as being like "vertebrae" in the spine of the play's unfolding event.

Yet another way of thinking about beats would be to think of your scene as a flow of energy (the "through-line of action") which flows to a point, then turns and flows in a new direction until it finally reaches its main turning-point, the crisis of the scene. Each turning point is a "beat change," a point at which one of the characters has made a choice which forms a new objective or a radically new strategy. In this way, beat changes can be defined as *moments at which a character chooses to change objectives or strategy in order to move the action in a new direction.*

Notice that a beat changes even if only one of the characters changes their objective or strategy. The important thing is that the energy of the *scene* turns in a new direction as a result of their choice; everyone in the scene works towards that choice, and everyone supports the change when it occurs, even if it is not instigated by their character.

In this way, everyone in the scene works to share a sense of the architecture provided by the playwright and works together through the early stages of rehearsal to discover the beat changes in the scene. This is called doing a *breakdown* of the scene.

As an example of a breakdown, let's examine the scene from *Death of a Salesman* which we have mentioned several times before. Willy, unable to go on driving as much as his job requires, goes to see his boss, Howard, who is the son of the former owner of the firm. Willy enters somewhat hesitantly and finds Howard playing with a new toy, a wire recorder. Howard wants to avoid this unpleasant confrontation (we learn later that he has already decided to fire Willy and has been putting off telling him) so he goes on playing with the recorder and forces Willy to listen to his children's and wife's innane recordings. Like a good salesman, Willy listens dutifully and even flatters Howard, while trying four times to bring up the reason for his visit. This is all one beat which lasts for several minutes; it contains Willy's action of trying to get Howard's attention without alienating him, versus Howard's counteraction of avoiding Willy by playing with the recorder. The crisis is finally reached when Howard tries to change the subject by asking, "Say, aren't you supposed to be in Boston?" Thus Howard remains "on top," and Willy stays on the defensive.

In the second beat, which is short, Howard attacks by demanding to know, "What happened? What're you doing here?" Willy reacts weakly, but manages to state his case: "I've come to the decision that I'd rather not travel anymore." He reminds Howard that he had promised to find him "some spot for me here in town," but Howard responds, "Well, I couldn't think of anything for you, Willy."

The main issue of the scene is now on the table: Willy *must* get off the road, but Howard refuses to help. Three beats follow in which Willy tries different strategies to change Howard's mind. Threading through this section is the recurrent action of bargaining, and in each instance Willy lowers the salary he is willing to accept in return for a spot in town.

In the third beat, he begs: "God knows, Howard, I never asked a favor of any man. But I was with this firm when your father used to carry you in here in his arms." He offers to take a cut in pay to sixty-five dollars a week, and when Howard still refuses he lowers his price: "Howard, all I need to set my table is fifty dollars a week," but Howard counters, ". . . it's business, kid, and everybody's gotta pull his own weight."

In the fifth beat, Willy tries to make Howard understand why his job is so important to him by telling him how he decided to become a salesman, and even lowers his price to forty dollars a week, but Howard, who is really the "kid" in this relationship, responds, "Kid, I can't take blood from a stone."

In the sixth beat, Willy grows desperate and demands justice, reminding Howard of his thirty-four years with the firm and of promises that Howard's father had made him; Howard simply walks out: "You'll have to excuse me, Willy, I gotta see some people. Pull yourself together."

Howard leaves, and we sense that Willy is worse off than before. There follows a brief interlude in which Willy thinks that he sees his old boss sitting in his chair, and is then frightened by accidentally turning on the wire recorder (which symbolizes Willy's inability to deal with the changes going on in the world.) This interlude serves to prolong and heighten the sense of crisis, which happens immediately.

Howard reenters, and Willy, knowing that he has made a terrible mistake, tries to put things back the way they were by saying, "I'll go to Boston." The scene is now at its main crisis as Howard chooses to fire Willy: "Willy, you can't go to Boston for us."

There follows a beat which flows from the crisis. Willy absorbs the fact that he's being fired and starts to beg, but Howard refuses to take responsibility, and asks, "Where are your sons? Why don't your sons give you a hand?" Of course, the last thing a proud man like Willy could do is to accept help from his sons:

WILLY:     I can't throw myself on my sons. I'm not a cripple!"
HOWARD:    Look, kid, I'm busy this morning.
WILLY:     (*Grasping* HOWARD'S *arm*) Howard, you've got to let me go to
           Boston!
HOWARD:    (*Hard, keeping himself under control*) I've got a line of people to
           see me this morning. Sit down, take five minutes, and pull yourself
           together, and then go home, will ya? I need the office, Willy.

Thus a fairly long scene (some ten minute's playing time) can be understood as being comprised of just five beats and an interlude leading to its main crisis, followed by one beat of "denoument." At the end, as with most scenes, we are left wondering "What will happen now?" so that we are led forward into the scenes to follow.

Notice that in each beat there is a central conflict between the objectives of the characters. These mini-conflicts may take the form of action versus obstacle, or action versus counter-action. For example, Willy is trying to get Howard to pay attention to him, while Howard is trying to avoid what he knows will be a painful confrontation. We can speak, therefore, of a beat as having its own central conflict and crisis.

Note also that within each beat the characters have a single objective or point of reaction. It is this fact that permits you to translate the architecture of the scene into the thoughts and actions of your character. You *as the actor* understand this structure and design the consciousness of the character so as to contribute to it; then, as you play the scene, you can surrender your immediate awareness *to the character's consciousness* knowing that what your character thinks, says and does will serve the scene.

If all the actors have worked together to develop a shared understanding of the scenario, the rhythm of the scene will be strong and clear. It is as important for actors to agree on the phraseology of their shared action as it is for members of an orchestra to work together to fulfill the phraseology of a piece.

To summarize, there are three main qualities of all beats:

1. A beat has a central conflict of its own, which drives the transactions between the characters;
2. It has its own clear shape and specific moment of crisis;
3. The crisis is a choice made by one of the characters which creates a new objective or different strategy.

### Exercise 62:
### Beat Breakdown

A. ANALYSIS
Using the same scene you developed in the last Lesson, work with your scene partner to do the following:

1. Make a scenario of your scene, as in the example above.
2. Select one important beat:
   a. define its central conflict;
   b. specify its moment of crisis;
   c. decide who makes the choice which is the crisis.
3. Examine how this beat grows out of the preceding beat and flows into the following beat.

## SCENE STRUCTURE

There are a number of other ways to define scenes. One of the oldest is the "French scene," which merely marks the entrance of a major character, and is a virtually useless device for the actor (the plays of Moliere, for instance, are divided in this way). Short plays like *The Zoo Story* and even some longer plays, like those of Beckett, may not be divided into scenes at all, though you can usually identify units of scenic action within them; the section in which Jerry takes the bench away from Peter might be thought of as one "scene," for example.

We will define a scene in the same way we defined a beat; each scene is a major item in the "scenario" of the entire play, each has its own central conflict, and each has its own clear shape and scene crisis. Though a scene can nearly stand on its own (whereas a beat cannot) it must also propel us forward into the next scene, so it will rarely have a strong climax.

Another important quality of a scene is that it will contain a *change in the situation* which causes the play to move in a somewhat new direction. The change may be some new piece of information, a change in relationship, or a new event. You can identify the most important aspect of a scene by asking yourself, "What would happen if this scene were cut from the play? What would we lose that would make it impossible for the plot to progress?" The answer is the main event of the scene, and your playing of the scene must achieve this event above all.

In the scene between Willy and his boss, for example, the major change in the situation is that Willy is fired. As a result, he has no way of fighting for his self-esteem because the only way he knows how to is through selling. He is forced, for the first time, to confront himself directly. All his life, he has known himself as a salesman; now that he cannot know himself in this materialistic, external way, will he be able to find his spiritual, inner self?

Beside identifying the main event of the scene, you will also benefit from identifying the exact moment of crisis. You will find it easier to identify the crisis if you think *backwards* from the main event, looking for the moment in which the outcome hangs in the balance. In this scene, that moment occurs when Howard finally decides that Willy must be fired and Willy cannot dissuade him.

Having identified the main event and moment of crisis, now identify each of the beat changes, as you did in the previous exercise, and see how each beat change contributes to the flow toward or away from the crisis. You now have a complete *scenario* of the scene.

When the actors have developed a shared understanding of the structure of the scene they can best begin to explore it in detail. This understanding will probably not be a verbal one, but rather a shared *rhythmic* experience of the rise and fall of the scene's energy. Structure lives as a sort of underlying "dance" in the flow of the scene: you feel the energy moving toward the crisis and then flowing naturally from it.

This sense of the underlying structure of the scene is especially important in film and television work when a single camera is used. A short section of the scene is usually shot from an overall point of view; this is called the "master." Several "takes" may be required before everything works, and then closer individual shots are taken, called "coverage," which are later to be inserted into the master by the editor. Several "takes" of each are usually required, and the whole process can take many hours. Not only must your performance be consistent from take to take, your close-ups must also "match" the master as to timing, position, expression, etc. This is made even harder by the fact that scenes, and even coverage within scenes, are often shot out of sequence. All this means that the film actor *must* have a firm sense of the structure of the scene, and how every moment fits into it, in mind.

In both film and stage work, the scenario is a kind of "map" which traces the energy-flow of a scene and permits all the actors to support one another in their journey through it. Sharing such a map makes your rehearsal exploration much more effective, and because you have less fear of becoming lost, your work can be more creative and enjoyable. Most important, the shared map helps you each to experience the natural shape and momentum of the scene as a single, rhythmic event. One symptom that the scene has started to "play" in this way is that it will seem shorter to you when you perform it.

### Exercise 63:
### The Scenario

Working in collaboration with your partner, answer these questions about your scene:

1. What is the major change in the situation of the play which occurs in this scene? How does this change cause the plot to progress?
2. What is the central scene conflict?
3. Examine the beat breakdown you made in the previous exercise; which beat contains the crisis of the scene? How do all the previous beats flow toward it, and how do subsequent beats flow from it?
4. Rehearse the scene on the basis of this analysis.

# Lesson
# Thirteen

# The Superobjective
# and Through-Line of Action

In the last lesson, you learned that a play is structured on levels: individual transactions make up beats, beats make up scenes, and the scenes form the overall shape of rising and falling action which give unity to the whole. Your character has objectives which correspond to each of these levels: in each individual transaction you will have an *immediate* objective; the flow of immediate objectives leads toward a *beat objective*; the objectives of each beat in sequence lead toward a *scene objective*; and the scene objectives can be seen as springing from a deep, overall objective which is the character's "life goal" or, as it is usually called, their *superobjective*.

For example, consider again the scene from *Death of a Salesman* in which Willy Loman goes to see his boss in order to get a job in the home office. Willy finds him engrossed in his new recorder, and is told, "I'll be with you in a minute." Being a good salesman, Willy tries to get his foot in the door by engaging Howard in conversation and asks, "What's that, Howard?"

At this moment, Willy's *immediate* objective is *to get Howard to talk to him by asking about the recorder*. Once he accomplishes this, he hopes he can move on toward his *beat* objective, which is *to bring up the subject of his assignment in a friendly way*; he would then hope *to persuade Howard to give him a spot in town* since he'd "rather not travel anymore," and that is his *scene* objective. His objective in this scene is connected directly to his *superobjective*: since he can no longer drive, he must get a spot in town in order to go on selling, and selling is the only way he knows how to pursue his life goal or superobjective, which is *to prove himself worthy by earning money and respect.*

You see that Willy's objectives on each level work together in a logical way, his immediate objective leading toward his beat objective, his beat objectives being steps toward his scene objective, and the scene objective as springing directly from his superobjective.

If we were to follow each of Willy's immediate objectives through the play, we could see how he is led from objective to objective in pursuit of his superobjective. The logic of this sequence of objectives striving toward the superobjective is called the *through-line* of the character's action.

Stanislavski once said that each individual action committed by a character fitted into this through-line, like vertebrae in a spine, hence the through-line is sometimes also called the "spine" of the role.

> In a play the whole stream of individual minor objectives, all the imaginative thoughts, feelings and actions of an actor should converge to carry out this superobjective. . . . Also this impetus toward the superobjective must be continuous throughout the whole play.[1]

Identifying your character's through-line of action as tending toward a superobjective can help you to better understand each of your specific actions, connecting each momentary action to the character's deepest needs and desires. It can also help you to see how the sequence of objectives has a single driving force; thus you can "play through" each moment and achieve both unity and momentum (what we call *pace*) in your performance.

Let's examine each of these concepts in detail.

## THE SUPEROBJECTIVE

A character's superobjective may be conscious or (more commonly) unconscious. Either way, it functions as an underlying principle which affects all of their actions, and sets the tone of their attitude toward life.

Willy Loman, for example, is presented with two alternative attitudes toward life. He could, like his brother Ben, strike off on some bold venture and be the "master of his fate"; or he could, like his neighbor Charley, accept his life as it is and find inner peace. But Willy lacks the courage to follow his brother's example, and lacks also Charlie's sense of self-identity. Willy has opted instead to earn his place in the world through selling. In the scene with Howard, Willy describes the moment he formed this superobjective:

. . . I met a salesman in the Parker House. His name was Dave Singleman. And he was eighty-four years old, and he'd drummed merchandise in thirty-one states. And old Dave, he'd go up to his room, y'understand, put on his green velvet slippers—I'll never forget—and pick up his phone and call buyers, and without ever leaving his room, at the age of eighty-four, he made his living. And when I saw that, I realized that selling was the greatest career a man could want.[2]

Eventually, however, Willy is no longer able to sell either his products or himself. His last "sale" is his suicide, and the insurance money is the last paycheck he will "earn." It will give his family the financial independence he has so long sought as a measure of his worth.

What drives the entire play is Willy's constant search for the success that will prove he is a worthy person; his tragedy is that he defines his success by the external measures of esteem and possessions. We can summarize Willy's superobjective as "to prove myself worthy by earning money and respect." Each scene, each beat, each moment of the role and every aspect of Willy's psychology can be understood as reflecting this superobjective.

Because it is so important to the theme of *Death of a Salesman*, Miller was explicit about Willy's superobjective; most plays are not so specific, even in the case of the major character. In most cases you must *deduce* your character's superobjective from their behavior in their circumstances. Tom in *The Glass Menagerie*, for example, clearly needs to make a place for himself in the world, but he cannot do this unless he escapes his role as the "provider" for his mother and helpless sister. Tom's superobjective therefore translates into the specific need "to leave home without guilt." The through-line of his scene objectives, his beat objectives, and each of his immediate objectives can be seen as being driven by this superobjective.

It is possible for the superobjective of a character to change in the course of the play under the pressure of extraordinary circumstances. King Lear begins his play intent upon retiring from the responsibilities of kingship so that he can enjoy his last days "unburdened" and basking in the love of his family and subjects. In the course of his suffering, however, he learns that he has been ignorant of true love, and he surrenders his self-centered superobjective in favor of a desire for universal justice and the simple, personal love he feels for Cordelia at the end.

It may be difficult to find the superobjective of minor characters, since the playwright has not provided much information; here you can be inventive, so long as your understanding of the character enables you to serve your dramatic function within the play without distortion, and without throwing the play out of focus by calling undue attention to yourself.

Even more difficult may be those plays in which the internal life of the characters is purposely mysterious, as those by Pinter, Beckett, or

Shepard. It may be useful to you as an actor to discover some sense of superobjective for such characters, but it would be disastrous if you were to "play" the superobjective and reveal it to the audience. All great plays have some measure of mystery at their heart, and it is a mistake to "pluck it out" by exposing things that the playwright meant to remain obscure.

Though you may develop some idea about your character's super-objective before rehearsals start, it is dangerous to become too set in your thinking; these early ideas need to be tested. Ideally, the sense of super-objective will emerge gradually from your experience of the specific actions of your character. Let your sense of the superobjective be the result of your rehearsal exploration, not a substitute for it.

## FINDING AND PERSONALIZING
## THE SUPEROBJECTIVE

Once you have begun to identify the superobjective, you must *personalize* it; you must come to care as deeply about it as your character does. Since the superobjective of most characters is fairly "universal" this is usually not difficult; like Willy Loman, we all want to be thought of as worthy, and we can all "identify" with Willy on this basis, however much we can see that Willy's way of pursuing self-esteem is mistaken.

In some cases, however, the precise manner in which a character manifests the superobjective may be so foreign to you that it presents difficulties. Isabella in Shakespeare's *Measure for Measure* is faced with a choice between sleeping with the Duke or seeing her brother executed for a trivial crime. Isabella, who is about to become a nun, believes that losing her virginity in this way would damn her, and she fully expects her brother to be willing to die in this cause, thereby winning a place in heaven. When he isn't, she angrily condemns him. If you are playing Isabella, it may be difficult for you to identify with such strong and inflexible religious values.

In such a case, you may have to find some analogous superobjective which can motivate you as strongly as your character's does her. In the case of Isabella, you might consider what action is so loathsome to you that you would ask your brother to die before you would do it; then, "substitute" this in your own mind for Isabella's situation.

Such substitutions may be useful, but they carry the danger of bring-ing inappropriate personal material into the performance. It is better, if possible, to simply surrender yourself to your character's situation and be-lief system. Remember our version of Stanislavski's "Magic If:" if you were in the character's situation, and if you made the same choices, who would you become? You have a vast personal potential; somewhere in you the religious fanatic, the saint, the mass murderer, the courageous hero, the snivelling coward are all waiting to be realized.

**Exercise 64:**
**The Superobjective**

Using the same scene you have worked on in previous Lessons, answer the following questions:

1.  Examine your character's actions: can you see a superobjective toward which they are tending, whether the character is conscious of it or not? Consider how this superobjective enables your character to fulfill his or her dramatic function.
2.  Define the superobjective using a transitive verb phrase with qualifiers.
3.  Look through your script: are there any actual lines that sum up your character's superobjective?
4.  Now consider ways of personalizing this superobjective, so that you feel it with the same intensity as does your character.

Now rehearse your scene again and find how the superobjective is expressed in it.

## THE THROUGH-LINE OF ACTION

It is neither easy nor necessary to describe the through-line of a role in words; it is more important to *feel* the sequence and flow of the role, and the "logic" by which one action leads into another as steps tending toward the superobjective. For this reason, the through-line will usually emerge gradually as the individual actions are explored and experienced in rehearsal.

The sense of through-line provides a background against which immediate objectives may be understood; as it becomes clear, each moment in your performance begins to "fit" with every other in a harmonious way; you can feel the spine of the role developing. Moments which seem incomprehensible at first begin to fit into the flow of the whole, like steps in a single journey. When finally the whole is in place, each moment of the performance will cumulatively support every other moment, and you will be moved naturally from one to the other by a sense of necessity.

In a production of Brecht's *Mother Courage*, for example, the actress playing the role of Kattrin, the mute daughter, needed help with her last scene. In it, Kattrin climbs atop a hut and beats a drum to warn the nearby town of an impending attack. The soldiers coax and threaten her, trying to make her stop drumming, but she refuses and is shot. Obviously, her choice to sacrifice herself in order to warn the town is the most important choice she makes in the play; it is also the crisis of the entire play, which embodies the play's meaning: we have created a world in which love for your fellow man is suicidal.

Knowing its great importance in the play, this actress was having terrible difficulty with this final choice. Rehearsal after rehearsal, she tried different ways of climbing the ladder, different ways of drumming, different ways of thinking through the choice. Nothing worked, and she was in despair.

Her mistake was in thinking that the problem was in this climactic scene; her real problem was that she had not yet found the through-line which would bring her to this moment properly. She had to examine each moment of her role, each of her previous actions and reactions, to see how it contributed to this final action, since this final action embodied the ultimate development of her character.

The dramatic purpose of Kattrin's character, then, is to provide one glimmer of selflessness against which we can judge the callousness of a world in which love has been sacrificed to economic necessity. Her superobjective, which we learn in various scenes, is to have a child which she can care for; the fact that there are children in the town is crucial, because by sacrificing her life for them she is winning her superobjective in the only way which the world of the play makes possible.

Having understood this, the actress began to go through rehearsals, moment by moment, asking herself, "what do I see going on at this moment that will eventually contribute to my beating that drum?" Each of her moments, beats and scenes were quickly understood as contributing to this through-line, and then climaxing in her final choice. Soon, that final choice became not only easy, but unavoidable!

When your character has such a climactic action it must be the "payoff" resulting from careful preparation. You may reap only what you have previously sown, and this cumulative effect is achieved by sensing the through-line and fitting each individual action into its proper place in the sequence.

We should note that unlike this example, a character's through-line may not be a "straight line." The character may try one thing, then another; they may need to discover an effective course of action through trial and error. Think of the through-line as the motivational energy driving your character forward toward their superobjective; every time they have to choose what to do, they will choose the thing that seems *at that moment and in that circumstance* to move in the desired direction, even if they later discover that they were wrong.

Perhaps the greatest value in experiencing the through-line is that you will find how each moment of your performance is driven by your character's deepest energies. In *The Glass Menagerie*, Tom introduces his sister Laura to Jim, the Gentleman Caller. This simple introduction ("Jim, this is Laura; Laura, this is Jim") can be seen as part of Jim's through-line of action moving toward his superobjective:

*Immediate Objective:* To get Laura and Jim off to a good start;

*Beat Objective:* To lay the seeds of a relationship between them;

*Scene Objective:* Hopefully to bring another man into the house permanently;

*Superobjective:* Because if there were another man in the house, I could leave home without guilt since Mother and Laura would be "looked after," and I could get out of here and find my own identity.

This is how the through-line of action brings unity and momentum (*pace*) to every moment of your performance. Once you have fit each moment into its place within the structure of the whole during your rehearsal preparation, you are then free in performance to give your full attention to playing each moment, secure that it will also be serving the play as a whole.

### Exercise 65:
### The Through-line

A. Examine the sequence of your character's objectives within your scene; do you see its logic as a reflection of an underlying movement toward a superobjective?

B. In each individual transaction, try to feel the connection of the immediate objective to the beat objective, the scene objective, and to the superobjective.

C. Run the scene without stopping and feel the momentum of the sequence of objectives.

## PACING THE SCENE

You have seen how a sense of through-line and superobjective can provide unity and momentum to each momentary transaction of your performance. When the actors experience how each of their individual actions contribute to the flow of the whole, the performance will take on a momentum that provides a sense of urgency, significance, and rising dramatic tension.

As in our Impulse Circle exercise, the actors will no longer have to make the scene happen, the scene will make itself happen! Each actor will receive more energy from the whole than they give to it, and the whole will be greater than the sum of its parts.

On the other hand, a scene lacking in momentum feels "flat" and fails to compel our attention: we commonly call this a lack of *pace*. Note that "pace," meaning the *momentum* of the action, is different than "tempo," which refers only to its *speed*.

When a scene lacks pace, there is a temptation to speed up or artificially "hype" the action; this is always a mistake. Good pace results only from the natural flow of the action according to its own internal logic; this natural connectedness is realized only when each transaction of reaction and action between the characters is real and complete. Rushing or forcing the scene only blurs these connections and harms the pace.

Paradoxically, poor pace is usually best corrected by "taking the time" to reestablish the connections within the scene, since a well-written scene contains all that is needed to achieve good pace.

The best source of pace is the underlying conflict of the scene itself. Whatever form the conflict has been given, it provides momentum by driving the conflicting forces against one another as the need for a resolution grows. If you can experience the conflict in this way, it can provide momentum as part of the intrinsic reality of the scene, thus avoiding an artificial heightening of energy by rushing or forcing your action.

More difficult are those scenes in which there is no obvious source of pace since there is no strong conflict between the characters. In such cases, the situation or locale of the scene may supply a sense of urgency: there may be an *external deadline* that requires that an objective be achieved as quickly as possible, such as someone coming, or the fear of discovery.

More commonly there is an *internal deadline*, such as the need to do something before you lose your nerve, to say something before breaking into tears, etc.

In some cases, since no playwright is always perfect, it may be necessary for the actors to invent some external or internal source of momentum for a scene. This might involve redefining the given circumstances to provide urgency. Another strategy is to invent some surface activity such as sewing, smoking, drinking, eating, or playing cards, that might help you to channel your energy outward and thereby move the scene forward.

On the other hand, it may be that at moments of great tension or emotion, *containment* and *stillness* will produce better pace than activity. Some actors tend to thrash about during the monumental emotional crises of classical tragedies, and this tends only to dilute and belittle the passion of the scene. Remember that activity "spends" energy and that you must invest your stage energy with great discrimination; it is often true that "less is more," *if* it is the right "less."

One important element of good pace is *cuing*, the way in which one character begins to speak after another has finished. In real life, if you and I are discussing something, I listen to you in order to understand the idea you are trying to express. When I have grasped that idea, I form my response and am usually ready to begin answering *before* you have actually finished your sentence. Listen to real-life conversations; do you hear how we actually overlap one another's speeches slightly, or at least are *ready* to respond before the other person has stopped talking?

This kind of overlap may actually be appropriate in naturalistic plays where the flow of the dialogue is meant to be like that in real-life. In non-naturalistic plays, however, especially in verse plays, we must respect the dialogue rhythm as structured by the playwright. But even here the energy which drives one speech must be aroused before the previous speech has ended. Even necessary pauses for thought between speeches must be filled with the energy which connects one speech to another; such pauses, by the way, must be rare so as to stand out in contrast to the normal flow of the dialogue.

To sum up, a scene will move with good pace naturally when you and your partners have experienced the through-line of your action, have recognized those conflicts or conditions that drive it forward with a sense of urgency or significance, and deliver your lines with good cuing.

Remember that the real source of a scene's pace is within the reality of the scene itself, not in any external technique applied by the actors. Any action, any piece of business, any emotion, or any character trait that impedes the pace of the scene should be discarded. As Stanislavski was fond of saying, "cut 80 percent!"

### Exercise 66:
### Pacing the Scene

Examine your scene with your partner, looking for those aspects of the situation which provide urgency or a sense of deadline and thereby contribute to the scene's momentum:

1.  The physical environment: time, place, and so forth.
2.  The social environment: customs, the presence of others.
3.  The situation: internal or external factors which create urgency or tension.
4.  The conflict between you.

Now rehearse your scene to achieve good pace, and practice your listening and responding skills to produce good cuing.

# Lesson
# Fourteen

# Emotion and Personalization

In the previous lesson, we said that you must *personalize* your character's objectives on every level and come to care about them as much as the character does. In this lesson, we will explore ways of doing this through various emotional techniques.

What is emotion? The root meaning of the word is *an outward movement*. It is any activity that expresses the immediate condition of our organism and is directed toward the outside world. This doesn't mean that emotional activity is always meant to be communicative; rather it arises automatically out of our efforts to relate to life. There are times, of course, when we wish to make our feelings known to others, but the feelings themselves have arisen in the course of our interaction with the world as we move outward and encounter either the satisfaction or frustration of our intentions.

In everyday life emotion serves many purposes. First, most forms of emotional expression are *safety-valve actions* that provide a release of tensions (pleasant or unpleasant) before they can build up to a point that would be injurious. Since our organisms tend to seek equilibrium through the release of tensions, emotions are one of our basic adaptive mechanisms.

Second, emotion is a *symbolic activity*. It serves to let us "act out" our feelings as tangible behavior. As we said earlier, most forms of emotional behavior are symbolic variations of activities that were at one time practical in nature.

Finally, some psychologists view emotions as a form of *value judgment* which we pass on our actions. Pleasurable emotions arise from those actions that we feel are "successful" in attaining a desired goal; painful emotions arise from those actions that are "unsuccessful." Specifically, when we try to attain an objective and are successful, we become happy; when we try to attain an objective and fail due to our own actions, we are sad; when we try to attain an objective and are prevented by circumstance or by someone else's actions, we become angry; when we try to attain an objective and fail, and don't know why, we become afraid.

From all these points of view, emotion is tied inextricably to action; it arises automatically from any significant confrontation with the world. So it is on stage: as actors, we do not create emotion; rather, emotion arises of its own accord out of our involvement in our action.

## THE GENESIS
## OF EMOTION IN ACTION:
## WORKING FROM THE OUTSIDE IN

Near the turn of the century two psychologists, Fritz Lange and William James, independently developed a theory of emotion of special interest to the actor (Stanislavski was familiar with it). This theory holds that what we call emotion is our recognition of a bodily condition which is itself a response to some external situation.

Let's say you are stepping off a curb when out of the corner of your eye, you see a car rushing toward you. Immediately you leap back out of danger. You are afraid, but you did not jump because you were afraid: you reacted to the signal of danger with a direct motor response; in the terms we have been using, it was an "automatic action." Your body automatically prepared for "flight or fight," as the psychologists say. Only then, with your heart pounding, adrenalin flowing, your breath short, did you recognize your own condition and call it "fear." Your emotion did not cause your action, your action caused your emotion!

This view of emotion can help to explain how emotional experience is communicated from actor to audience. It begins with simple physical imitation, which is unconscious and involuntary: the spectator's muscles empathically mirror the actor's physical state. If I watch you and your back is bowed and your chest collapsed, *my* back starts to bow and my chest collapses in a tiny but measurable way. Because my muscles are responding similarly to yours, the emotion connected with that physical state is inspired in me.

In this way I share your emotion directly, rather than simply observing it. If you are Willy Loman, shuffling across the stage at the start of the play, back bowed and chest collapsed, I participate physically in your exhaustion and dejection *even if I do not understand it conceptually.*

This same process applies to you as you play the character. If you adopt your character's action and enter fully into their physical condition, the fullness of the specific emotion required will grow within you!

Therefore, you needn't be concerned with emotional behavior as such; if you are able to pursue your character's action and physical condition with full involvement, the emotion will arise and it will be communicated to your audience. As some directors say, "Do the act, and the feeling will follow."

We should specify this idea further, however; if you do the *correct* act in the *correct* way, then the *correct* feeling will follow. In this way, your own emotional response to what you are doing serves to guide you in checking the correctness of your action. This is what the experienced actor means when he or she tries something and then says "It didn't feel right"; this is not a judgment about an emotional state, it is an evaluation of the action itself through its resultant emotion.

Another way of putting it is to say that your aim as Willy Loman is not to be dejected, but rather to find the specific quality of action and physical condition which produces the feeling that you understand the play to require at that moment. Your search for this action is guided by the script which provides not only specified actions, but a whole range of implied physical conditions embodied in its rhythms, emphases, images, and overall structure (we will explore these in detail in the next Part.)

You should consider the playwright's stage directions as well; in the sample speech from Albee's *The Zoo Story* (Appendix One) you will notice stage directions like *(JERRY is abnormally tense, now. . .)* and *(Much faster now, and like a conspirator).* You and your director may eventually choose to disregard such specifics in your particular production, but you must consider the internal state which the playwright meant for them to imply, and experience it in some other form.

My own preference is to respect the stage directions of most writers, in the same way that a musician would respect the diacritical markings for tempo and volume in a musical score. There is a moment in Chekhov's *The Three Sisters*, for example, when a stage direction says that Natasha "stamps her foot;" this functions like a sforzando in music, and if the actress ignores it, the scene will be incorrect.

By participating physically in such specified externals, we find the character's inner state to be engendered in us. As Plato noted two thousand years ago, the actor mimicking the gestures of an angry person tends to become angry.

**Exercise 67:**
**Working from the Outside In**

Examine your scene again, paying special attention to the external actions
(words, gestures, movements) and the physical condition suggested for
your character. Rehearse it so as to involve yourself in these externals as
fully as possible; surrender to the experience which they produce in you.

You should remember that emotion on stage is not always expressed in the
way it might be in everyday life; the form which any emotional expression
takes on stage must be consistent with the demands of the play's style.
Characters in Shakespeare and Chekhov might need to express similar
emotions, but the form in which the emotion would be expressed would
be different in each case.


## THE GENESIS OF EMOTION IN THOUGHT:
## WORKING FROM THE INSIDE OUT

As we said earlier, emotion arises out of our attempts to cope with the
world, and is in part our way of evaluating these attempts. In this sense,
emotion arises from action. But thoughts themselves are "acts," and our
evaluations of action are colored by our expectations and attitudes. The
school of psychotherapy called "cognitive therapy" is based on this fact:

> The first principle of cognitive therapy is that all your moods are created
> by your "cognitions," or thoughts. A cognition refers to the way you look at
> things—your perceptions, mental attitudes, and beliefs. It includes the way
> you interpret things—what you say about something or someone to yourself.
> You feel the way you do right now because of the thoughts you are thinking
> at this moment. . .
>     . . . The moment you have a certain thought and believe it, you will
> experience an immediate emotional response. Your thought actually creates
> the emotion.[1]

For example, suppose you want to become an actor and are reading this
thinking, "Hey, that sounds good; Benedetti's approach could really help
me!" This positive thought will make you feel good. If, on the other hand,
you are thinking, "This is too silly, I could never do it," then your feeling
will be negative.

Psychologists who treat depression have noticed that depressed people are seldom less "successful" in objective terms than many who are not
depressed; the difference lies more in the way they subjectively view themselves and their lives. They "send themselves messages" which are negative,
and every hint of failure confirms this negative self-attitude.

Some people hold a view of themselves as being unworthy: like Willy Loman, they can't accept praise or success which they don't feel they've "earned" through great effort, and they often can't accept the love which others may feel for them, as if this too must be "earned."

I have noticed that many actors feel unworthy as people; perhaps creating a stage performance is their way of "earning" the attention and praise from others which they find it difficult to accept in everyday life. While this is a powerful motivation for an acting career, it is a dangerous one: a person who feels unworthy of attention tends to "do too much" on stage as a way of "earning" the right to the audience's attention. Think about yourself: is what you do on stage rooted in your need to "earn" our attention? Are you sending yourself the message that "you better do something or they won't like you!"

Of course, cheerful and optimistic people are also sending themselves messages; they tend to evaluate their transactions with the world in more positive terms, like "I'm getting better at it," or "What I do makes a difference." Therapists know that identifying the negative self-messages and replacing them with realistically positive ones can change the way we feel.

In developing the emotional life of a character, it may be useful to examine the character's attitude toward themselves. Willy Loman is no less "successful" in objective terms than is his neighbor, Charlie, but he feels like a failure whereas Charlie feels like a success. Willy is constantly sending himself the message that he has to earn the respect of others and even the love of his own sons; he tries to do this by "selling" himself. He refuses to admit, as Charlie urges him to do, that he is a worthwhile human being. Willy has accepted the materialistic attitude of his society, and measures his personal worth in external terms: the size of his paycheck and the approval of others. Charlie, on the other hand, is able to accept his life and himself without external validation.

The messages which someone sends themself express a dominant attitude toward life which is clearly reflected in that person's superobjective. Willy's superobjective is "to prove myself worthy by earning money and respect"; the underlying assumption is that he is *unworthy*. He has created an unconscious attitude toward himself which we call his *self-image*.

We tend to become strongly attached to our self-image, even when it is negative. Much of Willy Loman's behavior seems perversely dedicated to proving his own unworthiness, just as Blanche Dubois behaves in ways that prove that she needs "to depend on the kindness of strangers." This kind of repeated pattern of behavior based on the self-image is called in Transactional Analysis the *life script*; this term implies that we live out our own self-image in a way that makes it a self-fulfilling prophecy.

To sum up: A character's superobjective is related to their self-image, which is in turn reflected in the choices they make in "acting out" their life script. Let's apply these ideas to your scene.

**Exercise 68: Self-image:**
**Working from the Inside Out**

What is your character's dominant self-image? What messages do they send themselves? Enter into your character's frame of mind and complete these phrases just before doing your scene:

1. The most beautiful part of my body is. . . .
2. Happiness to me is. . . .
3. The thing I most want to do before I die is. . . .
4. The most embarrassed I ever was. . . .
5. The ugliest part of my body is. . . .
6. The thing I like best about myself is. . . .
7. Pain to me is. . . .
8. My mother. . . .
9. The thing I regret most is. . . .
10. The most secret thing about me is. . . .
11. I can hear my father's voice speaking through my own when I tell myself. . . .
12. Love to me is. . . .
13. The thing I am most proud of is. . . .
14. Every time I don't get what I want I tell myself. . . .
15. If you could hear the music in me. . . .
16. I want my epitaph to be. . . .

Immediately enter into the scene and allow these feelings to effect it.

As you have seen in the last two exercises, it is possible to work *either* from the inside out *or* from the outside in. Emotion arises automatically out of your involvement in *both* the actions *and* thoughts of your character. Though you may find one approach more powerful for you than the other, most actors work simultaneously from the inside out and from the outside in!

## EMOTIONAL RECALL
## AND SUBSTITUTION

As emotion arises from your involvement in the actions and thoughts of your character, it often brings up associations or memories of past situations in your own life in which you experienced similar emotions. The formation of connections with the character's situation can be an enriching aspect of the acting process; we refer to this process as *personalization.*

Stanislavski experimented with the idea that the actor could develop their store of emotional memories as a resource for the acting process, much as a painter learns to mix colors:

> The broader your emotion memory, the richer your material for inner cre-
> ativeness. . . . Our creative experiences are vivid and full in direct proportion
> to the power, keenness and exactness of our memory. . . . Sometimes mem-
> ories continue to live in us, grow and become deeper. They even stimulate
> new processes and either fill out unfinished details or suggest altogether new
> ones.[2]

Stanislavski worked in the theatre at a time when psychology was emerging
as a specialized field, and he was deeply interested in it (Pavlov was a friend
who contributed to his thinking). One idea from early Russian psychology
which appealed to him was the notion that every cell in the body had a
capacity for memory, so that the recall of emotional states had the potential
to energize the actor in much more than a "mental" way.

We would not entirely disagree with this idea today, though we have
other ways of understanding the function of memory. One contemporary
school of thought, called "Psychocybernetics," describes the operation of
memory as serving the needs of survival. Your mind tends to record events
which, for various reasons, might be useful as a basis for future action.
They remain "on file," ready for recall should a similar situation occur,
when we can repeat (or avoid) actions that were in the past successful (or
unsuccessful).

For example, you probably suffered some physical injury, discomfort,
or severe psychological distress at some time in your childhood, and you
have probably "filed" certain prominent details of the event. These details,
or things which merely remind you of them, may continue to evoke feelings
when they recur, even when the new situation is quite different from the
original, or when the original has been lost to consciousness. In this way,
some events and details continue to evoke strong responses even when there
is no longer a direct link to the original situation. (Smells are especially
powerful in evoking memories.)

There are several techniques by which stored memories may be evoked.
Common to all of them is the crucial ingredient of *relaxation*. When we
relax, the subconscious becomes more accessible and we become more responsive to it. One of the easiest of these techniques involves *visualization*.
By relaxing deeply and entering into a visualization of the character's situation, the actor can invite associations from their store of memories. These
associations, or "recalls," automatically become attached to the character's
actions and situation; it is neither necessary nor desirable to "play" them;
they are simply allowed to "be there."

Another recall technique which may be useful in certain situations
involves making a mental *substitution* of someone from your own life for
one of the other characters in the scene. If you are supposed to be terribly
afraid of another character, it might be useful to recall someone frightening
from your own life and "substitute" them for that character.

Such a "substitution" is a special kind of emotional recall, and will
often arise naturally as you work.

Recalls and substitutions needn't be rooted in real events; *fantasies* sometimes supply more powerful material than memories of real events. I once played Lear, and found that Cordelia's dead body "became" the body of my son; my son was neither dead nor as old as Cordelia, but my love for him, and the grief I would feel should he die, helped me to feel as if I were in Lear's situation.

As useful as the processes of emotional recall and substitution may sometimes be, they are dangerous and can easily be misused. First, while recalls may be useful for opening an initial connection into the character's experience, you must go beyond this initial connection into the *specific* experience of the character within his or her given circumstances; if you do not, your response may be merely personal without serving the needs or style of the play.

Second, memories can be very powerful, and those which have not yet been fully assimilated can easily overwhelm artistic control. If you "fall into" your personal memory, you will no longer behave as if you were the character but will merely behave as yourself; you will also be out of the "here and now," cut off from your given circumstances and your partners by your absorption in the memory you are reliving. Lee Strasberg liked to say that seven years was a good length of time for a recall to have "matured," but since some memories grow stronger with age there is no guarantee that time alone will provide mastery over them.

Third, substitutions especially can become an obstacle to vivid contact with your scene partners. No one ought to have to be on stage with someone who is looking at them but "seeing" someone else. How much better to find the necessary qualities in the actor who is actually playing the role!

For all these reasons, I stress that though recalls may be useful as training and rehearsal devices, they are absolutely *not* intended for use in performance.

My own feeling is that a conscious use of emotional recall is neither necessary nor desirable, and note that Stanislavski himself eventually abandoned the technique. Personalization is a natural process (unless it is inhibited by internal censorship) and memories and associations arise naturally in the course of preparing a role; not much is gained by using this process in a premeditated way, and much can be lost. Most of all, one risks that omnipresent danger, *self-consciousness*. David Mamet said it best:

> The laws of attention which are true off stage are true *on* stage. The self-concerned person is a bore and the self-concerned *actor* is a bore. And whether the actor is saying, "I must play this scene in order to be well thought of," or, "I must remember and recreate the time my puppy died in order to recreate this scene well," makes no difference. In both cases his attention is self-centered, and in both cases his performance will tell us nothing we couldn't have learned more enjoyably in a library.
>
> Acting, as any art, must be generous; the attention of the artist must be

focused outward—not on what he is feeling, but on what he is trying to accomplish.[3]

## Exercise 69:
## Emotional Recalls
## and Substitutions

A. Place yourself comfortably at rest and do the Phasic Relaxation exercise.

B. Now go through your scene mentally; picture the entire circumstance and live through your character's actions as if you were actually doing them in those circumstances. Let your body respond freely.

C. As you live through the scene, notice the emotional associations that arise. Do you remember events from your past? Do the other characters remind you of people you have known? Avoid internal censorship; release into these memories fully.

D. Now examine the most significant of these recalls. Ask yourself the following questions about each memory:

   1. Where in my body is it located?

   2. What is it like? How big is it, what color is it, how much does it weigh?

   3. When I relive this event or recall this person, how does my body feel?

   4. Are there ideas, attitudes, or beliefs connected with this memory?

   5. Do I recall making any choices at this time, even unconsciously, which have effected me since?

   6. Are there images from even earlier times in this memory? If so, experience these: continue to allow such images to flood up and take you back further and further in time.

E. Review this exercise and evaluate any connections which were made; are they useful to the scene? Do they need to be specified or altered to meet the exact demands of the scene or style of the play?

F. Rehearse your scene and simply allow these associations to "be there."

## THE ROLE OF EMOTION
## IN PERFORMANCE

Finally, we must say something about the way in which you will experience your character's emotions in repeated performances.

By now, you have understood that you don't need to feel or even think a certain way in order to do something; rather you can come to feel a certain way because of what you are doing and thinking. This means that you don't need to achieve any particular level of emotion in order to give a satisfactory performance; rather the performance itself can give you the emotion. Young actors sometimes think that they must recreate the character's emotion in order to generate each performance "truthfully," but this is an exhausting and unreliable way of working.

We may sometimes be tempted to admire the emotionality of the actor who loses control and is overwhelmed on stage, but the display of emotion for its own sake is never our true purpose. The great actor aspires to use emotional technique to realize the truth of the character according to the demands of the play; the ultimate test of a performance is not only its emotional power, but the completeness with which it contributes to the whole play as a work of art; emotion is a means to this end, never an end in itself.

This was the position to which Stanislavski came by the end of his life. He insisted that emotion had to be fully experienced in rehearsal and was crucial in establishing the sequence of actions, rhythms, and thought patterns which he called the *score* of the performance; but in the performance itself, he said, it was the score which in turn generated impulse and feeling in the actor. In his last book, *Building a Character*, Stanislavski summed up his system this way:

> Our art . . . requires that an actor experience the agony of his role, and weep his heart out at home or in rehearsals, that he then calm himself, get rid of every sentiment alien or obstructive to his part. He then comes out on the stage to convey to the audience in clear, pregnant, deeply felt, intelligible and eloquent terms what he has been through. At this point the spectators will be more affected than the actor, and he will conserve all his forces in order to direct them where he needs them most of all: in reproducing the inner life of the character he is portraying.[4]

The important idea here is that in performance, "the spectators will be more affected than the actor." This is necessary for several reasons. First, strong emotion will interfere with your craftsmanship; as Stanislavski put it, "a person in the midst of experiencing a poignant emotional drama is incapable of speaking of it coherently."[5]

Second, it is unreliable to depend on emotion to generate a performance that must be done repeatedly on schedule. Stanislavski used the example of the opera singer who, at the moment the music requires a certain note with a certain feeling, cannot say, "wait a moment, I'm not feeling it yet."

Finally, and most important, your aim is the creation of a *transparent* performance, one through which we receive a clear view of the play. If your performance calls undue attention to itself, you have failed. As an audience member I am not here to watch *you* weep; I am here to weep *myself*.

Your experiences so far with the action and emotional responses of your character have probably begun to give you a vivid sense of his or her personality: it is now time to examine characterization *per se*, working from the foundation we have already laid.

# Lesson
# Fifteen

# The Body and Character

In everyday life we can sense the way a person's body reflects not only their immediate mood, but their basic attitudes and values as well. We call this "body language."

The reading of "body language" has become an important skill in our culture. Singles use it to identify likely partners, lawyers to select jurors, salespersons to determine their strategy toward a customer, interviewers to help evaluate applicants, and politicians to project desirable qualities of personality. In general, we tend to trust body language as a more accurate expression of personality than spoken language: do you remember the Hostess/Guest scene in Part One, in which we observed body language expressing feelings that were in direct contradiction to the words being spoken?

The theatre makes special use of this "universal physical language." The image of Willy Loman walking with bent back, shuffling through the opening scene of *Death of a Salesman* communicates a vivid sense of Willy's situation to audiences in Chicago or Peking; so, in their own way, do the formal, precise gestures of the Kabuki actor as he employs the conventions of his theatre to express real action and emotion.

## PERSONALITY IN THE BODY

Our contemporary interest with "body language" is a recognition of the fact that many aspects of personality actually come to be carried within the structures of the body. This is reflected not only in posture and gesture, but also in actual structural changes in the body. These expressive physical patterns are caused by the cumulative effect of repeated behavioral patterns, especially those in which we suppress or "hold in" certain impulses and reactions.

As Alexander Lowen, a psychoanalyst who works in the field he calls "Bioenergetics," puts it:

> The muscles can hold back movements as well as execute them. . . . Consider the case of an individual who is charged with rage and yet must hold back the impulse to strike. His fists are clenched, his arms are tense and his shoulders are drawn and held back to restrain the impulse.[1]

If rage is suppressed in this way often enough, the muscular tension in the hands, arms, and upper back becomes chronic. Because of this long-term tension, the muscles and other tissues in these areas eventually harden, losing their flexibility and sensitivity. The rigidity of these areas will eventually affect the person's posture and movement, and a trained observer can diagnose the precise psychological pattern captured in the musculature.

Even without special training, though, most of us can form fairly accurate impressions of people who "harbor a lot of resentment," or are "sitting on a lot of grief," or who "are afraid of their own sexuality," to name a few examples.

In psychological jargon, the configuration of the body and its movement pattern are, interestingly for the actor, called the *character structure.*

The suppression of emotion is not the only way character structure is created. The influence of heredity, the infant's mimicry of the parents' bodily motions, and patterns of social response (like the teenager's slouching) can all become "built in" to the body. Perhaps in your adolescence you were motivated to play the "tough" by thrusting out your chest, or your pelvis, or your jaw. Years later, even though this social motivation has ceased to operate, you may find these earlier muscular patterns still operating, literally "built in" to your body by habit, the shoulders still pulled back, the pelvis tilted to one side, the chin still thrust forward. These muscular patterns might have become expressive of your personality and continue to influence the ways in which you confront and react to life, and those whom you meet might initially think, "boy, does that person have a chip on their shoulder!"

Such a long-term postural pattern eventually alters the muscles and connective tissues so that it becomes part of the body's structure. Effected areas can become rigid, hard, overdeveloped, and cold (due to poor blood circulation) or, conversely, collapsed and weak through disuse. Some therapists call such semi-permanent alterations in the body's structure an *armor.*

We will return to this relationship between the structure of the body and personality later, but for now, bring your awareness to your own "character structure." Your habitual physical patterns are part of your personality, and it will be helpful to your development as an actor to bring these patterns within your conscious artistic control. Moreover, you must begin to restore yourself to an undistorted or "neutral" condition. If you do not, you may carry your uncontrolled physical habits and body structure into every character you play, appropriate or not.

### Exercise 70:
### Your Character Structure

Working with a partner or before a large mirror, assume standing alignment and check yourself: is one shoulder higher than another, or wider? Does your pelvis rock to one side as you stand? Perhaps your chest is somewhat sunken, drawing your shoulders forward; or, in the other extreme, the shoulder blades are pinched together and the shoulders drawn back. As you move, do you see parts of your body that are being held? Everyone has symptoms of this kind; find yours.

You can use these symptoms to trace habitual bundles of tension or to identify disused areas of your body; try to relate each of your alignment symptoms to the habitual posture or inhibition that produced it.

Do not be overly concerned with your findings; everyone has some distortion from "perfect" alignment, and such distortion is not in itself a major obstacle to your development as an actor unless it is extreme. As you continue your daily exercise program, remain aware of the structures you have noticed; and in your daily life as well, "catch" yourself when you notice yourself falling into the old habits. A "trigger" word that you say to yourself, like "lengthen" or "level," can be valuable. Do not, however, *force* yourself into a new alignment; merely try to stop doing whatever you are doing to misalign yourself, and let the body's natural structure reassert itself. This is a very gradual process of *undoing,* and over a period of months you may begin to notice change.

These suggestions pertain only to common and mild misalignments. If you have a severe problem, or wish to pursue this work further, you may want to consult an expert therapist. The Alexander Technique is one of several good therapies that help to align and liberate the body; other recommended techniques include Structural Integration (Rolfing), Patterning, Bioenergetics, and even deep massage such as Shiatsu. You should consult only licensed, reputable practitioners by contacting state or national accreditation centers for each type of therapy, or by consulting your physician. Avoid home remedies.

## THE CHARACTER'S CENTER

You experienced your own bodily center in Part One. Though it may move in various emotional states (we can be "up" one day and "down" the next) each of us has a location which is our normal center. The location of our energy-center, and the quality of the energy it contains, can be a profound expression of our attitude toward life. In our creation of a dramatic character we work to discover a physiovocal center which is consistent with the character's attitudes and behavior.

We can suggest five primary character centers that by bodily logic and by cultural tradition, are each associated with a different sort of person: head, chest, stomach, genitals, and anus. (See Figure 26.) Let's look briefly at each.

The *head* centered person may be thought of as cerebral, "other worldly," flighty, scattered or off-balance. This sort of person always seems "ahead of themselves." Their energy seems to come out through their eyes or their mouth; if they're passive, they may do a lot of watching; if they're active, they may do a lot of talking or be very aware of oral activity of all sorts, which may be their way of sublimating their sexual energy ("Chew, chew, chew," are the first words Amanda speaks in *The Glass Menagerie*.)

The *chest* centered person might have a lot of "heart" and be quite sentimental, or might be the reverse and be proud and "militaristic."

The *stomach* person is usually carrying the badge of self-indulgence; they may also be good-natured, easy-going, and nurturing; they often make good parents.

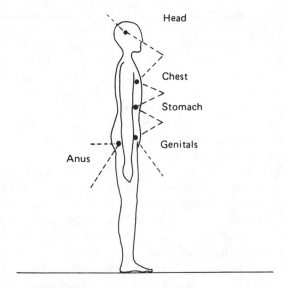

**FIGURE 26.** Primary Bodily Centers.

The *genitally* centered person might be libidinous, or contrarily naive in the "farmer's daughter" sense.

The *anal* person seems severe, sexually withdrawn, often stingy ("constipated"), dogmatic, and rigid in their behavior.

We have all known people who tend to relate to the world from one of these centers; observe some of your acquaintances from this point of view. Think also of some specific dramatic characters and imagine how this idea of centers would apply to each. What center might Amanda have in *The Glass Menagerie*? Falstaff in Shakespeare's *Henry IV*? Peter in *The Zoo Story*?

When we sense that someone is operating from one or another of these bodily centers, we tend to expect them to behave in the ways described above, so the placement of the character's center is a powerful tool of characterization. Moreover, if a character undergoes a radical change in the course of the play, it is possible that their center will shift. Think of King Lear; he could be played as a man who is driven out of his mind and into his heart!

More important than its influence on an audience is the power of the bodily center to effect you as you work on the role, moving you toward a transformational experience of character. You will find that the bodily movement of your character is a powerful force in the development of characterization, and bringing your own center into conformity with your character's center is perhaps the most fundamental physical characterizational choice.

### Exercise 71:
### The Character Center

Examine Figure 26; try "putting on" some of these character centers. Experience your impulse as initiating in them; move about and enter into improvised relationships. See what attitudes are evoked in you.

Consider various characters from plays you have read; which center seems right for each? Which center might be right for Jerry in *The Zoo Story*? For Peter? For Charlie in *Death of a Salesman*? For Amanda in *The Glass Menagerie*? Do any of these characters undergo changes which might result in a shift of their center?

## THE FLOW OF BODILY ENERGY

As we have said, the body takes on the qualities we associate with various kinds of characters through the repetition of certain physical responses to the stimuli of life. We will now trace the bodily path of the process of stimulus and response.

Once a stimulus has been received, it evokes a response that begins in the character's physiovocal center. As it moves outward toward the world, it can be directed, altered, or impeded as it passes through the structures of the body. We will trace this flow and the pathways it may take.

As you are reading this, recall a moment from the scene you have been rehearsing when you committed some strong physical action. Take a moment to relax and recall the experience as vividly as you can, so that it feels almost as if you were doing it again right now.

Feel the energy which is in your center; what is your level of arousal? Is it a high charge, or a low charge? We call this its *dynamic*.

Next, follow this energy as it flows away from your center; is it moving predominantly upward or downward or equally in both directions away from your center?

Notice that the musculature of your body offers two energy pathways running up and down the body. One pathway runs along the back of your body, another along the front. Because the muscles of the back are large and strong, the rear pathway usually carries your aggressive and sexual energies; the muscles and tissues in the front of your body are softer and more accessible or vulnerable, so that the front pathway usually carries our "tender" feelings. Which pathway are you using now?

Consider whether the energy is impeded or even blocked from flowing through certain areas of your body. Some of the most common points of blockage are the jaw, nape of the neck, small of the back, across the chest, or between the shoulder blades. You can perhaps feel such blockages of this energy within your own body; are the blocks, if any, habitual to you, or did you intuitively create them as part of the character?

Finally, become aware of how the energy leaves your body: is there an area or part of the body through which it tends to exit?

You now have traced the pathway by which any motion or sound which you produce must begin in a deep center and move through the various energy pathways of the musculature until it erupts into the outer world. When it does, it carries with it the tone, color, and shape of the interior world through which it has passed. Through this process, our physical and vocal expressions become a means by which we "turn ourselves inside out" and make a public expression of our private world.

You can see from all this that the quality of the movement and sound produced by the body is deeply expressive of our psychological orientation to the world. We have all learned to read these signs and our everyday language reflects this process: we speak of the happy person as "being on cloud nine," while the depressed person is a "drag." Consider, as one fundamental example of this, a person's walk. An insecure person, with a weak sense of self-identity, tends to be unstable, to "walk on eggshells." We speak of such a person as a "pushover," someone who "won't stand on their own two feet." In the opposite extreme is the "pushy" person who carries their weight on the balls of their feet and whose energy flows up the back into the aggressive stance of a fighter, and who walks as if they were punishing the floor and expected everything to get out of their way. It is not surprising that Sir Alec Guiness has said that he knows he has found the essential ingredients of a character when he has found his walk.

## PHYSIQUE AND PERSONALITY

As we said earlier, repeated patterns of behavior may begin to alter the very structure of the body. We come to hold our energy in a way that effects the contours of our body, so that the body soon comes to announce the nature of the energy which inhabits it. The Elizabethan idea of reading character in the body (e.g., "this is the forehead of a murderer") was crude but entirely accurate in principle.

When we meet someone we tend to form a distinct impression of their personality and mood from our observation of their overall bodily condition: this fact is especially important on stage, where audience's are encouraged to read the whole body more acutely than we do in real life. We will consider, then, how the contours of a character's body may communicate specific impressions of their personality.

We must first, however, distinguish between the way the body is held, which is called *alignment*, and the basic structure of the body itself, which is called *physique*. Certain physiques carry particular characterological associations within our culture: The large-abdomened *endomorph*, for example, is thought of as jolly, easygoing, and a good family type; the thin, wiry *ectomorph*, on the other hand, is expected to be nervous and compulsive, while the muscular *mesomorph* is expected to be a little like Stanley Kowalski.

These body types are of limited importance in the theatre. To be sure, it might be unreasonable to cast an endomorphic actor as the mesomorphic Stanley, but within such broad limits it is possible for almost any physique to capture the psychophysical essence of a role on the stage. Though Lee J. Cobb and Dustin Hoffman have very different physiques, they were each successful in the role of Willy Loman.

The camera, on the other hand, has no tolerance for fundamental adjustments of physique which, despite the most skillful makeup and costuming, usually read as false. Insofar as this is true, films and television must be "type cast," and serious film actors intent on creating roles for which their physique may not be quite right must go to lengths as extreme as those which Robert Deniro, for example, pursued for his role in *Raging Bull*.

## BODY ALIGNMENT
## AND CHARACTER

Bodily alignment, as opposed to physique, can be successfully adjusted both on stage and for the camera. Let's look at the specific qualities which are commonly associated with various bodily alignments. Examine Figure 27 and consider the qualities which each body suggests.

The first body, which features rounded shoulders and back, can have two very different qualities. When it is based on a low energy level, it is called the *oral* body. The chest is collapsed, the arms express yearning. The legs are weak, making the body unstable and poorly grounded. Aggressive energies at the rear are blocked, and a great deal of grief is held in the pit of the stomach.

On the other hand, when this structure is based upon a high energy level, it is called *masochistic*. The shoulders are rounded because of the overdevelopment of the muscles in the upper body, giving a gorilla-like hulking aspect. The bound-in aggressions of this type are turned inward upon the self; notice that the energy pathway along the back begins to approach a circle.

The second body is sometimes called the "militaristic character" because it resembles the stance of a soldier at attention. It is the most hostile of all alignments. The shoulders are thrown back and an enormous amount of anger is stored in the rigid area between the shoulder blades, the result of a long pattern of inhibited striking. This body is firmly rooted but so rigid in response that it is awkward, even mechanical. Aggressive energies

**FIGURE 27.**   Basic Character Alignments.

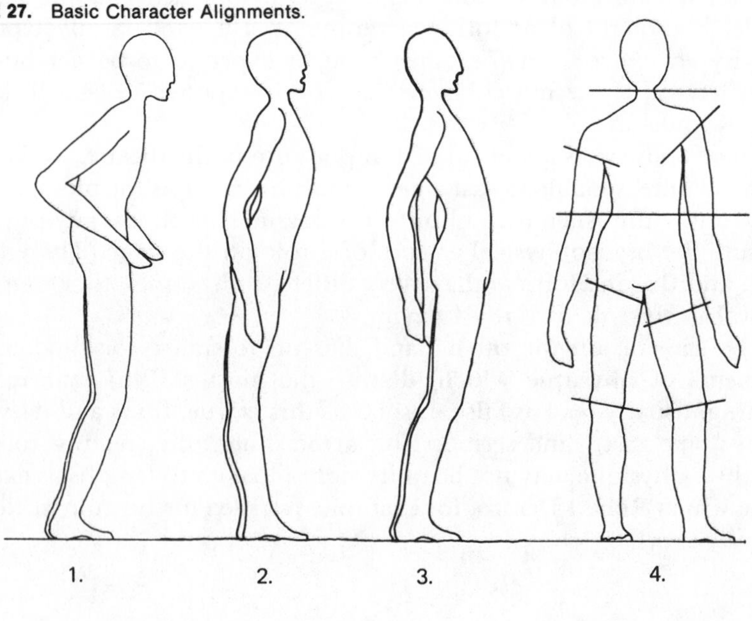

1.          2.          3.                    4.

stored in the back dominate, and the tender areas in the front of the body (chest and gut) are made hard. Small wonder that we train soldiers to stand this way and to not think for themselves.

The third body is clearly belly-centered. This "heavy" character responds with great equanimity and could be called the "aw shucks" body. We usually think of such characters as unaggressive (the sway back blocks the aggressive energies of the rear body) but jolly and sentimental (as the preponderance of the frontal energies would indicate).

The last body is called *schizoid*. Here the parts of the body at all the major joints are disassociated so that the person is literally "in pieces" and, as we say, "the right hand doesn't know what the left hand is doing. The head is often cocked in a birdlike way. This body is very unstable and poorly grounded; it lacks grace in movement.

## CHANGES
## IN BODILY ALIGNMENT

Although a bodily configuration may be deeply embedded in someone, it is still liable to surprisingly rapid change. I have seen extraordinary and permanent changes occur in people's body's almost instantaneously as a result of powerful life experiences or through therapy. Likewise, the bodies of dramatic characters who undergo radical changes in the course of their plays would believably change. The Willy Loman we see at the beginning of his play should not be the same Willy we see in his better days during the flashbacks, nor at the end when he is about to kill himself. Likewise, imagine the robust King Lear at the beginning of his play, and again after his ordeal in the storm when his daughter has to help him to walk. Do you see how such changes express not just the character's physical condition but psychological and even spiritual changes?

Remember, then, that the theatre is a bodily place. All its meanings, philosophical or psychological insights, emotions and all that may be communicated by a play, reach the spectator through the physical sensations which you, the actor, will generate. The "instrument" that creates the experience, your organism, is identical with the "instrument" that receives the experience, the spectator's organism, and there is an automatic and unconscious process by which your physical condition is mirrored in the deep muscles of your audience; whatever your physical condition is doing to you, it will also do to them. It is a real power: use it well!

Following is an exercise that will review all the material we have covered in this Lesson. It will help you to more sharply define the physical aspects of the characterization you have been working on throughout this Part.

**Exercise 72:**
**A Journey**
**into a Character Structure**

In this exercise you will create the experience of "living inside" the body of the character you have been developing in the previous exercises. You will do this by making a series of simple choices as outlined below.

Allow at least one hour for this exercise, and do it all in one session. The exercise has three ground rules:

1.  Use the full range of everyday movements (walking, sitting, getting up and down) throughout the exercise; do not remain still for too long. Use the voice throughout as well; count, say the alphabet, say your lines, or whatever comes to mind.

2.  In each item, make your choices on the basis of what "feels" right; explore the whole range of choice before you settle on what seems to fit your subject. Remember: the basis for the choice is how the energy flow *feels* inside the body, not what "looks" right or what "ought" to be right. Allow your mind to just settle back and witness.

3.  The choices are cumulative; stick to the sequence given. After you have made a choice, move on to the next and trust the body to retain the first.

Here are the choices in sequence:

1.  ATTITUDE TOWARD GRAVITY: As in Exercise 16, experiment with your character's "root." Alternate from "plowing" to "floating" to "flying," and the stages between; select the attitude toward gravity which feels right.

2.  CENTER: Review your choice of your character's center from the previous exercise; make it more specific.

3.  DYNAMIC: Experience the energy flowing from center as a low charge or a high charge and the stages between; listen to the changes in the voice.

4.  ENERGY PATHWAYS: Determine the way energy flows within this body.
    a.  Is it deep in the core or near the surface?
    b.  Is it upward or downward from center?
    c.  Is it mostly along the front or the back of the body?

6.  BLOCKAGES: Are there places in this body where energy is blocked? Try blocking each of these locations and see if it feels right; if it does, allow the block to remain:
    a.  eyes
    b.  jaw
    c.  head/neck
    d.  space between the shoulder blades
    e.  space between the breasts
    f.  pit of the stomach
    g.  small of the back
    h.  genitals (how are they held?)

7. BODILY ALIGNMENT: Try on each of the four alignments discussed:
   a. oral
   b. masochistic
   c. militaristic
   d. "aw shucks"
   e. schizoid

Now, allowing the body to hold whatever it retains of these choices, stand with your partner or, better, in groups of four or five. Speak directly to each of these persons with the following phrases, and allow a new spontaneous ending to erupt each time you repeat the phrase as you go around the group. If a spontaneous ending does not arise, simply say "pass."

When I wake up in the morning,. . .
Ever since I was a child. . .
When I look in the mirror. . .
Leisure to me is. . .
I can remember. . .
The child in me. . .
I need. . .
I hate. . .
Strength to me means. . .
Weakness to me means. . .
Right now I am aware. . .
Sometimes I want to cry out to people. . .
Pain to me is. . .
I love. . .
If I could be free to do what I want to do. . .
My body. . .
If you could hear the music in me. . .[2]

At the conclusion of the exercise, watch yourself for a time in a mirror, if possible. Then use the Phasic Relaxation exercise to "erase" the character structure you have created.

Share your experiences of this exercise. What did you learn about your character that you never knew before? What did your body teach you? Learn to treat the body as a source of discovery; there is much about acting which must be found only in physical experience.

# Summary to Part Two

# An Action Checklist

In Part One you prepared your body and voice much in the way a gardener prepares the ground prior to planting a seed. In Part Two you developed a way of experiencing action which is the seed from which the created role will spring; as you enter into the actions of your character within the given circumstances, "as if" they were your own, the transformational process begins to work upon you. In the next Part, we look closely at the dramatic text which inspires and guides this transformational process.

Before we do, however, we will summarize what we have learned about action in the following checklist.

**Exercise 73:**
**An Action/Character Checklist**

The following checklist covers the questions you should be asking yourself in the earliest phases of your rehearsal process.
I.  **The Givens: What, Who, Where, When:**
    A.  WHAT happens in this scene?
        1.  What is the *main event* of the scene? How does it move the plot of the play forward?
        2.  What *changes* as a result of this scene?
        3.  How does this scene grow out of preceding scenes? How does this scene lead into following scenes?

    B. WHO is in this scene?
        1. What is the *general* relationship?
        2. What is the *specific* relationship?
        3. Does your relationship *change* in this scene?
        4. What is discovered about your character in this scene?
    C. WHERE is this scene?
        1. How does the *physical* environment influence what happens?
        2. How does the *social* environment influence what happens?
    D. WHEN is this scene?
        1. How does the *historical* time influence the scene?
        2. How does the *season of the year* influence the scene?
        3. How does the *time of day* influence the scene?

II. **Scene Structure**
    A. What is the *main conflict* of this scene? How does it relate to the overall conflict of the play?
    B. What is the *scenario* of the scene, beat by beat? Be specific about the moment of choice that makes each beat change.
    C. What is the *crisis,* the event which determines the resolution of the conflict?

III. **Action Analysis:**
    A. Describe your main dramatic function within the play:
        1. What does your character do that moves the *plot* forward?
        2. What is the principal way in which your character contributes to *meaning* of the play?
    B. Express your *superobjective* as a transitive verb phrase with qualifiers.
    C. What is your *scene* objective in this scene? How does it relate to your superobjective and through-line in the play?
    D. Examine the sequence of your *immediate* objectives through the scene. Express each in a transitive verb as "SIP" (singular, immediate, and personally important); try to think of each as a desired change in the other character.
    E. Trace each *choice* which leads to the formation of these objectives:
        1. What is the *stimulus* for each?
        2. What *attitude* or need does the stimulus arouse?
        3. What are the *alternatives not chosen* in each case?
        4. What is it about the other character that makes this choice seem to be the right one?
        5. What activity results from this choice?
        6. Is your action direct or indirect? Is subtext is at work in your actions?
    F. What is the crucial choice for you in this scene? How does it relate to your crucial choice in the play?
    G. Do you undergo a change in the course of the play? How can you enhance the arc of the role by physical adjustments?

# Introduction to Part Three

# Text Analysis

A playwright is moved to write by a living experience or idea which we will call the *vision* behind the play. We can all learn to share the vision of the play if we develop the ability to reach for it through the text. Though the vision itself is the power behind the words, the playwright selected and combined certain words in certain ways, created certain characters in certain situations, and gave the whole play a certain structure, in order to embody the vision. Therefore, we can best reach back to the vision by reversing this process and working through these details of language, character, and structure.

This is a more reliable and fruitful approach than trusting only your subjective response to the play. While you certainly need to have strong feelings about the role, you must be careful to guide and correct your response by an informed and detailed study of the specifics of the text. All sensitive readers have a personal relationship to a good play, but the actor has a greater public responsibility; you owe it to your playwright, your audience, and to yourself as an ethical artist to present the play for what it really is, not simply to use it as a vehicle for your own feelings about it.

## LEVELS OF CLOSE
## TEXT ANALYSIS

In the previous Part, you came to understand the structure of a scene; in this Part, you will examine the details of the dialogue which you speak within that scene.

Unlike the novelist, the playwright does not speak directly to you in order to describe a character; the character must speak for itself, and ultimately, the dialogue will be all that is left of the fullness of the author's conception of that character. For you as an actor the words you will speak are the *residue* of a complete state of being. It is your job to *rejuvenate* this residue within the fullness of your own body and consciousness, and in the way that will best serve the vision of the play.

We will examine the text from several points of view:

1. Diction: the words themselves as units of meaning and their arrangement, or syntax, as a reflection of the character's mental processes;
2. Rhythm: the shaping of the language into rhythmic units, and the relationship of rhythm to meaning, emotion, and character;
3. Melody: the sound values of the words, and the way they support meaning and emotion;
4. Imagery: the sensations imparted by the words;
5. Figurative language: the patterning of words to achieve special meanings.

You will examine each of these aspects of the text in the following lessons, but remember that each is only a different point of view toward the same whole; a play cannot actually be broken into parts. In analysis you take the play apart to see what "makes it tick"; eventually you must reassemble it in your performance and make it run again "under its own power." In other words, *analysis must lead to synthesis*.

Although a well-trained actor can read in a script specific clues about rhythms, inflections, emphases, and all sorts of characteristics needed to create the role, a good play is not really like a blueprint or a coloring book; acting is not a matter of simply recognizing the playwright's outline and then "filling it in." The creation of a role is always a collaboration between you, the playwright, director, your fellow actors, and eventually the audience. The real answers to acting problems are found only in actual rehearsal and performance, when the play has a chance to live. Effective analysis can make the job easier and produce better results by guiding and motivating the living exploration of rehearsal.

Analysis, then, will not provide answers as much as it will identify the important questions and possibilities to be tested in rehearsal and performance.

## THE ROLE OF ANALYTICAL
## THINKING IN ACTING:
## RIGHT AND LEFT BRAIN FUNCTIONS

As we begin this Part on text analysis, let's consider the role of analytical thinking in the acting process.

In order to understand the proper role of analysis, you must consider the ways in which you think, and the ways in which your thinking is integrated with your behavior, for your analysis is valuable only insofar as it enriches the living experience of the scene through your actions.

The key to understanding how analysis can enrich action lies in understanding the different sources of these two modes of activity. Researchers have found that the brain is divided into two halves, or *hemispheres*, which seem to specialize in different kinds of thinking. The left hemisphere is the side which is mainly involved in analysis and other rational activity; it is adept at dealing with particulars in a logical and sequential way, and many of its functions can be mimicked by a computer. Most significantly for our purposes, the left side is the center of language and is the side which will primarily receive and interpret the text of the play.

The right side is more intuitive and operates in spatial, holistic, musical, symbolic and emotional terms. For this reason, it is often referred to as the "artistic" side in contrast to the more "scientific" left side. In general, we could say that the left side is in charge of "thinking about," and the right is in charge of "doing."

You can see at once that acting requires the cooperation of both hemispheres. It is important to realize that at any given moment one side is dominant over the other; we don't seem to function equally on both sides at the same time. Therefore, we must understand when we should be "thinking about" and when we should be "doing," and put ourselves into the proper frame of mind for each.

We can say in general terms that the acting process *begins* in the left hemisphere, which receives the language of the text from which all other understandings of the role are derived. During the rehearsal process, we switch between the two at various times, but when we are actually *playing* the scene we are working from the spatial, musical, emotional, and intuitive functions of the right hemisphere. In this phase of the work, most of your discoveries are made by "accident," that is, by *intuition*, which is the specialty of the right hemisphere.

These intuitions are guided by the understanding you have gained through analysis, and during the rehearsal process they are evaluated by the left hemisphere which edits and shapes the final result. Finally, the performance itself is generated out of the right hemispheres, with the left passively witnessing the experience in order to improve it for the future.

Because our educational system concentrates on left brain functions (which are measured by most tests) we often come to think of "intelligence" in left-brained terms, and even mistrust the intuitions of the right hemisphere. When you say that you want to "understand" what you are doing when you act, for example, you are probably referring to these left-hemisphere functions, but there is much about acting which is outside the province of the left hemisphere and can be "understood" only in the spatial/musical/emotional terms of the right hemisphere. This kind of understanding lives only in the *doing* of it.

Actors who are afraid to commit to an action until they "understand" it will probably never come to understand it! At some point, then, you have to just *do* it without knowing what you're doing!

This is why you must remember that analysis of the text is a a valuable *preparation* for the acting process, but cannot be a *substitute* for the real experience. Nor is it necessary for you to "understand" what you are doing in order to do well; rather you come to understand fully through the doing.

## SAMPLE ANALYSES
## AND EMBODIMENT EXERCISES

As each lesson in this part introduces one of the five aspects of text analysis, sample analyses will be given to demonstrate the principles being discussed. The same two speeches will be analyzed in each lesson: one is from a classical play, Shakespeare's *King Lear*, and the other from a modern play, Edward Albee's *The Zoo Story*. These speeches will be found in Appendix One, and both plays should be read in their entirety before continuing in this Part.

In addition, you should have material of your own which you will analyze throughout these lessons. Choose a speech, preferably one from a scene and play you know well, about one minute long or less; it should have rich language, if not poetry as such. One of the best choices would be one of Shakespeare's Sonnets.

You will find it useful to prepare four triple-spaced copies of your speech to be used in the analyses that accompany each lesson. Be sure to type it exactly as it is printed.

In order to translate the results of your left-hemisphere analysis into a right-hemisphere spatial/musical experience, each level of analysis will be accompanied by an exercise translating that element of the text into a deep-muscle movement/sound exercise. I call these exercises *embodiments*.

These embodiment exercises are not meant to be performances, but rather experiences which *sensitize* you to an aspect of the text. Each is a chance to take what you have learned from analysis and turn it into a deep-muscle physical experience. There it will live in you without conscious awareness and will enrich your "normal" delivery of the scene. Your speech should be thoroughly memorized before attempting the embodiment exercises since they demand full concentration and complete freedom of movement.

# Lesson
# Sixteen

# Diction

"Just say the words." This was the motto of a long tradition of British acting, and it is advice that one still hears today among film and television actors. You will see in the next four lessons that "just saying the words" when properly understood is no simple matter: it is in fact a profound way of involving yourself in the life of the character.

You must first understand what "the words" mean, and why the playwright has chosen to have your character express themselves in precisely the way they do. A character's choice of words is called their *diction*, in the sense of *diction*ary.

There are many factors influencing a character's diction: their educational and social background, the nature of their mental processes, the immediate situation, etcetera. Understanding your character's diction is important to you, not only because you have a responsibility to communicate the meaning of your lines accurately, but also because it reveals the way your character thinks and feels, and their values and background as well. In fact, speaking your character's words is the first and one of the most powerful ways that you enter actively into the life of your character.

Diction can be approached on four levels: the literal meaning of the words, or *denotation*; the emotional associations which the words carry, or *connotation*; the *germinal idea*, the basic idea which the words express;

and any hidden meanings which may be lurking beneath the words in a *subtext*. Finally, since the meanings of words are profoundly effected by the way in which they are arranged, you must consider also the *syntax* of the speech.

## DENOTATION

Linguist Edward Sapir once said that "language is the medium of literature as marble or bronze or clay are the materials of the sculptor."[1] Words, however, are different from the sculptor's clay or the painter's pigment in that they carry meanings of their own, at least partly independent of the way in which the writer has used them in this instance. This literal, dictionary meaning is called *denotation*.

Meaning is not a static thing; there may be several possible definitions for a word, and the meaning of even common words in popular usage often changes. Topical and colloquial speech may change its meaning very quickly, and doing a play only ten years old may require some investigation of the meaning of words and expressions. You must be sure that the meaning you take for granted today is not a distortion of the playwright's original intention.

It is surprising how many actors think they can get along on their intuition of the exact meaning of the words they speak. Such actors may commit themselves to partially or completely erroneous line readings without ever suspecting that anything is amiss. For example, Juliet coming out on her balcony says, "O Romeo, Romeo? Wherefore art thou Romeo?" and many young actresses deliver the line as if Juliet were wishing that Romeo were there, in the sense of "Romeo, where are you?" But knowing that "wherefore" originally meant *why*, we see that she really is saying, "Why are you named Romeo, member of a family hated by my own?"

Another aspect of denotation is *colloquial* usage and *slang*, which is common in plays since characters often speak in the highly informal, conversational language of a particular time and place. Calling a beautiful woman "a dish," for example, or "a real tomato," or her legs "a pair of gams," summons up 1930's America in a very specific way. In *Hamlet*, Shakespeare uses a slang pun for serious effect: Hamlet, meeting Ophelia, tells her "Get thee to a nunnery," and in this tortured speech uses the word repeatedly: sometimes he means "convent" (that is, "get yourself to a safe place") and sometimes he means, in Elizabethan slang, "brothel" (that is, "you are a whore, go where you belong").

Good dictionaries will help you to be sure about denotation. For modern plays, the Merriam-Webster third unabridged edition will be useful. For old (English) plays, the Oxford English Dictionary (the O. E. D.) lists the changing meanings of words with the dates of their currency. There are even dictionaries of slang and bawdy sayings.

Of great value to the actor are the carefully noted editions of great classical plays with glossaries, or with a "running gloss"; there are also *variorum* editions of Shakespeare's plays, with explanatory notes and excerpts from important critical commentary, line by line (these are quite out-of-date, but thankfully new editions are now being prepared). Acquaint yourself with these resource materials!

## PUNS

Of all forms of writing (except for lyric poetry) playwrighting uses the fewest words to achieve the greatest effect; this requires a tremendous amount of *condensation* of meaning, and you will see that playwrights use a variety of devices to pack extra meaning into their dialogue. One such device is punning. Though puns have been called "the lowest form of humor," they are used by great writers for both serious and comic effect.

A pun depends on placing a word that has more than one denotation in a context where both meanings could be applied. A "mark," for example, might be a marking, a bruise, or a kind of money. In Shakespeare's *Comedy of Errors*, a play filled with puns, one of the heroes has entrusted his money to his servant and later meets his servant's twin brother, who knows nothing about the money:

> Master: Where is the thousand marks thou hadst of me?

> Second Servant: I have some marks of yours upon my pate,
> Some of my mistress' marks upon my shoulder,
> But not a thousand marks between you both.
> If I should pay your worship those again,
> Perchance you will not bear them patiently.

From a modern source, we see the same delight in punning when we examine the names of Beckett's characters in *Endgame*: Hamm (ham, the decaying and impure meat), and Clov (clove, the spice traditionally used with ham for flavor and preservation); ham is meat that comes from an animal with a cloven hoof, and Clov is indeed the "feet" of Hamm; Hamm actor, the tragedian, and Clov (clown), who together are the two masks of drama and the two faces of mankind. Hamm keeps his parents in garbage cans; they are named Nell (nail) and Nagg (*Nagel* means "nail" in German) and they are repeatedly "pounded down" by the overbearing Hamm (hammer), as is Clov (*clou* means "nail" in French.) All these meanings, wonderfully appropriate to the play, are incorporated through puns.

The tradition of character names which indicate personality by punning is very old; don't underestimate the value of such information. Imagine the qualities implied by names like Dikaiopolis (righteous citizen), Hotspur, Mistress Quickly, Sir Foppington Flutter, Mrs. Malaprop, or Willy Loman.

## CONNOTATION

*Connotation* refers to the emotional and attitudinal associations that words carry. Unlike denotation, which is determined by common usage, the connotative possibilities of words can be highly personal and variable. You need to consider context in order to determine which of the connotative possibilities of a word might be appropriate. In rich, skillful language, words will be selected in order to utilize more than one of their connotations, thereby supplying various levels of emotional impact.

Like people in real life, dramatic characters use connotation as a way of revealing their attitudes and feelings toward something or someone; connotation is therefore closely tied to the emotional life of a character. When Blanche Dubois arrives at her sister's apartment she describes it thus:

> Only Poe, only Mr. Edgar Allan Poe could do it justice. *(She gestures toward street)* Out there, I suppose, is the ghoul-haunted woodland of Weir.

Her feeling that the neighborhood is dank and depressing is clear enough, but we must also realize the level of education and imagination captured not only by her reference to Poe, but also to the painter Weir, whose imagery is perfectly suited to the place. The contrast to her less elegant sister, Stella, is highlighted by Stella's bluff, prosaic reply, "No, honey, those are the L and M tracks." Later, when Blanche describes Stanley as "swilling and gnawing and hulking," we understand not only her attitude toward him, but also something about the quality of her mind as expressed by these animalistic but poetic images.

As in this example, the physical sensations evoked by words are an important part of the connotation and demand from the actor a strongly physical response. By recreating in yourself the physical qualities of "swilling and gnawing and hulking" as you speak these words, you will find yourself thrust into Blanche's emotional attitude toward Stanley.

The capacity of language to evoke physical sensation as a way of expressing the character's emotional attitude is a powerful device. Remember that a playwright knows that these words will be spoken aloud by an actor trained to respond in a total way; as you will see more completely in the lesson on imagery, the physical sensations evoked by the language are a way for the playwright to reach deeply into your being. Read aloud this description of death, spoken by Isabella's brother in the prison scene from *Measure for Measure*: feel the physical sensations it evokes and how powerfully they can generate his feelings about death in you.

> Ay, but to die, and go we know not where,
> To lie in cold obstruction and to rot,
> This sensible warm motion to become
> A kneaded clod; and the delighted spirit
> To bathe in fiery floods, or to reside
> In thrilling regions of thick-ribbed ice,
> To be imprisoned in the viewless winds
> And blown with restless violence round about
> The pendant world; or to be worse than worst
> Of those that lawless and incertain thought
> Imagine howling; 'tis too horrible.

You don't need to be afraid of death in order to say this speech; the speech can terrify you on its own!

## THE GERMINAL IDEA

As we discussed in Lesson Six, a character's speech is the result of a process of verbalization whereby a preverbal seed or *germ* of an idea is developed into a full verbal form created to capture the specific shade of meaning and feeling desired. This process sums up the character's mind and personality, so it is essential that you be able to relive the process of verbalization.

In order to do this you must work back from the final verbal form provided by the playwright, to the preverbal thought and feeling from which the words can spring. In the example of Blanche seeing her sister's place for the first time, you might begin with a germinal feeling of revulsion and disappointment: "How awful!" The awfulness of the place gives rise to two specific emotional associations: "It feels dank, dark, and frightening, like a Poe story, or just like that dreadful painting by that insane Mr. Weir." She then forms these thoughts into a statement specifically designed to communicate to her sister Stella. Perhaps these artistic allusions are also designed to remind Stella that they share a sophisticated educational and social background in which Stella's present circumstances were acknowledged only as the subjects of demented imaginations.

As you relive your character's process of verbalization, from the germinal idea and feeling to the final expression, you will begin to participate actively in their mental processes and feelings. Only when you have done this can you truly speak their words as if they were your own; until then, you are merely parroting someone else's words, learned by rote. As long as you speak someone else's words, you will be speaking "in someone else's voice:" you will sound stiff, mechanical, and false.

To sum up: Your ultimate objective in the study of your character's diction is to marry your mind to their mind, and to make their voice your own.

## PARAPHRASE

The study of diction involves an understanding of what you are saying in its historical, social, and psychological contexts. Consider each of these questions:

1.  What were the meanings of the words when the play was written?
2.  What do they mean when used by my character in their situation?
3.  What feelings or meanings might be hidden beneath these lines as a subtext? Remember that subtext must be deduced from an understanding of the situation and action, as you learned in Lesson 11.

One very good way to be sure you have asked yourself these questions is to do a *paraphrase*. This is a process in which you return to the germinal meaning of your lines, and then restate them in your own words as if you were translating from one language into another. Obviously, much of the emotional tone, connotations, mood, and poetic richness of the original will be lost; but even this will make you appreciate the subtleties of your character's language, and you will at least have made sure that you have seriously considered the possible meanings of each word you speak. A complete paraphrase will require examining each of the four levels of diction: the denotative, connotative, the germinal, and the subtextual.

A paraphrase on the *denotative* level, especially of poetry or poetic prose, will usually be longer than the original. This is because good dramatic speech, and poetic speech in particular, involves condensation and intensification of meaning; in your paraphrase, you are releasing these impacted meanings and allowing them to "expand" back to their original mass. Doing this will help you to realize the economy of the original, the rightness of every word in its place.

For example, in the scene from *Measure for Measure* which we mentioned above, Isabella is faced with a terrible choice: in order to save her brother's life, she must sleep with the Duke's deputy. About to become a nun, the loss of her chastity would mean eternal damnation to her, and so she cannot save him. She goes to see him in the prison and tries to break the news gently, but he is desperate:

CLAUDIO          Is there no remedy?

ISABELLA
None but such a remedy as, to save a head,
To cleave a heart in twain.

CLAUDIO          But is there any?

ISABELLA
Yes, brother, you may live;
There is a devilish mercy in the judge,
If you'll implore it, that will free your life,
But fetter you till death.

CLAUDIO          Perpetual durance?

ISABELLA
Ay, just—perpetual durance, a restraint,
Though all the world's vastidity you had,
To a determined scope.

A literal denotative paraphrase of these lines is:

CLAUDIO          Is there a way to make this right?

ISABELLA
No way, except one that, in order to save your life,
Would break one's heart.

CLAUDIO          But is there any?

ISABELLA
Yes, brother, it is possible for you to live;
The judge is offering the kind of deal that the devil would,
And if you'll beg for it, you won't be killed,
Though you would remain in prison for life.

CLAUDIO          Life imprisonment?

ISABELLA
Yes, exactly—imprisonment forever, and such an imprisonment that even
if you could travel anywhere in the world, you would still be penned in.

On the *connotative* level of paraphrase, you try to translate the emotional
tone of the lines into words and phrases which you might speak if you were
feeling the same way. For this scene, a connotative paraphrase might look
like this:

CLAUDIO          Please tell me there's hope!

ISABELLA
    The only hope of saving you is so terrible
    That it makes me sick to think of it.

CLAUDIO       I don't care how terrible it is;
    If there's any chance I want to know about it.

ISABELLA
    All right, I'll tell you; there is one chance.
    The judge has offered a hellish deal
    That could save you, but the life it would give you
    Would not be worth living.

CLAUDIO       God, life in prison?

ISABELLA
    Yes, life in prison, but not in the way you think; it's not a physical prison,
    It's a *worse* prison that you could *never* escape from,
    Because it would be inside you.

On the *germinal* level, reduce the number of words as far as possible to get to the preverbal germ. This scene might be reduced to:

CLAUDIO       Save me!

ISABELLA
    It's too terrible.

CLAUDIO       Save me anyway!

ISABELLA
    It's not worth it.

CLAUDIO       Please!

ISABELLA
    It would cost you your soul!

On the level of *subtext*, you express the hidden message that you deduce to be lurking behind the language. For this scene, that might be:

CLAUDIO       I'm so frightened; can you save me?

ISABELLA
    You look too desperate; you might make the wrong choice
    If I tell you now.

CLAUDIO       Look, this is my life, I'm not playing games!

ISABELLA
    I can't lie, I'll have to at least admit there is a chance,
    But I'm not going to tell you exactly what it is
    Until I see that you are man enough to do
    The right thing.

CLAUDIO          What the hell are you saying?

ISABELLA
I'm going to try to make you understand that your
Immortal soul is at stake. Please don't lose it
By being a moral coward. You couldn't bear to live
With the guilt, and I'm not going to do it anyway!

Try reading the original lines aloud with the understanding that this
four-level paraphrase has given you.


## SYNTAX

Syntax refers to "the due arrangement of words to show their mutual
relation in the sentence." This idea of "mutual relation" is expressed in
an old theatrical maxim that a good delivery of a line will "throw away"
or de-emphasize about 80 percent of the words in order to give the proper
emphasis to the remaining 20 percent in which the germinal meaning of
the line is crystallized.

This is only to say that the intelligibility of our speech depends
more on the "shape," patterning, or mutual relation of words than on the
meaning of individual words alone.

In music, instrumentalists are sometimes told by their teachers, "Don't
play the notes, play the music!" This means understanding the shape
and sense of a whole phrase as a unit and not simply as a succession of
individual notes. The actor's problem in the delivery of lines is like the
musician's problem of phraseology: it is from the shaping of the larger
thought units of phrases, sentences, and paragraphs, that meaning best
emerges.

It is the nature of our language that "idea units" (sentences or independent phrases) have a conventional structure which automatically provides emphasis for certain words: the most common structure is *subject,
verb, object,* as in

I come to bury Caesar. . .

"I *(subject)* come to bury *(verb)* Caesar *(object).*" In a longer sentence
which contains phrases that qualify the subject, verb, or object, you must
"highlight" the root sentence so that it can be felt running through the
whole. Consider this speech:

ISABELLA
Ay, just—perpetual durance, a restraint,
Though all the world's vastidity you had,
To a determined scope.

Can you pick out the root sentence here?[2] She is explaining exactly what she means by "perpetual durance," and what she is saying is "perpetual durance (is) a restraint to a determined scope." The verb, *is*, is implied; the predicate nominative, "a restraint to a determined scope," is split by a parenthetical aside, *Though all the world's vastidity you had.*

Try reading the speech aloud and stress the subject, "think" the missing verb, and vocally put the parentheses around the aside:

> Ay, just—a **perpetual durance**, a **restraint**—(Though all the world's vastidity you had)—To a **determined scope**.

Notice how you had to suspend the thought after "restraint—" by ending on a rising inflection, then drop your tone to set off the parenthetical aside, and then resume the main thought by returning to the pitch level of "restraint." This is how we turn the structure of the language our character speaks into a full physical action.

Playwrights can achieve special effects by departing from the traditional sequence of subject, verb, object and employing instead an *inverted* syntax. For example,

> Though all the world's vastidity you had,

is arranged *object, subject, verb*: we would normally say,

> Though you had all the world's vastidity,

Even though this arrangement is as rhythmically correct as the original, notice that it fails to drive the point home to Claudio, which the first does by placing "you had" at the end of the line.

Beside inverted syntax, there are two other types of word patterns that are commonly used in plays: *periodic* and *balanced*.

In *periodic* structures, a sequence of various elements "pile up" upon each other until the fullness of the accumulated meaning is revealed at the end. This structure is particularly appropriate to the painting of word-pictures, where the total effect is achieved through a "funding" or combining of a number of descriptive elements. An excellent example of a periodic structure which creates a funded verbal picture is this description of Cleopatra's barge as it sails down the Nile in Shakespeare's *Antony and Cleopatra*:

> The barge she sat in, like a burnish'd throne,
> Burn'd on the water. The poop was beaten gold;
> Purple the sails, and so perfumed that
> The winds were love-sick with them; the oars were silver,
> Which to the tune of flutes kept stroke, and made

The water which they beat to follow faster,
As amorous of their strokes.

Do you feel the way the images of this speech begin to form one total picture?

In *balanced* syntax, elements of the sentence are placed against one another and meaning is revealed by contrast. The contrasted elements need not be opposite to one another, only different. You can see this sort of structure at work in this famous speech by Marc Antony from *Julius Caesar*:

Friends, Romans, countrymen, lend me your ears;
I come to bury Caesar, not to praise him.
The evil that men do lives after them;
The good is oft interred with their bones;
So let it be with Caesar. The noble Brutus
Hath told you Caesar was ambitious.
If it were so, it was a grievous fault;
And grievously hath Caesar answer'd it.

Again, do you feel the balancing of the contrasted words, *bury* and *praise*, *evil* and *good* in the first four lines of this speech? Notice also in the last two lines how the repetition of the word *grievous*, with a shift in meaning, develops Antony's argument. Read it aloud: Understanding how the meaning is localized in these contrasted words, use pitch and volume to emphasize them; support the comparison in your deep muscles so that we can *feel* the comparison as well as hear it.

This ability to translate the verbal structure of the speech into a total vocal and physical experience is a critical skill for the actor; it forms the connection between the playwright's structure and the physical life of the role. The ideal connection goes from the page to your mind, next from your mind to your body and voice, then through the audience's mimicry of your muscular condition, and finally back into their minds. *Through your own physical embodiment of the structure of the speech, you turn it into a kind of "dance" that your hearers can share.*

## SAMPLE DICTION ANALYSES

(Refer to sample speeches, Appendix One.)

### *King Lear:*

The periodic syntax of the four lines develops a vivid cumulative picture of poverty. *Poor* in the first line is not simply a term of pity but refers literally to those who suffer poverty. The theme of the speech is economic and social injustice; the plight of the poor is made vivid by highly physical connotations. *Wretch* originally referred to an exile who had been driven out of his native country, so "wretches" are not only unfortunate persons but also those who are helpless and alone; the poor are, in this sense, politically disenfranchised as well as miserable. *To bide* connotes not only endurance but a sense of expectation, the poor waiting to be lifted out of their misery.

The *pitiless storm* in which Lear finds himself also comes to signify the lack of pity shown to the poor by society. When he says "wheresoe'er you are" (whether you are in my storm or not), Lear makes it clear that he refers not only to the actual storm he is in, but to the pitiless storm of human life in general. Pity also connotes piety or moral rightness, a quality lacking in Lear's society. *Loop'd and window'd raggedness* depicts the holes in the clothing of the poor and refers us back to *naked*.

The physical connotations of all these words develop a feeling of defenselessness, exposure to the elements, and helplessness, as well as a sense of spiritual desolation. In line 6, he suggests the remedy: "Take physic, pomp." *Pomp* refers to the vain splendor of the rich, and *Take physic* connotes that this concentration of riches is a disease that must be cured. *Physic* (in the sense of physician) refers to healing and especially to the giving of purges by bleeding or enemas. The image of pomp taking physic graphically reveals how Lear now feels about the rich, as well as his new realization that wealth needs to be dislodged and allowed to flow freely to all levels of society.

This image is supported by *shake the superflux to them*, which means "scatter your surplus wealth to the poor." *Shake* also gives the physical connotation of shaking a tree so that the ripe fruit falls out of it to be eaten.

In the last line, Lear suggests that *heaven* itself would seem to be *more just* if man treated man humanely.

A literal, *denotative* paraphrase of this speech might look like this:

1. Poverty-stricken, defenseless, and helpless people, whether you are in this actual storm or not,
2. Who are awaiting the end of this inhuman and unjust misery,
3. How will you be able, without adequate shelter and food,
4. With your tattered clothing, to withstand
5. This incessant deprivation? I was once rich, a king, in a position to help,
6. And I was blind to your plight. The splendor of the rich must be dislodged;
7. The wealthy must open their hearts to the suffering of the poor
8. And redistribute the excess wealth now in the hands of the few
9. And thereby make the universe appear fairer than it does now.

A connotative paraphrase might be:

Oh, you poor victims! How can you stand this unbearable poverty, this terrible pain?
I was so blind; you rich bastards, see this!
Feel it! Do something about it!

The germinal idea is really summed up in those three powerful words,

Take physic, Pomp!

***Zoo Story:***

"Realistic" prose is often less compact than poetry, but can be just as rich in associations. At the beginning of this speech, in which Jerry tries to describe his life to Peter, the diction is almost severe in its stark, straightforward simplicity.

In lines 1-3, Jerry is trying to get started, searching for a way of explaining his problem. In line 4, he begins enumerating the things he has tried to relate to, and he is soon describing his world, the world of his rooming house and apartment. The theme of coping, of "dealing" with things recurs, and the connotations of most of the words reflect a sense of basic physical inhibition, which relates to the search for identity through contact with others. The important thing about the pornographic playing cards in line 13 is that they are associated with an unlocked strongbox (they are a form of sexual contact that is accessible).

Around line 14, Jerry has really "tuned in" and his thoughts are flowing in longer phrases, an outpouring of pent-up frustrations with the connotations becoming richer and more physical. In the next phrases, love triggers a sequence of *vomiting* (symbolic rejection of nourishing contact with life), *crying* (a vocal gesture of frustration in this context), *fury* over the disappointment of the realities of sex, the exaltation of the love act as transcendent of the circumstances in which it occurs, and *howling because you're alive* as the ambivalent awareness of the pain of existence (compare Lear's "Howl, howl, howl, howl.")

Finally, God, who symbolizes for Jerry contact between people, is connected to A COLORED QUEEN (a black homosexual) and A WOMAN WHO CRIES WITH DETERMINATION. The COLORED QUEEN is a symbol of ephemeral sexual contact, preoccupied with maintaining an illusion of femininity by plucking his eyebrows. The WOMAN WHO CRIES WITH DETERMINATION, and whose sorrow has become the only possible gesture toward life, is a symbol of heterosexual contact, remaining inaccessible BEHIND HER CLOSED DOOR. Jerry's inability to open the door to human contact will lead him to his final, desperate act, a suicide which has an implicitly sexual connotation as he thrusts himself on the knife held by Peter.

**Exercise 74:**
**Diction Analysis**
**and Embodiment**

A. ANALYSIS

In this and the next three Lessons, you will be doing close text analyses of the sonnet or verse speech you have selected. Type it carefully triple-spaced, exactly the way it appears in the original, with all the same line endings, punctuation, and capitalization. It will be useful if you make four copies of it.

Using one of these copies, write a paraphrase on each of the following levels:

1. Between the typed lines of the speech, write your paraphrase on two lines. One line is for literal denotation, expressing the precise meanings of the words;

2. The other line is for emotional connotation, use colloquial language which is natural for you to capture the feeling of the speaker;

3. In the right-hand margin, write the germinal idea of each speech in the fewest words you can;

4. In the left-hand margin, express the hidden meanings or subtext, if any.

B. EMBODIMENT

Using your paraphrase as a basis, do each of the following exercises:

1. In an extemporaneous but accurate way, perform the speech in paraphrase. You should understand the ideas behind the words well enough that you can recreate it in your own words.

2. Speaking the words as written, use free-flowing dance-like movements and emphatic gestures to make the syntax as vivid as possible for yourself; feel all the main parts of each sentence, and all the words that are contrasted or have special meaning.

One note of caution: Remember that acting is reacting, so keep the dramatic situation from which the speech comes alive in this exercise. If you are addressing someone else, have a partner "stand in" for that character. Feel your actions in pursuit of your objective moving through the words toward them, so that *speaking becomes a form of doing!*

# Lesson
# Seventeen

# Rhythm

Rhythm is perhaps the single most powerful aspect of stage language. It functions in three primary ways: to support meaning, express personality, and to express emotion.

Though rhythm is the most physical and least "intellectual" aspect of language, it is closely tied to and supportive of meaning. It functions not only as tempo (fast or slow), but also in the variations of tempo and force that give emphasis to certain words, images, or other elements of language.

In addition to supporting meaning through emphasis, rhythm is also highly expressive of personality. The blustery, pompous person has a rhythm of speech much different from the thoughtful, introspective person. Even nationality and social background affect rhythm: the Irish, for example, tend to speak each thought on one long exhalation of breath, imparting an unmistakable rhythm to their speech. Good playwrights build these rhythms into the language which their characters speak, so that a character's speech rhythms are appropriate to their personality and social background. Your analysis of these rhythms will aid you in forming your characterization.

Emotions also have recognizable rhythmic implications. All emotion causes measurable changes in the tension of our muscles, and this has a direct effect on our speech. Take anger as an example: as anger rises in us, the body becomes tense, especially in the deep center where the largest muscles mobilize themselves for action. Tension in the interior muscles is communicated directly to the diaphragm, limiting its movement and forcing us to take shallow breaths. Since we need to oxygenate the muscles for defense purposes, we compensate by taking more short breaths. Tension, spreading to the pharynx, causes an elevation of pitch, and coupled with the increased pressure of the breath stream, this results in a "punching" delivery and increased volume. The vestigial biting and tearing of the jaw related to anger encourages us to emphasize hard consonant sounds, so that our speech may become, in rage, similar to the snapping and growling of an angry animal.

By responding sensitively to the rhythms and sounds the playwright has built into your character's speech, and by experiencing them fully in your own muscles you will find them a powerful aid in entering into the consciousness of your character. As Stanislavski said,

> There is an indissoluble interdependence, interaction and bond between tempo-rhythm and feeling. . . The correctly established tempo-rhythm of a play or a role, can of itself, intuitively (on occasion automatically) take hold of the feelings of an actor and arouse in him a true sense of living his part.[1]

## RHYTHM IN POETRY: SCANSION

We will turn first to the analysis of rhythm in poetry since it is more obvious and regular than is prose rhythm. The heightened rhythmic patterning of poetry is a great help to the actor; it makes the analysis and delivery of the speech more specific. (Remember, however, that rhythm is just as carefully structured in good prose as it is in poetry, and most of the principles of rhythmic analysis apply equally to both.)

First, can you easily tell the difference between poetry and prose? If you will look at a few pages of Shakespeare's plays, you will notice that some lines stop before they get all the way to the right-hand margin; this is the poetry. The lines that are printed in solid blocks, with each line going all the way to the right, are the prose. Can you guess why they are different in this way?

The lines of poetry are written according to a predetermined pattern; each line is allowed a certain number of syllables, so they do not go all the way to the right-hand margin. This *line length* is the basic regulator of poetic rhythm.

In order to understand how the length of the poetic line is established, we must first understand how the words and syllables that comprise the line are patterned. The term for analyzing the rhythm of a line, syllable by syllable, is *scansion*.

All words are made up of one or more syllables, some of which are emphasized or *stressed* ("punched," as the Romans put it) and some are relatively *unstressed*. When these words are joined into a poetic line, their stressed and unstressed syllables work together to form an overall rhythmic pattern within that line. The first step in scanning a line, then, is to identify the stressed and unstressed syllables. Take this famous line from *Romeo and Juliet* as an example:

But soft! What light through yonder window breaks?

We know for a start that the pronunciation of multisyllabled words determines the placement of stresses, though in rare instances we may be required to use an unusual pronunciation for the sake of poetic metre. We put a line called a macron ( — ) over the stressed syllables and a semicircle called a breve ( ˘ ) over the unstressed ones:

But soft! What light through yŏnder window breaks?

Next, we can deduce that the meaning and syntax of the line require emphasis on the words "soft," "light," and "breaks." As we said in the previous lesson, subjects, verbs and objects are usually emphasized, especially when an unusual syntax brings attention to them; here, *light* is the subject, *window* is the object, and the verb *breaks* is at the end, getting special emphasis.

But sōft! What līght through yŏnder window brēaks?

Filling in the remaining unstressed syllables, we see this pattern emerge:

Bŭt sōft! Whăt līght thrŏugh yōndĕr windŏw brēaks?

Though we have marked syllables as either stressed or unstressed, these are only very general categories, and there is actually a great deal of variation within each. If we were to read all stressed syllables one way and all unstressed another, the result would be a monotonous singsong. Only a few of the stresses in each line are actually *major* stresses. In this line, for example, we would probably read only *soft, light,* and *breaks* as major stresses. At the same time, an unstressed syllable like *What* certainly receives more emphasis than the unstressed syllable *der*.

Some systems of scansion actually recognize four different levels of stress rather than just two. Using such a system, with 4 being the heaviest stress and 1 the lightest, this line would look like this:

2   4   1   4   2   3   1   3   1   4
But soft! What light through yonder window breaks?

Even though it is more accurate, this type of system is too complex for most actors to use easily. For our purposes, it is enough to recognize a general pattern of alternating stressed and unstressed syllables, remembering that stress is *relative to adjoining syllables* and that not all stressed syllables nor all unstressed syllables are equal to one another.

The rhythmic pattern of this line can be identified by using the most common system of English poetry, *foot scansion.* To use foot scansion, one arranges the stressed and unstressed syllables into units called *feet.* There are a limited number of these units of stressed and unstressed syllables established by tradition, and they work very much like measures in music. If I write ( ♩ ♩ ♩ ) in music, you recognize it as a measure of waltz time. The same is true of our arrangement of syllables. If I write *But, sŏft!*, it is recognized as a foot called an *iamb.*

The traditional feet used in English verse are six in number and look like this:

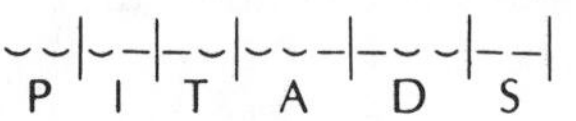

ᵛ ᵛ | ᵛ – | – ᵛ | ᵛ ᵛ – | – ᵛ ᵛ | – – |
P      I      T        A          D        S

**FIGURE 28.** Traditional Poetic Feet.

You can remember the names of the traditional feet by remembering the nonsense word PITADS. The first letter of PITADS, P, stands for the weakest foot, the *pyrrhic*, which has only two unstressed syllables, ( ᵛ ᵛ ). The second letter, I, stands for the most common foot, the *iamb*, which has an unstressed syllable followed by a stressed one ( ᵛ – ). The third letter, T, stands for *trochee*, the opposite of iamb, ( – ᵛ ). A is for *anapest*, which is different because it has three syllables, two unstressed and one stressed ( ᵛ ᵛ – ). D is for *dactyl*, the opposite of the anapestic, ( – ᵛ ᵛ ). Finally, S is for *spondee*, the strongest foot of all, with two stresses, ( – – ).

If we look again at our line from *Romeo and Juliet*, we see that it divides regularly into iambic feet, and we mark those feet with a vertical line just like a measure line in music:

But, soft! What light through yon der win dow breaks?

Notice that the division of feet does not necessarily coincide with the division of words. When foot divisions *coincide* with word divisions, the result is a *heavy* meter in which the regularity of the rhythm is pronounced; it is usual in Shakespeare for simple, emphatic feelings like joy or rage to be expressed in heavy meter.

When foot divisions and word divisions *conflict*, the result is an *internal tension* within the line, and some particular quality, image, or idea is emphasized by the irregularity. Shakespeare often used this kind of inner tension to express conditions of inner conflict or uncertainty in his characters (many of Hamlet's speeches contain such tension, for example).

In the line from *Romeo and Juliet*, another function of foot divisions can be seen: The line breaks more heavily after the key words, *soft*, *light*, and *breaks*, and this helps shape the meaning of the whole.

Notice that like most of Shakespeare's poetic lines, this line has exactly ten syllables, and the ten syllables are divided into five iambic feet. We therefore call this meter "iambic five-meter," or *iambic pentameter*. If there were more or less than five feet, we would call it *trimeter* (3), *tetrameter* (4) or *hexameter* (6). We identify the meter by combining the name of the predominant kind of foot with the average number of feet per line: Iambic tetrameter, for example, would be a meter that generally had four iambic feet in each line, as in this speech from the end of *A Midsummer Night's Dream*:

> Now, until the break of day,
> Through this house each fairy stray,
> To the best bride-bed will we,
> Which by us shall blessed be;
> And the issue there create,
> Ever shall be fortunate.

In these lines, there is a missing syllable at the beginning of each line:

(˘)
N̄ow, | ŭntīl | thĕ brēak | ŏf dāy,

Missing syllables should be treated like rests in music. In this case, the rest emphasizes the end of the lines and thereby accentuates the rhyme.

Notice that in this example we might have placed the missing syllable at the end of the line, making the lines scan as *trochaic* instead of iambic:

N̄ow, ŭn | tīl thĕ | brēak ŏf | dāy, (˘)

Try reading the line with this feeling, and you will see that it makes a big difference. In this example, the trochaic meter doesn't really fit the line or the mood of the speech. The iambic reading has a momentum that flows from the unstressed syllables up to the stressed ones and is therefore called a *rising* meter. A trochaic line has the opposite tendency and is called a *falling* meter. The happy sentiment of these lines encourages us to scan them with a rising feeling. Falling meter is sometimes used to express sadness, as when King Lear, with his dead daughter in his arms, says:

> . . . . She'll come no more
> N̄evĕr, | n̄evĕr, | n̄evĕr, | n̄evĕr, | n̄evĕr.

Iambic pentameter is the most common English meter. When it does not rhyme, it is called *blank verse*. When each successive pair of lines rhyme, it is called *heroic couplets*. Shakespeare will usually end a scene with a couplet or even a triplet.

A word of caution: the meter, in either prose or poetry, does not necessarily affect the tempo of the speech. Just as waltz time can be played quickly or slowly and still be 3/4 time, a passage of iambic pentameter can be read at any tempo. The meter establishes internal relationships of syllable to syllable, while tempo is determined by meaning, emotion, and character.

## METRICAL VARIATIONS

We name poetry by the dominant kind of meter it possesses, expecting that there will be variations. For example, we call Shakespeare's poetry "blank verse" or "iambic pentameter," even though there are some lines with more or less than ten syllables, and there may be many feet that are not iambic.

Some variations are more common than others. In *Romeo and Juliet*, Juliet exclaims:

> Gállŏp ăpāce, yŏu fīerў-fŏotĕd stēeds!

If we scan for pronunciation and meaning, we get:

> Gallop apace, you fiery-footed steeds!

When we divide this into feet, we get:

> Gállŏp | ăpāce, | yŏu fī | erў foot | ĕd stēeds!

Two irregularities are immediately obvious. The first foot is not iambic, it is trochaic; since a trochee is an "upside down" iamb, this is called an *inverted* foot, and is a common variation in the first foot of a line. It is also fairly common to find a spondee in the first foot since both these variations are used to get a line off to a strong start.

Notice that the rhythmic pattern created by "Gallop apace" is a perfect rendering of galloping!

The fourth foot is also not iambic, but *anapestic*. There is a great deal of argument among scholars about whether three-syllable feet (the anapest and dactyl) are "proper" in English poetry. Most critics feel that they are not, and that the poet wanted the line read to conform to the two- syllable pattern demanded by convention. Nevertheless, we ought to determine each case on its own merits, not by an all-inclusive rule; let's do so here.

If you pronounce all three syllables in *fiery*, you will find that it stands out somewhat from the dominant meter. Your impulse is to speed up these three syllables into the space of two, thereby maintaining the basic beat of the line. This speed is certainly appropriate to the meaning of "fiery": it also extends the feeling of "galloping," and this might be a good reason to preserve the extra syllable. If we do, the line has one syllable more than the basic ten syllable pattern and is called *hypermetrical.*

On the other hand, many scholars would say that this extra syllable should be removed so that the line conforms to the regular iambic pattern. This can be done by the process of *elision.* You *elide* a syllable by slurring or gliding over it as you speak it, so that it is minimized *though not eliminated altogether.* You can see that it is easy to glide over the middle syllable of *fiery* and say the word as if it had only two syllables, *fi-ry.* If you do this, the meter of the line becomes perfectly regular.

One of the best arguments in favor of such an elision is that hypermetrical lines usually contain words that are easy to elide, and so must have been chosen for this purpose by the poet. Theatrical tradition is also in favor of making these elisions.

In actual practice, this is a decision which must be made by the director, since any given production must be consistent on this matter, one way or the other.

Elision is sometimes marked by the printer, and sometimes not. When you see a word printed "Heav'n," it may or may not be a proper elision. Only your own analysis will tell you, since these typographical markings were not made by the playwright.

## SHAPING OF POETIC LINES

We have now identified two levels of poetic rhythm that involve individual syllables and words. There is a larger rhythmic pattern that the poet establishes by manipulating the endings of the lines. The general ten syllable length of the pentameter line establishes a dominant rhythm; by varying this dominant rhythm the playwright achieves special emphasis and effect.

One way poets achieve special rhythmic effect is by breaking up the flow of the line. A strong pause that interrupts a poetic line and sounds like a "false line-ending" is called a *caesura.* It is usually marked by a semicolon, colon, or period. For example:

Tŏo līt | tle cāre | ŏf thīs. ‖ Tāke phȳ | sĭc, pōmp;

I use a double foot line to mark caesuras.

Lines may end on either stressed or unstressed syllables; most common are those ending on stresses, which are called *masculine* endings. An unstressed syllable at the end of the line is a *feminine* ending. Such a final "feminine" syllable is usually an "extra" syllable and was not meant to be elided:

He was a thing of blood whose every motion
Was timed with dying cries. Alone he enter'd
The mortal gate of the city, which he painted
With shunless destiny. . .

In these lines from *Coriolanus*, we feel the effect of the extra last feminine syllable driving us on into the next line, supporting the vigor and determination of what is being described. As in this example, hypermetrical feminine endings in Shakespeare almost always appear in clusters of two, three, or more.

When lines "run on" into each other, as these do, they are called *enjambed* lines. Enjambed lines are the opposite of end-stopped lines. Several lines may be enjambed to form a larger rhythmic unit, and these will usually form units of thought (see the Lear Sample Analysis to follow).

One extremely interesting manipulation of poetic lines is in the *sharing* of a line between characters. Look again at the speeches from *Measure for Measure* which we analyzed in the last lesson.

CLAUDIO     Is there no remedy?

ISABELLA
    None but such a remedy as, to save a head,
    To cleave a heart in twain.

CLAUDIO     But is there any?

ISABELLA
    Yes, brother, you may live;
    There is a devilish mercy in the judge,
    If you'll implore it, that will free your life,
    But fetter you till death.

CLAUDIO     Perpetual durance?

ISABELLA
    Ay, just—perpetual durance, a restraint,
    Though all the world's vastidity you had,
    To a determined scope.

You notice how Claudio's lines are printed in from the margin, directly beneath the end of Isabella's preceding line. This is because the two characters are "sharing" one line of iambic pentameter between them. If you scan the first instance, you get one feminine line:

To cleave a heart in twain. / But is there any?

These shared lines encourage the actor playing Claudio to "jump in" quickly on top of Isabella's endings, and this would certainly be appropriate to his desperate frame of mind. Shared lines can often be used in this way, though this is not an inflexible rule.

We have seen that the various levels or layers of poetic rhythm exist simultaneously, and their interaction produces a contrapuntal richness which provides emphasis and texture. We can list these layers of rhythm from the smallest patterns to the largest:

1. The arrangement of stressed and unstressed syllables;
2. The division of these syllable patterns into feet, and the tension between word division and foot division;
3. Variations within the basic foot pattern;
4. The placement of caesura within the line and the manipulation of line-endings to form larger patterns;
5. The groupings of several lines into verse paragraphs.

## PROSE RHYTHMS

A skillful playwright utilizes rhythm extensively, whether they are writing prose or poetry. Prose rhythms are usually not as heightened or formalized as those of poetry, but they operate on the same principle of variety within regularity. Just as there are levels of poetic rhythm, so there are layers of prose rhythm which we will call *cadences*.

The basic rhythm of prose, like that of poetry, is established by the alternation of stressed and unstressed syllables. While they are not regular enough to be named by tradition, the sensitive reader will quickly sense the "beat" underlying a prose speech. We will call the basic rhythm established by the flow of syllables the *syllabic* cadence.

Look at the following example from Samuel Beckett's *Endgame* and scan it as if it were poetry; you will see that Beckett uses the pattern of duple and triple rhythms (as if they were iambs and anapests) to great effect. After scanning it, read it aloud for full rhythmic effect.

> One day you'll be blind, like me. You'll be sitting there, a speck in the void, in the dark, forever, like me. (pause) One day you'll say to yourself, I'm tired. I'll sit down, and you'll go and sit down. Then you'll say, I'm hungry, I'll get up and get something to eat. But you won't get up. You'll say, I shouldn't have sat down, but since I have I'll sit on a little longer, then I'll get up and get something to eat. (pause) But you won't get up and you won't get anything to eat.

The rhythmic flow of these syllables is surely as powerful as any formal poetry ever written.

Next in the hierarchy of prose cadences is the *breath* cadence. The evolution of our written language was greatly influenced by the way we speak; most simple sentences can be said on a single breath. If a sentence becomes too complex for one breath, we break it up into phrases which form *breath* cadences. These breath cadences are sometimes marked by commas, semicolons, or colons (in music, the comma is still used as a breath mark).

Playwrights, since they are writing for the speaking voice and not just the eye, manipulate breath cadences to guide the actor into a pattern of breathing; we have already seen how the rhythm of breath is a primary factor in the generation of emotion. Try reading the Beckett quote above with a small breath at every comma, a full breath at each period, and a large breath at each (pause). What emotional experience results?

Note that breath cadences are also important in poetry, often coinciding with caesuras and end-stopped lines, and influence your breathing in the same way.

A still larger prose pattern is developed by the length of sentences, the ends of which are marked by a strong pause indicated by a period, question mark, or exclamation point. This is called the *terminal* cadence. In longer speeches it is especially necessary to organize the thoughts of the speech into rhythmic groupings according to terminal cadences.

Radical changes in the terminal cadence are usually our best indicators of changes in tempo; shorter terminal cadences usually indicate a faster tempo, longer ones a slower tempo, though again, this is by no means a hard-and-fast rule. Terminal cadences are also of great importance in poetry as organizing factors and tempo indicators.

Finally, sentences are grouped into units of meaning which are called *paragraphs* in prose. In most dialogue, each *speech* acts as a paragraph. We get a good impression of the tempo of a scene by looking at the density of the printed script; a mass of long speeches suggests a different tempo than, for example, the extremely short back-and-forth exchange of some farce. We call this the *dialogue* cadence.

A summary of these cadences, which apply as well to poetry as to prose, are listed here from the smallest rhythmic units to the largest:

1.  syllabic cadence;
2.  breath cadence;
3.  terminal cadence;
4.  dialogue cadence.

Notice that levels 2 and 3 may be the same in simple declarative prose.

## YOUR BASIS FOR ANALYSIS

Remember that the rhythm of speech does not absolutely determine meaning or even emotion; as you begin to analyze rhythm, you will see many possibilities, and you will probably be puzzled about which of them to select.

Your choice must be based upon your understanding of the meaning of the line and your evaluation of the relative importance of its various elements, taking into account the demands of character, situation, and emotion. Nevertheless, a detailed analysis of the rhythms of a character's speech should begin to impart to you a sense of the personality of the speaker.

In our everyday life we have an intuitive and highly developed sense of the communicative value of sound and rhythm which together form the *melody* of speech. It is what gives our speech its color and individual flavor, and it helps us to catch implications, sarcasm, and all sorts of connotative values that round out our daily speech and make it expressive.

In a well written play, these aspects of speech have been incorporated into the structure of the lines in a selected and heightened way. Through careful and informed analysis, you can unlock these inherent values of tone and rhythm: if you can surrender yourself to experience them fully as muscular actions, you can bring them back to life for yourself, and through your experience for your audience as well.

## SAMPLE RHYTHM ANALYSES

*King Lear:*

1. Poor na | kĕd wrē | tches, where | sŏ e'er | yŏu āre,

2. Thăt bīde | thĕ pēl | tǐng ōf | thǐs pīt | ilĕss stōrm,

3. Hōw shāll | yŏur hōuse | lĕss hēads | aňd ūn | fĕd sīdes

4. Yŏur lōop'd | aňd wīn | dŏw'd rāg | gĕdnēss, | dĕfēnd yŏu

5. Frŏm sēa | sŏns sūch | ăs thēse? || Ō! Ī | hăve tā'en

6. Tŏo līt | tle cāre | ŏf thīs. || Take phy | sǐc, pōmp;

7. Ĕxpōse | thysēlf | tŏ fēel | whăt wrē | tches fēel,

8. Thăt thōu | măyst shāke | thĕ sū | pĕrflūx | tŏ thēm,

9. Aňd shōw | thĕ hēa | vĕns | mōre | jŭst.

Examine the above sample scansion for metrical variation. Notice especially the use of spondees in the first feet of lines 1, 3, and 6. There is also a pair of spondees in the fourth feet of lines 5 and 6. The speech has a strongly emphatic quality, and the heaviness of these stresses contributes to the strong feelings Lear expresses.

In line 2, we follow custom by eliding *pitiless*. The fact that we "mispronounce" the word when making the elision helps call attention to it. Line 4 appears to have a hypermetrical feminine ending, with the final *you* being the extra syllable. There are two reasons for this: first, the leftover beat moves us on strongly into the next line, and this is one of only two enjambed lines in the speech; second, the word *you*, which appears in some form in lines 1, 3, and 4, shows Lear's concern for others. At the beginning of the play, he was self-concerned, but through his suffering he has learned concern for others. His realization of his past lack of compassion is crystallized in this speech.

The elision of "taken" into *ta'en* in line 5 is marked by the printer. Nevertheless, we might argue with it; there are only two run-on lines in the speech, lines 4 and 5; line 4, directly preceding, uses a hypermetrical feminine ending to urge us past the line-ending and on into the next line. Therefore, it might be consistent to utilize the same device in line 5 and leave *taken* as a hypermetrical feminine ending, especially since feminine endings usually appear in clusters. The decision, however, is yours. (This may seem like a ridiculously small point, but crucial meanings sometimes turn on minute details.)

The terminal cadences and placement of caesura in this speech are intriguing. The first four and one-half lines are one long and cohesive sentence. There follows the short sentence, *O! I have ta'en/Too little care of this.* Though it is broken up by the line endings, this sentence reads as if it were one line of iambic pentameter formed between the caesuras in lines 5 and 6. Next is the short phrase *Take physic, pomp,* which is itself broken by a slight pause. The remainder of the speech is one sentence, which flows smoothly until we come to the last line.

These terminal cadences break the speech into three units of thought and emotion: in the first four lines, Lear's attention is on the poor. In line 5, he realizes his own guilty share of things with *O! I have ta'en/ Too little care of this.* In the remaining lines, Lear turns his attention again to others, those who are rich as he himself once was, and he prays that they will act as he did not.

The last line is particularly interesting. *Heaven* could be elided to Heav'n, which is a common Shakespearean elision (though it is difficult to pronounce) and the line could scan as regular iambic trimeter:

Aňd shōw | the hēavens | mŏre jūst.

This seems like a terribly weak ending to such an important and deeply felt speech. I suggest that by the shortening of this line, Shakespeare indicates that he wants it "stretched out" to fill the time usually taken by a full five feet, as if the two missing feet functioned like quarter rests in music. He is, in a sense, giving the actor time to complete the emotional flow of the speech.

I have therefore scanned the speech to use implied pauses, which produce an iambic line:

Aňd shōw | the hēa | vens | more | just.

This results in a reading that emphasizes the concept of justice, provides a strong rhythmic finish for this crucial speech, and makes positive use of the line's irregularity. Again, there are no absolute rules about such matters.

Accepting this scansion, we see a beautiful shaping of the whole speech. Since caesuras give the effect, in reading, of "false" line endings, and strong run-on lines obscure actual line endings, we could print and read the speech like this:

> Poor naked wretches,
> Wheresoe'er you are,
> That bide the pelting of this pitiless storm
> How shall your houseless heads and unfed sides,
> Your loop'd and window'd raggedness,
> defend you from seasons such as these?
> O! I have ta'en too little care of this.
> Take physic,
> pomp;
> Expose thyself to feel what wretches feel,
> That thou mayst shake the superflux to them,
> And show the heavens
> more
> just.

As it is printed here each line represents a breath cadence. Read it aloud, taking a breath for each line, and see what effect this has on you; what emotion begins to result? Do you see which ideas and feelings are emphasized by this shaping of the whole?

### The Zoo Story:

As in the speech from *King Lear*, cadences play a crucial role in shaping here. The syllabic cadence is heavily stressed, since the preponderance of words are of one syllable. The effect is emphatic.

The breath cadence is probably the most important rhythmic device in this speech. At first there are "dead ends" in Jerry's thinking, which Albee has indicated by ellipses (. . .). The speech begins with these fragments as Jerry searches for words to describe his feelings; then, as his thoughts begin to flow, the breath cadences begin to lengthen and swell, reaching a prolonged climax in lines 18-20, and the use of capital letters as volume and emphasis markings supports this. The speech then dies away in a few final gasps, finishing with a heavy sigh. This overall pattern suggests the rhythm of sexual intercourse.

Try reading the speech aloud; suspend your breath sharply at each ellipsis (. . .), and take a new breath at each new sentence. A pattern like this emerges:

```
_____
_____ Soft
_____X_____X_____
_____X_____ Faster, Searching
5  _____X_____
_____X_____
_____X____
_____
_____X____ Building
10 _____X_____X____ Flowing
_____
_____
_____
_____
15 _____
_____
_____X with God_____
_____X_____ Loud and Continuous
_____
20 _____ Slowing
_____
_____X____with people._____ "Sighs Heavily"
```

Just as in the speech from *King Lear*, certain ideas are emphasized by being isolated as short units surrounded by longer cadences. The long, continual terminal cadence which begins line 10 runs until the semicolon in line 17 and is then followed only by the two words, *with God*. The question of God is the culmination of Jerry's verbal searching during the first part of the speech.

Once he has crystallized his feelings in this concept, the full outburst, the section in capital letters, is unleashed. Then, his energy spent, he says "with God who, I'm told, turned his back on the whole thing some time ago. . ." and he returns to his starting point, people.

### Exercise 75:
### Rhythm Analysis and Embodiment

A. ANALYSIS

Using one of the copies of your speech, analyze the rhythm of your lines using the system of marking we have explained. If it is poetry, mark the following:

1. Stressed and unstressed syllables;
2. Foot divisions;
3. Elisions;
4. Caesuras;
5. Run-on lines;

Whether your speeches are poetry or prose, also mark:

6. The breath cadences;
7. The terminal cadences;

And work together with your partner to examine:

8. The dialogue cadence.

Discuss with your partner the way in which these rhythms are appropriate to your characters, emotions, and situation.

B. EMBODIMENT

1. Using your analysis as a basis, create a dance-like version of the speech which exaggerates its rhythms. Move from your center; involve the deep muscles, not just the arms and legs. Speak the speech as you move, and allow your voice to be freely influenced by your movement. Give your entire body a chance to participate; do not limit yourself to "realistic" movement, or even to the way you might do the speech in performance.
2. Take a moment to "reset" yourself for the beginning of the speech, then do it in its "normal" form. How much of your body's memory of the embodiment carries over to enrich the speech in its traditional form?

The body will "remember" these experiences far better than the mind. In Stanislavski's terms, you are creating *sense memories* based upon the qualities of the text. Then, as you do the speech in a "normal" way, these bodily memories will automatically enrich your performance without conscious effort. Trust your body to remember the really important things, and let the rest fall away!

# Lesson
# Eighteen

## Melody

> Letters, syllables, words—these are the musical notes of speech, out of which
> to fashion measures, arias, whole symphonies. There is good reason to describe
> beautiful speech as musical.[1]

As Stanislavski indicates here, the actor must develop a heightened capacity
for the musical aspects of speech. We do this not only to produce beautiful
sound, but because we must express extraordinary levels of feeling and
experience. As he put it,

> Musical speech opens up endless possibilities of conveying the inner life of a
> role. . . . What can we express with our ordinary register of five or six notes?
> . . . We realize how ridiculous we are when we have to express complicated
> emotions. It is like playing Beethoven on a balalaika.[2]

A good playwright selects and arranges words not only for meaning, but
also for rhythmic and tonal values which support and enhance meaning,
character, and emotion. The music of speech communicates the speaker's
personality and emotion; it can also help to specify nuances of meaning.

Scholars have formed various theories about the relationship of sound
and meaning in language. One of these was the Roback Voco-Sensory
Theory. Experimental subjects were asked to tell which of several three-

letter nonsense syllables, like *mil* and *mal*, made them think of larger or smaller objects. As you probably would guess, *mal* seemed "bigger" than *mil* to most subjects. The theory explained this by noting that saying *mal* requires opening the mouth more than does saying *mil*, and so it carries the connotation of bigness.

The theory went on to suggest that much of language was formed by our association of the physical sensation of pronouncing certain sounds with the meaning of the sounds themselves. Words like "rough" feel rough when you say them, and "smooth" feels smooth, just as *rushing* rushes, *explode* explodes, and so on.

Roback's theory is limited, however, since many words do not seem to relate to the physical qualities of their pronunciation; for example, *small* is made up of "big" sounds, while *big* is "small."

Although the voco-sensory theory can thus be disproved as explaining the genesis of language, it can still be useful to us as actors. The physical sensations created by words as we speak them are often important to their *connotation* if not to their *denotation*; a good playwright will have selected words which have sounds that can be useful to you in supporting the meaning and emotional tone of your character's speech. As long as you remember that meaning is not *determined* by sound but rather is *supported* by it, you will be able to use the physical act of pronouncing a speech as a way to enhance the appropriate meaning and feeling.


## ONOMATOPOEIA AND ALLITERATION

When a speaker is responding fully to the sound value of the language, the melody of speech can also evoke sensations directly. Stanislavski reminds you that,

> To an actor a word is not just a sound, it is the evocation of images.[3]

This is most obvious in the case of words which have special sound values, and in cases where certain sounds have been emphasized through repetition.

*Onomatopoeia* refers to words whose sound resembles the thing they describe, like "hush" or "buzz." Whole speeches may be onomatopoeic, like Lear's

> Blow, winds, and crack your cheeks! Rage! Blow!
> . . . Spit, fire! Spout, rain!

Even without a specific use of onomatopoeia, a good writer will have supplied you with sounds you can use to emphasize the effect of a line.

When Juliet says,

> Gallop apace, you fiery-footed steeds,

we recognize that *gallop* can be pronounced so as to sound like a horse galloping and is onomatopoeic. Even *fiery* lends itself to being spoken in a fiery manner; the quick explosion of air from between your lips on the *fi* sound can be the sort of aggressive, bold action we connect with fieriness.

Notice how Shakespeare has reinforced the onomatopoeia of "gallop" by repeating the key sounds in other words: "Gallop apace," with its repeated *ah* and *p* sounds, sounds like galloping both rhythmically and tonally. Likewise, the repetition of the *f* sound in "fiery-footed" and the closely related *s* sound in "steed" helps reinforce the effect of fieriness and also relates fieriness to the feet of the horses, thus referring us to a quality of their galloping.

This repetition of similar sounds in words in close juxtaposition is called *alliteration*. We use the term broadly to refer to all closely repeated sounds, whether vowels or consonants, whether they occur as initial sounds or within the words.

We will also be interested in patterns of sounds that recur within a speech or even within a role even if they are not close enough together to be called alliteration. While individual cases of alliteration or onomatopoeia can be used for emphasis of particular points, such overall patterning of sounds on a larger scale produces an effect that good writers will use to help distinguish one character from another, one mood from another, or the changing of emotional states within a role.

You might find, for example, that the sounds of your character's speeches make a particular pitch range and inflectional pattern more natural than others, and that this pitch and pattern will be psychologically and physically appropriate to your role. The melody of your character's speech suggests vocal qualities of delivery, which in turn generate experiences in you which suggest aspects of characterization.

One of the most important functions of speech melody is that it serves as a link between the words of your text and your total physical performance. Any skillful playwright has incorporated in the words of the play a wealth of vocal actions that can lead you to a full involvement with the character. When you fully revitalize the melody of a speech, you find that the sounds help to make the feelings and meaning more vivid and more immediate. As Stanislavski said,

> When an actor adds the vivid ornament of sound to the living content of the words, he causes me to glimpse with an inner vision the images he has fashioned out of his own creative imagination.[4]

## SAMPLE MELODY ANALYSES

*King Lear:*

The melody of poetry is extensively patterned, and it is often useful to chart graphically the recurrent sounds by underlining, coloring, or some other device, so as to see the melodic pattern as a visual pattern.

In line 1, the falling vowel sound of *Poor* followed by the hard, almost cruel sound of *naked* set the mood. These sounds are not hard or soft but can be used to physicalize the meaning of each word. As you say *Poor*, the full weight of poverty and all that it means must be experienced. *Naked* must likewise be delivered with a vivid sense of nakedness, so that pronouncing these words becomes a vocal gesture strong enough to achieve the appropriate intensity of meaning and feeling.

*Wretches* is a somewhat onomatopoeic word; its sound is bitter and regurgitative as in "retching." *Wretches, wheresoe'er* is alliteration of the *w* sounds, extending the effect. *Wheresoe'er you are* is a triple repetition of *r* sounds.

In line 2, *bide, pelting,* and *pitiless* alliterate, tying these three aspects of the condition of the poor together. *Pelting* is onomatopoeic, and the physical and vocal gestures required to pronounce it "peltingly" carry a sense of physical cruelty over to *pitiless*, which contains roughly the same sounds, turning it into an especially ruthless and active lack of compassion and morality. Try continuing the analysis for yourself for lines 3-6.

In line 7, *Expose* is a sound that begins small and then opens, "exposing" the mouth, and this quality can be extended to our whole body and attitude so that Lear does physically *expose* himself *to feel what wretches feel,* the alliteration of the *f* sounds emphasizing the need to have compassion, to not be pitiless. Earlier, Lear called this speech a prayer, and a gesture of exposure from a prayerful attitude might be to throw the arms open into a pose reminiscent of the crucifixion, the pose of another man who exposed himself to feel what wretches feel.

The thought in lines 8 and 9 is emphasized by the balancing of the *sh* sounds in *shake* and *show.* Other qualities of these lines were discussed earlier.

*The Zoo Story:*

At the beginning of the speech, the emphasized sounds are clipped, either hard consonant and fricative sounds which combine with the broken rhythm to produce an irregular or staccato effect, emphasizing the halting quality of Jerry's thought. As the speech progresses, however, the beat and tone changes, deepens, and broadens into a howl. But as the speech progresses and his associations begin to pour out, the sounds likewise begin to elongate, until lines 18 and 19 are one prolonged tonal outcry.

There are words with onomatopoeic qualities in the latter half of the speech, and their qualities reflect Jerry's emotion: *bleeding, hard, oily-wet, wisp, vomiting, crying, fury, howling,* and so on. There is a surprising amount of alliteration as well: *wisp of smoke, pornographic playing, pretty little ladies aren't pretty little ladies, making money, COLORED QUEEN . . . KIMONO . . . PLUCKS.*

As we noted earlier, this speech is really a description of Jerry's world. The kinds of sounds we have noticed and the gestures they demand, should be used to make Jerry's response to that world vivid, as well as creating the world itself, with its illusions *(wisps of smoke; pretty little ladies aren't. . . ),* its pain *(vomiting, crying, fury, howling),* and its futile efforts at meaningful contact *(pornographic playing, COLORED QUEEN, WOMAN BEHIND HER CLOSED DOOR).*

### Exercise 76:
### Melody Analysis and Embodiment

A.  ANALYSIS
Analyze the patterning of sound in your scene. Mark it graphically on one of your copies of the scene, using underlining, colored pencil, or any other visual device you can invent which reveals the sound pattern.

Note the dominant sounds and consider their usefulness to support meaning, feeling, and the personality of your character.

B.  EMBODIMENT
1.  Recite your scene in monotone. Feel the impulse to break out of the monotone into melody. Where is this impulse the strongest?
2.  Sing it as if it were pure music. Forget that the sounds have any verbal meaning; invent a melody that stresses the sounds you have decided are most important.
3.  Now repeat your rhythm embodiment (Exercise 75) and exaggerate the sound values that are dominant in the speech as a kind of vocal music to accompany the "dance" of your embodiment. Notice what you discover about the interrelationship of sound, rhythm, muscular activity, and the meaning, emotion and character.
4.  Take a moment to "reset" yourself to the beginning, then perform the scene in a "normal" way: how much is carried over from your embodiment?

The melody and rhythm of your stage language are powerful sources of a sense of character. Remember the work you did on vocal gesture in Part One and the profound relationship between sound, breath, energy, and character; as we pointed out then, the word *personality* has a root meaning of *per-sona,* "through sound." The techniques of analysis you have experienced in these two lessons can heighten your intuitive participation in your character's sound and, through it, in their personality as well.

# Lesson
# Nineteen

# Imagery and Figurative Language

Drama is one of the most condensed and intensified forms of literature; what a novelist needs thousands of words to do, a playwright must pack into the dialogue alone. Besides the heightened use of diction, rhythm, and melody you have already considered, the skillful playwright gets an extra measure of impact and meaning in two additional ways: through the potential of language to evoke physical sensation, and by arranging words in special combinations that produce extra levels of meaning.

The creation of physical sensations through the evocative potential of language is called *imagery*, and heightened meaning achieved by special patterns of words is called *figurative language*.

## SENSE IMAGERY

In its most literal sense, an *image* is something imagined. The painting of "word pictures" is the most common kind of imagery, but language may appeal to any of our other senses as well. This speech from Shakespeare's *Antony and Cleopatra*, for example, describes Cleopatra's royal barge sailing down the Nile and is filled with images of many sensory types:

> The barge she sat in, like a burnish'd throne,
> Burn'd on the water. The poop was beaten gold;
> Purple the sails, and so perfumed that
> The winds were love-sick with them; the oars were silver,
> Which to the tune of flutes kept stroke, and made
> The water which they beat to follow faster,
> As amorous of their strokes. For her own person,
> It beggar'd all description. She did lie
> In her pavilion, cloth-of-gold, of tissue,
> O'erpicturing that Venus where we see
> The fancy out-work nature.

The picture of Cleopatra's barge drawn by these words is so vivid that we can "see" this *visual* image in the mind's eye. We can find examples of almost every other type of sense imagery in this speech as well. The image of the silver oars "which to the tune of flutes kept stroke" appeals to our hearing, and is called an *aural* image. The image of the "perfumed" sails which made the winds "love-sick" appeals to our sense of smell, and is called an *olfactory* image. The humorous reference to the water chasing the oars, as if the oars' strokes were lovers' caresses, and the smoothness of the fabric of Cleopatra's pavilion, awaken our sense of touch and texture, and are *tactile* imagery. The cooling breeze of the fans and the flowing warmth of Cleopatra's cheeks are contrasted *thermal* images. If only Cleopatra were (as she might well have been) dining upon some exotic delicacy, we might have been treated to some tasty *gustatory* imagery.

Throughout the description of the barge, we have a sense of its slow, gliding movement on the water, the softly billowing sails, and the rhythmic stroking of the oars. These images of movement are called *kinetic*, while images which refer to physical states that do not involve movement, such as our sense of Cleopatra's relaxation upon her cushions, are called *kinesthetic*.

Kinesthetic imagery often serves as a physical "background" for a speech, providing a general physical state that underlies all the other sensations the speech may contain. If, for example, we put ourselves completely in the place of the speaker and attempt to relive all his original responses, we would be aware of the feeling of the openness of the night air over the dark water and the cool breeze upon our face. This kinesthetic response helps us to recreate a scene as vividly as possible by imaginatively "putting us in the picture."

Shakespeare packed these sensations into the speech with such density that they begin almost to combine with one another; the sounds, colors, and smells begin to merge into one sensory experience. When a poet uses one sense to describe another, as in a "raging red," or a "sweet tone," it is called *synesthesia* (literally, "the bringing together of sensations"). While the description of Cleopatra's barge contains no synesthesia in the technical sense, its overall effect is synesthetic.

All these images have a luxurious and sensual quality appropriate to Cleopatra's character. Images often appear in such clusters of related sensations; compare the images of pain and exposure in the first section of Lear's prayer. Such clusters have a powerful cumulative effect, especially when they excite multiple sensory channels in the same way.

You may also notice sequential changes in a character's imagery which signal a change in their personality. In *King Lear*, for example, Lear's religious references at the beginning of the play are ornate allusions to pagan gods, and his images are of regal splendor. During his madness, his images become bestial, sexual, and scatological. By the end of the play they are simple and human; he no longer speaks of "Hecate" and "Juno," but simply of "God." He no longer speaks of himself as a "dragon and his wrath," but as a "fond, foolish, old man." This change in his imagery beautifully expresses his shift in personality.

There may even be a common *fund* of imagery related to a specific character; Lear's Fool uses a great many animal images; Goneril and Regan are often connected with images of monsters and reptiles.

Though imagery is especially prominent in descriptive passages (like the Cleopatra speech) it is also present in ordinary dialogue, in prose as well as in poetry, and is used by modern as well as classical writers. Try speaking aloud this speech from a recent play, Peter Barnes' *Red Noses*; in it, a Pope is speaking over the bodies of a troupe of clowns whom he has just had killed:

> Wind blow the poppy seeds over them and us, aaaaaawwh.
> *(He howls softly as the lights fade down)*
> Heaven is dark and the earth a secret
> The cold snaps our bones, we shiver
> And dogs sniff round us, licking their paws
> Monsters eat our soul
> There is no way back
> Until God calls us to shadow
> So we rage at the wall and howl.
> Go down, she said, go down with me.
> World go down, dark go down,
> Universe and infinity go down,
> Go down with me, aaaaaaaawwh.

Good delivery of imagery like this requires that you recreate the sensations as if they were happening for the first time. By fully reliving them in your own response, you will find the character's condition generated in you, and thereby in the audience as well.

Your aim is to help the audience to visualize and respond to the scene for themselves through the completeness of your embodiment of the sensations without calling undue attention to the images themselves. You want your delivery to remain "transparent" so that the action can be experienced *through* it. If your audience is more aware of your delivery than of the sensations you are describing, you will have failed in your purpose. As B. L. Joseph puts it in *Acting Shakespeare*:

> The actor's preparation is not aimed at making the audience conscious of the figures for their own sakes,. . . but to incorporate the technique into his playing, and affect them by the creation of his role.[1]

The best approach is to explore each image fully, recreating its sensation in physical terms either through fantasy or some overtly physical technique, then allow this experience to remain stored in the body as a specially created "sense memory."

## SAMPLE IMAGERY ANALYSES

### King Lear:

Notice how the imagery is emphasized by the rhythm and melody of the speech. The speech is about the poor, and the visual images make the poor vivid to the mind's eye: *naked wretches, houseless heads, unfed sides*, the hanging tatters of *loop'd and window'd raggedness*, and so on. Supporting this is the strong overriding tactile image, the pelting of the storm.

The periodic syntax of the first four lines causes these images to "fund" into a single impact. As you examine each visual image, you will find that they also have strong kinesthetic content: *naked, houseless, and unfed*. Lear not only makes us *see* the poor, he makes us *feel* what it is to be poor as well, as he himself does at this moment.

The context of this speech gives us a clear idea of its kinesthetic background, as the exhausted and weatherbeaten Lear uses a lull in the storm to pray.

Continue the analysis for yourself, recognizing each of the many sensations contained in the speech and identifying the way each supports and heightens the meaning.

### The Zoo Story:

This speech proves that even naturalistic prose can be as rich in imagery as poetry. As in Lear's prayer, Albee has provided a clear kinesthetic context for the speech, both in the situation and in the stage directions. Jerry, growing more and more tense, is heading for an explosion; the climax of this speech is one of the mini-crises leading up to his death.

Besides the obvious visual images, there are a good many other types. The touch of things seems important to Jerry, and most of the visual images have a tactile impact as well. Textures are contrasted in *oily-wet* and *wisp of smoke*. Next comes a sequence of kinesthetic and partly kinetic images: *vomiting, crying, fury, making money with your body, act of love, howling, WEARS A KIMONO, PLUCKS HIS EYEBROWS, CRIES WITH DETERMINATION*, and *turned his back*.

There is then a falling sadness at the end of the speech after Jerry has spent himself in this outcry. Notice that throughout, the images are drawn almost entirely from bodily and sexual sensations.

In both Jerry's speech and Lear's speech, the physically vivid imagery supports meaning and emotion. These speeches also demonstrate how different types of images work together, and how a single word often has several imagistic values within a single context.

### Exercise 77:
### Imagery Analysis and Embodiment

A.  ANALYSIS
Use a copy of your speech to mark its sensory images; use different colors or markings for different senses. Pay special attention to clusters and sequences of images, and to those images emphasized by sound and rhythm.

Consider how the images of the speech support meaning, emotion, and character. Go through the speech and find a way to relive each sensation.

B.  EMBODIMENT
1. Perform a slow word-dance of your scene and exaggerate in your physical responses the sensory impact of each image. Treat each image individually and fully relive the sensation of each. Experience also the flow of the images. How does this sensory content relate to the meaning and emotion of the speech? Be sure to involve the articulation of the words directly in your recreation of the sensations of the speech.
2. Take a moment and "reset" yourself to the beginning of the scene, then perform it in a "normal" way. Do the sensations you experienced the first time remain alive as sense memories?

## FIGURATIVE LANGUAGE

*Figurative* language is contrasted to *literal* language. When we speak literally, words can be taken at their face value. But when we speak figuratively, we combine words (place them into a *configuration*) to make them express more than their face value. Such a pattern of words to produce special meaning is called a *figure of speech*.

There are numerous figures of speech recognized in the field of rhetoric, which was in Shakespeare's time a subject studied by all schoolchildren. These were traditionally divided into three categories called "Figures of Word," "Figures of Sentence," and "Tropes." (For a complete discussion of these, see Bertram Joseph's *Acting Shakespeare*.) Only about a third of the traditional figures are of special importance to a working actor, however, and we will discuss these by dividing them into four categories of our own:

1. Diction figures, which require the selection and manipulation of specific word meanings;
2. Structural figures, which are products of special syntax;
3. Varieties of metaphor, which combine disparate elements to create new meanings;
4. Clusters of images and figures of speech as recurrent motifs.

*Diction figures*: You already know one of the diction figures, the *pun*. Another common diction figure is *allusion*, a brief reference to a person, place, or thing which the writer assumes will be known to the audience, who will then "fill in" the reference from their own knowledge. When Juliet, looking at the sky, says "Gallop apace, you fiery-footed steeds," Shakespeare assumes that the audience will know that she is alluding to the chariot of Apollo, which, according to myth, carries the sun across the heavens. Since she wants Apollo's horses to hurry, we understand that she wants night to fall as soon as possible because then Romeo will come to her.

Another diction figure is *hyperbole*, the use of conscious exaggeration for either comic or serious effect. Lear says, "Had I your tongues and eyes I'd use 'em so heaven's vault should crack," which is an exaggeration expressive of the magnitude of his grief.

*Structural figures*: Structural figures achieve their meaning by arranging elements of a line or speech so that they are contrasted or compared. These figures require a very active delivery which emphasizes the comparisons being made through your use of pitch and stress.

Perhaps the most important structural figure for the actor, and one of Shakespeare's favorite devices, is *antithesis*. This is the contrasting of two opposing ideas, usually within a single line or adjoining lines. The contrasted ideas will often be phrased in parallel structures with emphasized words or phrases carrying the opposing meanings. In this speech from *Romeo and Juliet*, Juliet has just learned that Romeo has killed her cousin Tybalt in a fight; naturally, she is torn between her love for Romeo and abhorrence of what he has done, and this ambivalence expresses itself in a series of antitheses:

O serpent heart, hid with a flowering face:
Did ever dragon keep so fair a cave?
Beautiful Tyrant: fiend angelical:
Dove-feathered raven: Wolvish-ravening lamb:
Despised substance of divinist show:
Just opposite to what thou justly seem'st,
A damned saint, an honorable villain:

Can you find each pair of contrasted elements? In this example, the contrasted elements make up the two halves of a balanced line; as you read them aloud, you will find yourself naturally expressing this "seesaw" structure in inflection, pitch, and gesture.

Notice the combination of some words with opposite meanings and connotations in a single phrase, like *damned saint* and *honorable villain*. This combining of opposite sensations or meanings within a single phrase is an especially intense kind of antithesis, and it's technical name is *oxymoron*. If we look at the structure of one of the lines that uses both antithesis and oxymoron, we see a pattern demanding great sensitivity from the actor:

Beautiful tyrant! fiend angelical!
    oxymoron      oxymoron

*Metaphor:* This is the broadest and most complex category of figurative language. While a metaphor is a specific kind of figure of speech, the metaphorical process is common to many related figures. All types of metaphor have one thing in common: they take disparate things or ideas and combine them in order to reveal a new meaning. This new meaning transcends the individual meanings of the two previously separate images, so that a metaphor crystallizes a wealth of meaning in a single image which is greater than the sum of its parts.

For example, when we say *he's a rat*, we have taken two different kinds of things and put them together in such a way as to make them seem identical. *He* (man) is one kind of thing; *rat* is another; but the metaphor *he is a rat* makes them identical. Of course, it is obvious that man and rat are not identical in *every* way, so the metaphor highlights only certain qualities that are shared by both, such as cowardice, dirtiness, guile, meanness, and so on. We therefore project these qualities of "ratness" upon the object of our metaphor, the man. The object of the metaphor (man) is called the *tenor*; the metaphorical word (rat) is called the *vehicle* because it "carries" the meaning of the metaphor.

We value metaphor because it can achieve new and often startling meanings through the combination of otherwise commonplace words. The more startling the combination, the greater the insight it may give us, and the best metaphors combine extremely dissimilar ideas. In *Othello*, for example, Iago sums up his moral code with a tremendous metaphor that combines the lowliest of real and perishable objects with the highest of abstract and timeless concepts: "Virtue? A fig!" Similarly, Falstaff comically dismisses "Honor" as a "mere 'scutcheon," an escutcheon being a part of a coat-of- arms.

Our delivery should make the surprise of such metaphorical combinations vivid by giving each of the contrasted words its full individual value, thereby heightening their dissimilarity rather than diminishing it.

In addition to pure metaphor, where dissimilar things are used as if they were identical, there are milder forms of this device, such as *simile*. Here the elements are not directly combined but only compared; they are shown to be similar, not identical. The comparison is usually expressed by a word such as "like" or "as." The description of Cleopatra on her barge, for instance, continues thus:

> . . . On each side of her
> Stood pretty dimpled boys, like smiling Cupids,
> With divers-color'd fans, whose wind did seem
> to glow the delicate cheeks which they did cool,
> And what they undid did.[2]

Here the "pretty dimpled boys" who fan the queen are compared to mythological figures, "like smiling Cupids." In paintings of Venus, goddess of love, cupids were often shown hovering near her. The picture of Cleopatra lying on her pillows with cupids about her is therefore a *simile* combined with an *allusion* to this myth, thereby endowing Cleopatra with superhuman beauty.

Two other types of metaphor are of special importance to actors. One is *personification*, which occurs when an inanimate object or abstract idea is described as if it were alive, as when Macbeth describes his own greed as "vaulting ambition, which o'erleaps itself."

If the abstract or inanimate thing is not merely made to seem alive, but is spoken to as if it were present, it is called an *apostrophe*. Edmund in *King Lear* apostrophizes, "Nature, thou art my goddess!" In apostrophe, you must "create" the imagined object of the speech by speaking to it as if it were actually present.

*Recurrent figures and motifs*: Figures of speech, like images, may appear in clusters, or recur throughout a role or play as *motifs*. The recurrent references to nature in various forms in *King Lear* are a good example, as are the recurring references to eating, drinking, illusion, and deception in *The Glass Menagerie*; the glass menagerie itself is a metaphor for the condition of the family, and Laura is compared to the unicorn who is "not like the others."

Such clusters and motifs can express dominant qualities in a character, or important thematic content. Often these motifs will not simply recur, but will change and develop within a play, providing concrete "touchstones" for the actor as the character develops, as in the earlier example of Lear's changing references to the gods. These figurative motifs, when carefully examined and physicalized by the actor, can help to realize many important aspects of a character. As B. L. Joseph puts it:

> When the actor asks why he as the character must use a particular image, he ought not to be satisfied with the answer that the image is important to the expressing of Shakespeare's theme. . . such answers are not to be ignored, but they should not be accepted as adequate. . . . The individual images [must be] related to the emotional life of the character who speaks them.[3]

## SAMPLE ANALYSES
## OF FIGURATIVE LANGUAGE

### *King Lear:*

The speech is structured as two apostrophes, one to the poor (lines 1-5) and one to the rich (lines 6-9), separated by a sentence where Lear's focus turns inward to himself. The shifts of focus from the poor, to himself, to the rich are supported by caesuras in lines 5 and 6 which break the flow of the speech and provide time for the necessary thought process.

In each section, you must visualize the lowly poor, then the exalted rich, and speak to them as if they were present with the attitude which Lear has toward them at this moment. This structure suggests the possibility of a physical change to delineate the three sections with their changing focus.

The sound and diction figures in this speech have already been mentioned, except for what could be considered a hyperbole in the last line, which reflects Lear's characteristically enormous scope of thought in showing the heavens themselves more just.

### *The Zoo Story:*

The speech revolves around several metaphors. In the early section there are two "submerged" metaphors: the first is in line 9 where toilet paper "is" a mirror. The usual mirror is one where we see our face, where the world enters us in breathing and eating; toilet paper is a mirror of the orifice through which the world leaves us as excrement, and occasionally, appropriately to Jerry's torment, as blood. ("Always check bleeding" refers to the custom of checking the toilet paper for blood which would indicate hemorrhoids.)

The second submerged metaphor is the strongbox. . . WITHOUT A LOCK in lines 14 and 15, a metaphor for accessibility, for the possibility of being "open," just as the woman's CLOSED DOOR is an antithetical image. Also, a strongbox that cannot be locked is useless, unable (like Jerry) to fulfill the purpose for which it was created: in fact, a strongbox without a lock is a powerful paradoxical metaphor for Jerry himself: open to contact, but at the same time hopelessly bound in.

Finally, the central metaphor climaxes the speech: GOD is A COLORED QUEEN and A WOMAN WHO CRIES WITH DETERMINATION BEHIND HER CLOSED DOOR. God, the fulfillment of all human aspirations, of all possibilities of goodness and perfection, is, for Jerry, the choice between illusory sexual relationships on the one hand, and complete isolation and determined sorrow on the other.

**Exercise 78:**
**Figurative Language**
**Analysis and Embodiment**

A.  ANALYSIS
Use one of the copies of your scene to visually highlight each figure of speech; consider each for its relationship to action, meaning, and character. Look also for recurrent figures in your role as a whole.

B.  EMBODIMENT
1.  Find ways to physicalize each figure of speech in your selection. Don't be tied to a realistic delivery: your aim is to make the figurative language as literal as possible, to "release" the wealth of meaning that has been condensed in each figure of speech. Again, remember to involve the physical act of articulation directly in your exercise; do not separate the words and the physical actions, but emphasize their interrelationship.
2.  Take a moment to "reset" yourself to the beginning of the scene, then perform it in a "normal" way and allow your body's memory of the polarization to influence the performance.

# Summary to Part Three

Our aim in this Part has not been a "literary" analysis but rather an understanding which enhances the living experience of a speech. It doesn't matter if you can correctly identify a kinesthetic image or a metaphor if you cannot experience them as aspects of your character's action, thought, and emotion. Remember that the ideas and sensations carried within your character's language are profoundly revealing of his or her way of thinking and feeling. As B. L. Joseph sums it up:

> . . . The poetic quality of the lines can be fully realized only when they are spoken in character; yet, on the other hand, the completely imagined and truthful character can itself be realized only when the qualities of the literary text are taken into account at some stage of preparation.[4]

This synthesis of the verbal form with the life of the character is the aim of your examination of the text. In a great play, each element is an organic, inseparable part of the whole: When we analyze the play, we choose to focus our attention on one aspect or another, but we must never lose sight of its place within the whole. In other words, analysis ("taking apart") is only a preparation for synthesis ("putting together") in the process of rehearsal, which is the subject of the next Part.

# Lesson Twenty

# Your Working Attitude

It is now time to consider how all the skills and principles you have studied so far will be applied in the actual process of creating a role. An effective work process depends on three things: a productive and creative attitude, a good method of work, and a clear sense of purpose. In this Part we will look at each of these things, beginning with your attitude within the working process.

Underlying all your work are certain basic attitudes which are reflections of the motivations which brought you to acting, your personal and artistic values, and your hopes for your future as an actor. These values and hopes effect profoundly the way you work, though their influence is often unconscious; getting in touch with them at the outset can help you to lay the basis for a more effective, pleasurable, and growthful working process.

## THE DESIRE FOR SUCCESS
## AND THE FEAR OF FAILURE

Perhaps the most fundamental motivations that can be observed in actors, like most people, are the desire for success and its flip side, the fear of failure. Everyone has both, of course, though one may be said to be dominant over the other in many individuals. Each is a powerful source of energy, but the differences between them are important.

At the 1984 Olympics in Los Angeles, the champion athletes were tested to see which were driven primarily by a desire for success, and which were motivated primarily by the fear of failure; it was found that over 70% were driven by success, while less than 30% were motivated by the fear of failure. While the study was not specific about the differences between these two groups of athletes, I would suspect that those motivated by fear of failure tended to be technically precise but cautious, while the larger group would include more "inspired" athletes who were greater risk-takers; the fear of failure encourages safe and conservative choices, while the desire for success can generate energetic and sometimes risky choices.

No one has ever tested a group of actors in this way, but I suspect that a larger proportion of actors would be found to be driven by the fear of failure. There are many unsuccessful or marginal actors, perhaps 80%, who hang on in the business for year after undistinguished year, whose work is competent but uninspired, who deliver reliable but cautious performances, and who simply don't seem to "go for it." Their motto seems to be "nothing ventured, nothing lost."

The fear of failure encourages the attitude that "I must do it exactly right," producing, at best, technical skill, precision and consistency. These are qualities which, in athletics, are rewarded for their own sake, but when you reach the top levels of competition the absence of creative inspiration is damaging; you can't win on technical points alone, you have to have the style points as well! In acting, the situation is even clearer: technical skill, while valued, will never entirely compensate for a lack of creativity. For the actor, technical skill is always the means toward the expression of an artistic vision.

An excessive fear of failure can cause you to censor creative impulses, fearing that "I'll look foolish." When you censor an impulse, you must literally "hold it in," and this causes muscular tension. It is no accident that we tell overly cautious people to "loosen up."

Finally, and most important, the fear of failure may cause you to continually judge your own performance to see if you are "doing it right," and this judgmental attitude encourages self-consciousness. You can't surrender to a character and be standing in judgement of your own performance at the same time!

### Exercise 79:
### The Fear of failure

Think back to your most recent work in an audition, rehearsal or performance: do you remember censoring yourself? Were you sending yourself messages like, "this isn't going to work," or "this might make me look stupid." What physical tensions resulted from "holding in" your impulses?

Next time you work, notice these moments of self-censorship as they occur: simply release the tension, take a breath, and get back to work.

## INTERNAL AND EXTERNAL
## MEASURES OF SUCCESS

A working actor needs the drive, courage and long-term tenacity that a strong desire for success can provide, but you must ask yourself what it is that constitutes true success. There are really two ways of measuring success: in purely internal, personal terms, and by external measurements like reviews, grades, and the response of the audience. Obviously, all actors are, and should be, concerned with both. What we need is perspective and balance between the two.

Most actors err on the side of emphasizing external measures of success over internal. Even if they have a sense of their own work, they usually don't trust it, and they feel so dependent on the opinions of others that a negative response from anyone damages their self-esteem.

Of course, it hurts any actor when their work is not received well. But the serious actor strives to balance the healthy desire for immediate success with the equally important long-range demands of artistic development. You should approach each new role, each rehearsal, and each performance, with a desire not only to please others but also a desire to *learn for yourself*. When evaluating the experience, you must not only ask "Did I do the job well," but also "Am I now a better actor for having done it?"

Winning parts, applause and good reviews, as important as these things are, is not enough. I know some actors, especially in film and television, who are wildly successful in commercial terms but who derive little personal satisfaction from their careers. The "business" demands that they use the same skills, role after role, and no matter how highly developed these skills may become, they can bring only limited artistic satisfaction.

Serious actors insist on continuing to develop and extend their abilities with disciplined regularity throughout their lifetime. There is no real substitute for meeting the day-to-day demands of rehearsal and performance; this is why the actor in a repertory company, preparing a continual variety of roles, may develop much faster than the actor who works in long runs, or repeatedly plays the same kinds of roles.

Most difficult is the situation of the film/TV actor who, unless they are among the less than 6% who work regularly, works only a few weeks out of every year. Classes, workshops, and little theatre roles are the only chance such an actor has to maintain and extend their skills. In the waiting room at a TV audition I heard these two jokes:

> Three actors were complaining about being out of work. "Heck," said the first actor, "I haven't had a part for four months." "That's nothing," said the second actor, "I haven't even had a decent *audition* for a year!" "I've got you both beat," the third actor said, "I haven't had a part for six years. It's gotten so bad, I'm thinking of leaving the business."

and,

Question: How many Los Angeles actors does it take to change a light bulb?
Answer: 20,000. One to change the bulb, and 19,999 to stand around and say,
"I could do that."

**Exercise 80:**
**Defining Success**

Think back to your most recent performance; did you have your own
independent evaluation of it? Did you trust that evaluation? How did the
comments of others effect you?
Did you distinguish between the short-term measurement of your
success in the role, and the long-term benefits of the work to you as a
developing artist?

## JUDGING YOUR WORK

When we began to study action, we said that one of the benefits of being
"in action," was being so completely caught up in what you were doing
that you had no awareness "left over" to be self-conscious. Even while you
are in action, self-consciousness can strike. "Hey," you say to yourself, "this
is pretty good!" and as you start to watch yourself, your experience becomes
disjointed and your activity becomes awkward; you start to lose rhythm and
focus. It is difficult to do something and to watch yourself at the same time
(this is what makes it so hard to be a student of acting; it is easier to just
act!)

So, here is the problem: how do you form a reliable judgement of
your own work without becoming self-conscious?

Athletes have this same problem. In his book, *The Inner Game of
Skiing*, author Tim Galway offers an explanation. He refers to the conflict
between two parts of ourselves which he calls *Self One* and *Self Two*. Self
One is our conscious awareness, our logical, controlled self. It is similar
to what Freudians call our "Superego," or Transactional Analysts call our
"Parent;" Philosopher Baba Ram Dass calls it "the knower that knows that
it knows."

Self Two, on the other hand, is our intuitive self, alogical, childlike
and sexy. Self Two is who we are when Self One gets out of the way, when
we forget to censor ourselves because we are completely involved, fascinated,
committed, or playful; in other words, in action.

Selves One and Two each have particular abilities, and both are
necessary to our success. Self One has many of the qualities we associate
with the left side of the brain: sequential logic, verbalization, a sense of
order. Self Two has many right-brain qualities; spatial and musical sense,

and control of complex motor skills. Self One can read a textbook about acting better than Self Two, but Self Two has to get up and do what Self One learned.

Unfortunately, Self One tends to be suspicious and even jealous of Self Two. For one thing, Self One doesn't usually believe that Self Two is very reliable or consistent; it thinks that Self Two works too much "by accident." Even when Self Two does something that Self One can't, like ski around a tree, Self One tries to take over and "understand" what has been done so that it can make it "happen again on purpose." Unfortunately, Self One can't handle as many simultaneous actions as can Self Two, so Self One usually crashes.

In the same way, actors sometimes discover wonderful things in rehearsal "by accident" (that is, intuitively). Self One immediately takes charge and tries to analyze these things so that it can "do them again on purpose;" this is why such moments are so difficult to repeat. It would be easier just to let Self Two do it again!

You grew up in an educational system that was designed by and for Self One, and which often discourages reliance on Self Two; Self Two does poorly on objective tests, for instance. You are now entering an artistic discipline which will require a lot more trust and involvement of your intuitive Self Two.

It is sometimes said that when we were children we were all "natural actors" because we "made believe" easily. While it is probably true that we lose some of this intuitive ability of Self Two as we grow up and our world becomes more logical and structured, it is possible (and necessary) for us to keep some of that "child" alive in us, and to give it the skill and discrimination of the adult. As an actor, you will rediscover your own childlikeness; cherish and nourish it, but also give it the skill and discrimination of an adult.

Sometimes we speak of Self Two as being our "real" or "authentic" self, but the truth is that we are both selves; your challenge will be to make them work together harmoniously and in mutual support. Acting is clearly a whole-self activity.

## ACTING AND DUAL
## CONSCIOUSNESS

Self One and Self Two, then, are at work simultaneously. For the actor, this is experienced as a dual consciousness, or perhaps even a triple consciousness. As George C. Scott once observed in an interview:

> I think you have to be schizoid three different ways to be an actor. You've got to be three different people: you have to be a human being, then you have to

be the character you're playing, and on top of that, you've got to be the guy sitting out there in row 10, watching yourself and judging yourself. That's why most of us are crazy to start with or go nuts once we get into it. I mean, don't you think it's a pretty spooky way to earn a living?[1]

The multiple consciousness of the created character existing simultaneously with the actor's personal identity and theatrical concerns, is similar to the ancient mask-wearer's experience of being "possessed" by the mask. This "being yourself and yet someone else" is a kind of controlled schizophrenia or, as the Greeks called creativity, a "fine madness." It is the quality that allows the actor to maintain artistic choice while simultaneously becoming the character. As the young actor Kostya in Stanislavski's *Building a Character* put it:

> "I divided myself, as it were, into two personalities. One continued as an actor, the other was an observer. Strangely enough this duality not only did not impede, it actually promoted my creative work. It encouraged and lent impetus to it."[2]

Multiple consciousness is a feature of all acting: no matter how realistic a play may be, the actor never entirely loses a sense of separate identity from the character. If the actor were to lose a sense of separate identity, they would also lose the ability to make aesthetic choice, and the "fine madness" of creativity would become ordinary insanity.

Nor can we ever entirely lose sight of the character as a separate being; without the "mask" of our character, we are no longer actors, though we may be performers in the sense of stand-up comics or political orators.

What you have committed yourself to, then, is to become an artist of personal reality. In your preparation and performance, you will redefine yourself and enter new realms of experience that extend and enhance your sense of aliveness. Your ability to "become anew" can move your spectators to a similar enhancement of their own spiritual vitality.

## YOUR ATTITUDE IN REHEARSAL

The interactive nature of drama means that your individual creation cannot be separated from the work of all the other actors and the director. Your attitude toward your fellow workers is as important as your attitude toward your own work.

Your working relationships will be most effective when they are based upon three principles:

1. Mutual commitment to the working relationship;
2. Mutual support for one another's individual objectives and methods;

3. Free and open communication so that problems can be thrashed out and thereby become opportunities for creative interaction.

Commitment to the working relationship is not the same thing as being "friends," and never should the need to be "nice" cause you to falsify your values or discipline. You want to work together because an effective professional relationship will enable each of you to do better work as individuals. While group membership requires generosity, good humor, and a spirit of reasonable compromise, it should *not* involve either a sense of personal sacrifice or the surrender of personal standards.

Support for one another's objectives and methods is the basis of respect. You might not share another actor's reasons for doing what they are doing, nor might you share their way of doing it, but you should respect their way of working and support them in their right to work that way. When your ways of working are different enough to cause a problem, negotiate compromises on both sides which, as much as possible, meet everyone's needs equally.

Finally, the possibility of free and open communication is critical to the negotiation of the inevitable problems that arise in any creative process. This doesn't mean that we say everything that's on our mind in the name of "honesty;" some things are best left unsaid and as Falstaff says, "discretion is the better part of valor." But the *possibility* of discussing problems needs to be felt by everyone, or an atmosphere of repression will develop and tensions will mount, perhaps to a boiling point.

Actors depend on receiving feedback to their work more than most other artists. The notes we get from our teachers, directors, and fellow actors are tremendously important in guiding our growth. Actors therefore have a solemn responsibility to provide accurate and useful feedback to one another. Beware the common pitfalls that impair the effectiveness of our working communications.

Here is an exercise exploring these as they were defined by my late friend and teacher, Dr. George Bach.

### Exercise 81:
### Communication Disorders

Think back over your working experiences. Have you suffered or been guilty of any of the following communication disorders?

1. FOGGING: Using generalities without referring to specifics. Example: "You need to work on your voice."
2. MIND-RAPING: Assuming you know what someone is thinking without bothering to check. Example: "Why are you hiding from us in this scene?"
3. DEFUSING: Excessive self-criticism that makes it impossible for anyone else to criticize you. Example: "I just couldn't concentrate at all today; I know the scene was terrible, but what did you think?"

4. DUMPING: Using criticism as an emotional release or as a weapon.
5. GUNNYSACKING: Saving up grievances until an explosion becomes likely.
6. NO TRESPASSING: When unstated rules exist within a group that certain people or certain issues may not be criticized.
7. HOLIER-THAN-THOU: Criticism of others for the purpose of avoiding criticism of self.
8. DOOMSAYING: Feedback which emphasizes only the negative without acknowledging the positive.

The most effective feedback we can give each other is based upon a few basic principles:

1. Say WHAT YOU SEE and HOW IT MAKES YOU FEEL. Don't say, "Why are you hiding from us," say, "I noticed that you rarely looked at your partner during this scene, and that made me feel as if you were hiding from us. What was going on?" Do you see the difference between these two statements?
2. Be CLEAR about your message BEFORE you deliver it.
3. Be SPECIFIC, SIMPLE, and DIRECT; use examples.
4. Pick an APPROPRIATE TIME to communicate.
5. CHECK to see if your message was received accurately.

Here is an exercise to practice these communication skills.

### Exercise 82:
### Attractions and Reservations,
### Agonies and Ecstasies

Join with one of your fellow workers to share impressions of your own and each other's work. Take turns completing the following statements, and in each case apply the five principles listed above.

A. My greatest agony about my own work just now is. . .
B. The greatest reservation I have about your work is. . .
C. The thing I feel best about in my own work is. . .
D. The thing that attracts me most about your work is. . .

Compare your feelings about praise and criticism. Which do you take more seriously? Did you learn equally from each?

Are you benefiting from the feedback of others enough? Or are you *too* dependent on them?

## YOU AND YOUR DIRECTOR

Finally, we must consider the special relationship between actor and director regarding their separate functions.

The director's main function is to guide the development of an overall interpretation for the entire ensemble. This is because any good play has many levels of meaning: *King Lear*, for instance, might be viewed as a play about old age, the responsibilities of kingship, the generation gap, or social injustice. Even if the cast were to agree that each of these is part of the play's total meaning, there might still be disagreement about the point of view or "focus" of your particular production. The director either provides this focus at the outset, or guides the cast in discovering it during rehearsals.

Your performances, like every other element of the production, must be aligned toward this central focus of interpretation. Even if your personal preference might be for a different interpretation or emphasis, once you have accepted the role it is your job to work effectively within the director's production concept.

Perhaps the most destructive attitude is that of the actor who becomes an apologist for their character, arguing from the character's point of view as if every scene "belonged to them." Group interpretation can be ruined by actors who insist upon adopting their character's point of view at the expense of the play as an artistic whole.

On the other hand, we do a great disservice to our director and fellow actors and ourselves if, out of our desire to avoid conflict, we fail to express ourselves honestly. An actor who is too pliable is as destructive as one who is too rigid. Your ideas will be appreciated by your ensemble if they are presented in a reasoned, timely, and respectful fashion. While a show must have only one director, everyone connected with it must feel the responsibility of providing ideas that may be of value.

There are many ways in which these responsibilities can overlap and where compromise will be necessary. The actor, intimately involved with the life of the character, possesses insights into the life of that character which are denied to the director. At the same time the director, with an overview and special responsibility for interpretation, has an objective point of view unavailable to the actor. In an effective working relationship, each will respect and value the special insights of the other and seek to join their points of view to the best possible advantage.

Even in the best situations there are times when insoluble disagreements occur. At such times you must remember that the director has assumed public responsibility for the interpretation of the play, while you have assumed public responsibility for the portrayal of your character within the context established by that interpretation. Once the director's interpretation has been clarified, it is the actor's responsibility to find the best possible means of implementing it; if this proves to be impossible, the relationship must be severed for the sake of the play. Except in the case of major "stars," this usually means that the actor gets fired.

Beside interpretation, another important function of the director is to establish a common approach in the conduct of rehearsals. Each director has a characteristic way of working, and it is easier for the actors to adapt to the director's method than for the director to adopt an individual approach to each of the actors. It is therefore part of your job to adapt, as much as is reasonable, to the director's approach, and to help the director develop the most effective channel of communication with you.

To sum up, you and your director are coworkers, not master and slave. Though you share many responsibilities, you have essentially different functions that are interdependent and equal. The director's first responsibility is to the overall patterning of the play as a theatrical experience; your responsibility is to bring your role to life so as to best contribute to that pattern. Therefore, it is ultimately the director's function to evaluate *what* the actor does, and the actor's job is to find *how* best to do it.

# Lesson
# Twenty-One

# Developing the Character

In life, our personality develops largely through our interaction with our environment. As infants our physical exploration of the world is the main process; as we grow older, our relationships with our parents and eventually with larger social groups shape us, as do the customs, taboos, and value systems of our culture. Our personality emerges from this accumulation of experiences and transactions and is continually evolving under the influence of ongoing experience.

It seems logical to assume that the personality of a dramatic character should evolve according to these same life principles and through the same ongoing process of physical exploration and social interaction. The rehearsal process, then, can be viewed as the condensed period of evolution and maturation of the dramatic personality.

For this reason, your primary aim in rehearsal is to open yourself to the specific experiences and transactions of your character within his or her given circumstances, "as if" they were happening to you. It is through these specific experiences that your character will develop and evolve in the same way that your own personality has grown and is continuing to grow in your world.

In short, *character grows out of action*. You don't need to worry about "being the character" first and then doing things "because that's what my character would do"; instead, *do* the things your character does in the way that they do them, and see who you *become*.

Every role will suggest experiences and behaviors similar to those you already know, and you will certainly want to use these established connections; but every role will also offer the possibility of reaching out into *new* modes of experience; of extending you into a new state of becoming. You possess a vast personal potential; if you can engage your own energy in your character's actions, and open yourself to their experiences and relationships within their given circumstances, you will find your own energy being transformed under the influence of those specific experiences.

This is the most exciting aspect of the actor's creative process!

## ROLE-PLAYING
## AS A LIFE PRINCIPLE

Much of our lives are spent acting, in the sense that we behave in certain ways in order to pursue our objectives, or in presenting a certain image of ourselves so as to get the response we want from others.

Those who study human behavior have described this process in various ways. Around the turn of the century, psychologist William James described our personality as a complex structure consisting of an "I" and a number of "me's." Each of us, he said, has a repertoire of roles, or "me's," which our "I" adopts in various situations. This morning, for example, I began as Loving Father as I got my children off to school; I switched to Knowledgeable Teacher during my morning class; I then became a Good Buddy as I talked about football with my office mates; finally, I was Experienced Director at rehearsal this evening.

Your roles as daughter, son, student, employee, friend, or lover, all call upon you to modify your behavior in different situations in order to achieve your particular objectives within those situations. If you have ever been forced to perform two different social roles at once, you know how radically different some of our "me's" can be (visits by parents to their children at school often occasion such uncomfortable situations).

According to William James, your "I" is your sense of the performer who plays the various "me's" and ties them together into one, multifaceted personality. As Shakespeare put it, "One man in his time plays many parts."

Much of our everyday behavior can be seen as supporting the roles we play: the way we dress, the way we carry ourselves, the car we drive, and the kind of work we do.

The fact that we are all acting most of the time does not mean that we are insincere: to behave in a way that will achieve our objectives in a given circumstance is a natural and necessary way of coping with life. Most of us adapt our social behavior to the demands of our situation automatically and unconsciously.

For instance, when we are in a group, we tend to "sort ourselves out" within a pattern of roles that are natural to the psychodynamics of all groups. Here is an exercise to explore this kind of role-playing.

### Exercise 83:
### The Social Rep Company

Form a group of six or less; choose a topic to discuss or a project for the group to plan (something the group might really care about, like a political issue or planning how to start a theatre).

Below are a list of six roles. Each person in the group will play one of these roles in the group discussion; every two minutes, pass your role to the person on your left; keep the flow of conversation going as the roles are passed, and keep going until everyone has played all the roles.

1. THE CHAIRMAN, who loves to organize the group;
2. THE VICTIM, who sees any group action as potentially threatening or unpleasant;
3. THE PHILOSOPHER, who loves to generalize and point out the deeper meanings of things;
4. THE DERAILER, who is forever trying to change the topic as a way of controlling the group;
5. THE DEBATER, who loves to argue and doesn't really care what position they take.
6. THE RED CROSS NURSE, who takes care of anyone who seems to need help whether they want it or not.

After everyone has played all the parts, share your experiences and perceptions: Why did these "characters" behave the way they did? What did they want? How did they present themselves and how did they treat others?[1]

As you played the various roles in the last exercise, you probably felt how easy it was to "become" them. Some may have been more uncomfortable or unfamiliar than others, but with practice any of them could become part of your social repertoire, a new "me" to be played by your "I." Just so, your evolving stage character is becoming a new "me" to be used for the particular purpose of rehearsing and performing the play.

## CHARACTER
## AND DRAMATIC FUNCTION

The conflict that drives the play is brought to life by the actions of the characters. The way the characters have been formed by the playwright is largely determined by the way the character's behavior must contribute to the progress and meaning of the play; we call this the *dramatic function* of the character.

You must remain aware of dramatic function throughout your work on a role. Too often actors approach their characters so personally that they begin to forget the larger purpose for which that character was created; but without the sense of function, you have no basis on which to evaluate the result of your rehearsal exploration. Which is the best way to play the scene? What qualities of the character are most important? These and all the other choices you will have to make must be determined according to the sense of function. In acting as well as in good design, form must follow function!

There are two main ways that a character may contribute to the play: by advancing the *plot* through their actions, and by contributing to the *meaning* of the play through the values which those actions express. You must be clear about each.

These two basic functions can take many forms. Some examples: on the level of plot, your character may commit crucial actions which drive the plot forward; it may serve as a "foil" to frustrate the intentions of another character; it may simply serve to provide some essential plot information, like the classical messenger.

On the level of meaning, your character may represent values which are meant to contrast the values of other characters; it may be the spokesperson for one of several conflicting points of view; it may serve to embody an element of a conflict within the main character; it may be a *raisonneur* who acts as the playwright's spokesperson.

No matter how "alive" your characterization may be, if it does not fulfill the character's dramatic function, you have failed. The entire play is lessened in this case, since a play, like any mechanism, works best only when every part has performed its job in its proper relationship with every other part. The ultimate expression of a character's life is to serve the life of the play!

### Exercise 84:
### The Dramatic Function

Consider the character you have been developing over the previous exercises: what is its dramatic function within the play?

A. If your character were to be cut, what would be missing from the plot? What actions would have to be given to another character in order for the plot to proceed?

B. How would the meaning of the play suffer if your character were cut? Is there some value or point of view expressed by your character which is essential? Would the meaning of the other characters be as clear?

Now that we have a sense of dramatic function, let's look more specifically at the qualities or *traits* which a character may be given by the playwright in order to believably fulfill this function.

## CHARACTER TRAITS

In order that a character may serve their purpose within the play believably, the playwright will have provided them with certain traits which make the required behavior and thought natural to them. Aristotle called these the character's "functional traits." Whatever other traits are suggested by the text, or whatever else you may invent in the course of rehearsal to "round out" the character, you must be primarily concerned with these functional traits.

We can classify all characterizational traits on four levels as outlined here by Oscar Brockett:

> The first level of characterization is physical and is concerned only with such basic facts as sex, age, size, and color. Sometimes a dramatist does not supply all of this information, but it is present whenever the play is produced, since actors necessarily give concrete form to the characters. The physical is the simplest level of characterization, however, since it reveals external traits only, many of which may not affect the dramatic action at all.
>
> The second level is social. It includes a character's economic status, profession or trade, religion, family relationships—all those factors that place him in his environment.
>
> The third level is psychological. It reveals a character's habitual responses, attitudes, desires, motivations, likes and dislikes—the inner workings of the mind, both emotional and intellectual, which precede action. Since habits of feeling, thought and behavior define characters more fully than do physical and social traits, and since drama most often arises from conflicting desires, the psychological is the most essential level of characterization.
>
> The fourth level is moral. Although implied in all plays, it is not always emphasized. It is most apt to be used in serious plays, especially tragedies. Although almost all human action suggests some ethical standard, in many plays the moral implications are ignored, and decisions are made on grounds of expediency. This is typical of comedy, since moral deliberations tend to make any action serious. More nearly than any other kind, moral decisions differentiate characters, since the choices they make when faced with moral crises show whether they are selfish, hypocritical, or persons of integrity. A moral decision usually causes a character to examine his own motives and values, in the process of which his true nature is revealed both to himself and to the audience.[2]

Let us examine each of these four levels of characterization more fully.

## PHYSICAL TRAITS

The first level is physical, and it is of primary importance to an actor since the external traits of body and voice communicate all the other levels of characterization.

The playwright will have specified the essential aspects of your character's physical traits. There are four main sources of such information in any text. First, the *stage directions* or *prefaces* by the author; in his preface to *The Zoo Story*, Albee specifies that Jerry is 38 years old. Do you see how this age is important to the exact quality of his desperate loneliness? It isn't the same play if you imagine Jerry as being only 22.

Next are traits *described by other characters*; of course, we must evaluate such descriptions and determine if they are accurate, or perhaps distorted by the other character's prejudice. In Shakespeare's *Henry IV, i*, Prince Hal gives an elaborate description of the war-like Hotspur as "a popinjay," but his view is obviously clouded by the jealousy he feels for Hotspur. Aside from such distortions, however, the statements of other characters can be a valuable source of information. "Yon Cassius," in *Julius Caesar*, probably *should* have "a lean and hungry look."

Many traits can be deduced from the *style of the play*; a character in a Restoration comedy, for example, had better not slouch around like a Sam Shepard cowboy.

Finally, and most important, are traits that are *implied by the action*; if you look at the most important actions which your character commits in the play, you will see that there are fundamental physical traits required in performing these actions believably. If Stanley is going to rape Blanche, for example, he probably should have some of the "gnawing and swilling and hulking" quality that Blanche says he has, even though we can be sure that she is exaggerating.

### Exercise 85:
### Physical Traits

Examine the entire play to find clues to your character's physical traits. Check each of the following:

A. The stage directions; what does the playwright specifically tell you about your character's age, body, etc?

B. Descriptions by other characters; what can you learn from what others say? Are their descriptions accurate, or prejudiced by their point of view?

C. What are the physical implications of the style of the play?

D. What are the implications of the action? Considering the most important things your character does, and what physical traits do they need to believably perform these actions?

## SOCIAL TRAITS

This second level of characterization places the character in their environment and in relation to the others in it. Such factors as educational and social background and type of work are important here. The fact that Stanley Kowalski is an ex-Marine sergeant, travels in his work, and is captain of his bowling team are all important to an understanding of his personality.

The most important aspect of social characterization, of course, is the relationship between the character and the other characters in the play. As we said at the start of this lesson, our personalities are largely shaped by our interactions with our world. Drama is an artistically heightened version of this social interaction; just as we are influenced greatly by those around us in everyday life, so a dramatic character is formed largely by the way they relate to the other characters in the play.

As we watch characters on the stage, we get a great deal of information not only from what *they* do, but also from how all the other characters *relate* to them. In fact, the common idea that the actor's job is to create their character is somewhat erroneous; it would be truer to say that each of the actors must create *all* the characters in the play. If you have ever been on stage with someone who failed to relate properly to you, you will know how difficult it is to overcome the false impression that another actor may create; audiences will place more credence in what they observe within the relationship than they will on individual action. In short, remember that *you create each other on stage more than you create yourself.*

For this reason, you must develop your characterization by relating to the personalities and actions of the other characters as they are developed by your fellow actors; no actor can work in isolation, and all characterizations must be designed to function in specific interaction with those of the other actors.

In *Death of a Salesman*, Willy has a relationship with each person in the play: father, husband, lover, neighbor, employee, salesman. We see Willy operating in each of these contexts, and each relationship reveals another aspect of Willy's character. Each of these relationships serves to penetrate the surface of his behavior and express the underlying truth of Willy's character, for he is all those things. In the terms that William James used, they are the "me's" of his "I." Each of these relationships must be cooperatively developed by the actors involved if the character of Willy is to live for the audience.

### Exercise 86:
### Social Traits

A. Examine the play for information about your character's social background. If no specific information is given, make the best inferences you can. Consider each of these categories:
1. Childhood environment;
2. Educational background;
3. Socioeconomic or class background;
4. Work experiences.

B. Consider your character's relationship to every other character in the play. How does each relationship reveal your needs, desires, and values?

C. Rehearse your scene with your partner: your aim in this rehearsal is *to create each other.*

## PSYCHOLOGICAL TRAITS

Here we are concerned with the process of thought which is the antecedent of action. As Oscar Brockett pointed out, "the psychological is the most important level of characterization." It is the level that justifies all physical and social characteristics. As Chekhov once said in a letter, "a playwright may invent any reality except one: the psychological." All characters must think before they act.

This is not to say that the psychology of character is always the most important element of the play as a whole. In plays where the external events of the plot (the "story") is the dominant element, the psychological aspect of characterization may serve merely to make the action believable. On the other hand, in plays featuring interior action (like those of Chekhov and O'Neill), the psychology of the characters may be the main interest of the play and the plot may be secondary.

Just as a character's body has certain qualities, so their mind has certain qualities. Consider the mental processes of the character you are developing; are they:

1. Simple or complex?
2. Fast or slow?
3. Rigid or flexible?
4. Precise or vague?
5. Reasoned or intuitive?
6. Global or sequential?

The last two items are qualities of "right brain" or "left brain" dominance which can be noticed in people. Right brain people tend to think globally ("the whole thing") in spatially and emotional terms, while left brain people tend to reason in a linear way ("one thing at a time") in verbal and logical terms.

If you want to give someone directions to your house, for instance, you should tell a left brain person to "go three blocks down, turn right, go to the second light, and turn left." A right brain person will have trouble with these kinds of directions; they will do better with a map. (One of the greatest difficulties in writing this book was to take the global and intuitive skill of acting and translate it into a linear, verbal sequence; hopefully, you are putting it back together in your mind as you read!)

Your examination of your character's action has already provided you with the basis for understanding their psychology; it is in reliving the "inner monologue" that links stimulus to response that you best come to understand the character's mind. Every phase of the process of action is expressive of character: consider the character you have been developing and ask yourself each of these questions:

1. To what stimuli do I most strongly react? To which am I unresponsive? How do my sensitivities reflect my life goal?
2. What is my dominant attitude toward the world? Am I optimistic or pessimistic, fatalistic or opportunistic?
3. What alternatives do I see as ways of fulfilling my needs? What alternatives do I fail to see?
4. What sorts of choices do I characteristically make in specific situations?
5. What is my characteristic way of manifesting my choices? How do I treat people?

You can see that each step in the flow of your action offers a wealth of information about the character's mind: more important, each is a way for you to enter actively into the experience of that mind.

### Exercise 87:
### Psychological Traits

A. Consider the way your character thinks: is their mind slow or fast, simple or complex, flexible or rigid, precise or vague, right-brain or left-brain dominant?

B. Select the most significant choices made by your character in the play; what does each tell you about the character's mind?

## MORAL TRAITS

This level refers to the character's values, especially their sense of right and wrong, of beauty, and their religious and political beliefs. When this aspect of character is important it will always relate directly to the thematic content of the play; the moral choice confronting Willy Loman, for example, is an embodiment of Arthur Miller's thesis regarding the erosion of spiritual values by our society's emphasis on material values as a measure of self-worth.

Your thinking about your character's superobjective has already brought much of their morality into focus; the superobjective, and the means used to achieve it, are the active expressions of the character's morality. Blanche Dubois, for instance, tries to use sex to achieve sanctuary, but we do not think of her as an immoral character, as Stanley does, because, unlike Stanley, we can understand the level of her desperation, and because we know that her affairs were hollow gestures which did not involve her essential self.

### Exercise 88:
### Moral Traits

Speaking as your character, answer the following questions:
1. My religious preference is. . .
2. I believe that when we die, we. . .
3. The greatest thing one person can do for another is. . .
4. The person I admire most is. . .
5. I would define a good person as someone who. . .
6. The person I detest most in the world is. . .
7. The most evil thing I can imagine is. . .
8. The most beautiful thing I ever saw was. . .
9. The ugliest thing I ever saw was. . .
10. The nicest place I ever visited was. . .
11. My political affiliation is. . .
12. The proper role of government is. . .
13. I am superstitious about. . .
14. After I die, I want to be remembered as someone who. . .

## ECONOMY OF CHARACTERIZATION

We have examined each of four levels of characterization. Each works in relation to the others, and the way they are put together reflects the purpose and nature of the play. Oscar Brockett explains this:

> A playwright may emphasize one or more of these levels. Some writers pay little attention to the physical appearance of their characters, concentrating instead upon psychological and moral traits; other dramatists may describe appearance and social status in detail. In assessing the completeness of a characterization it is not enough merely to make a list of traits and levels of characterization. It is also necessary to ask how the character functions in the play. For example, the audience needs to know little about the maid who only appears to announce dinner; any detailed characterization would be superfluous and distracting. On the other hand, the principal characters need to be drawn in greater depth. The appropriateness and completeness of each characterization, therefore, may be judged only after analyzing its function in each scene and in the play as a whole.[3]

It is a common impulse of actors to try to treat the maid who answers the door as if she were Lady Macbeth. This is not to say that the maid should not be fully characterized; she should be as fully characterized *as she needs to be.* Economy of characterization is to do everything that needs to be done, but no more.

Think of a great athlete whose performance you have admired. This person's "style," their grace and power, come from the complete efficiency with which every bit of their energy is focused on the job at hand. They do nothing that does not directly contribute to their purpose; this is their economy. If your purpose is to be a maid answering the door, then any energy directed toward creating qualities beyond those necessary for the fulfillment of this task is wasteful and distracting. An overly detailed performance is as disruptive as an incomplete one.

**Exercise 89:**
**A Character Checklist**

This checklist reviews the work of this lesson. Use it as you begin rehearsals to be sure you have all the information you need to begin work, then check again near the end of rehearsals to be sure that you have considered all the possibilities.

A.  What are the physical traits that influence your action?
   1.  Those specified by the playwright;
   2.  Those reported by other characters;
   3.  Those which can be inferred from the action.
B.  What are your social traits?
   1.  Your background and education?
   2.  Your socioeconomic class?
   3.  Your attitudes and behavior toward each of the other characters?
C.  What are your psychological traits?
   1.  Are your mental processes fast or slow;
   2.  Rigid or flexible;
   3.  Complex or simple;
   4.  Are you intuitive and global, or analytical and verbal?
D.  What moral, religious, or political values influence your choices?

# Lesson
# Twenty-Two

# The Rehearsal Process

Though there are various ways in which directors may choose to structure the rehearsal process, there is a common sequence to the way the work will usually progress. This sequence can be outlined as having nine phases:

1. Auditions and casting;
2. Preparation and homework;
3. Early readings;
4. Getting up and off book;
5. Exploring the action;
6. Establishing the score;
7. Making adjustments for performance;
8. Technical and Dress Rehearsals;
9. Growth after opening.

We will discuss each in order.

## AUDITIONS AND CASTING

Though not usually thought of as part of the rehearsal process, auditions are in fact a time when you may form an initial response to a role which will greatly influence your later work.

Auditions are a nerve-wracking but necessary part of the actor's life. If it is any consolation to you, directors are under even more pressure during auditions than are actors; the initial casting of a play is the most influential step in the formation of an interpretation, and yet the director must usually make this crucial decision with only minimal knowledge of the actors.

Most directors have developed their own auditioning techniques, some of which can be rather disarming, but in general we can divide auditions into types, the "general" and the "specific."

Most general auditions, sometimes called "cattle calls," are used for preliminary screening for a role, or for entry into a company. In such auditions, you will be required to present two selections of different types; usually these are monologues, though in some enlightened situations scenes may be used. You should develop a repertoire of at least three or four carefully chosen and prepared audition pieces, including comedy and tragedy, poetic and modern styles. About two minutes is a good length for each; shape each speech to have a satisfying ending, and in monologues where another character is assumed to be present, be careful to "create" the other person.

Your repertoire of speeches should be chosen to demonstrate your abilities to the best advantage, but most important, they should be material which you love; it will be a tremendous advantage to you if your positive feelings for your material outweigh your negative feelings about auditioning!

When auditioning for specific roles, you will probably be asked to read from the play at hand. In the live theatre, you will usually be able to read the entire play in advance and prepare a selection from the role. In film and television, you are often given only a single scene from the play and a short time for preparation (though it is a union rule that an entire script must be available if you ask to see it.) In the time available, your job is to find a playable objective in the material and to make that objective important to you through some kind of personalization.

Don't hesitate to ask questions about the character's given circumstances, about the contribution the character is expected to make to the show, or about the approach the director intends to take.

Some actors can give good cold readings with only a few moments work, but theatre directors are sometimes suspicious of this; many times these slick cold-readers fail to develop much beyond their initial reading. In television, however, quick results are required; here, casting is often done by producers who are more result-oriented than are directors.

Some otherwise competent actors are slow of study and these "late bloomers" are at a disadvantage in most audition situations. Fortunately, most directors want to know about your past experience and get some reliable references about your previous work. You must be prepared to provide this information in an organized and attractive resume.

Your 8 x 10 photo will assist the director in remembering you; it should be current and "neutral;" that is, it should look like you and not limit the impression it provides of you to one quality like "sexy," "likeable," or "dangerous."

Auditions will be much more enjoyable if you approach them without a sense of competitiveness. Think of them not as a contest with other actors but as an opportunity to communicate your potential to a director. Whether or not you are cast or get the particular role you wanted, auditions challenge you to face great pressure with integrity and a willing spirit.

Above all, do not take auditions personally. It usually requires many auditions before you will land a part (in film/TV about ·20 seems to be an average, in live theatre it varies tremendously). You can't take every rejection as a reflection on your talent. Auditions do not test your artistry so much as they test your usefulness to a director or producer for the specific role at hand.

Take the long view and remember that the opinion formed of you at an audition may be important at some future time; it is therefore important that you honestly present your best abilities and avoid falsifying yourself for the sake of the particular instance. The question young actors most often ask about an audition is, "What do they want?" A much better question would be, "How can I best show them what kind of actor I am?"

## PREPARATION AND HOMEWORK

Now that you have been cast in your role, you will do some important preparation before rehearsals begin. Analysis, private experimentation, beginning to learn the lines, and private rehearsal of special skills must be accomplished outside the rehearsal hall. Never should you waste the time of your fellow actors and director by failing to do your homework.

Remember that homework is a *preparation* for rehearsal, not a *substitute* for it. Your pre-rehearsal work identifies the alternatives that need to be tested and prepares you to explore them aggressively in concert with your fellow workers; it does *not* determine the form of the finished product. Unfortunately, some actors are so insecure that they prepare for rehearsal as if it were performance, creating a rigidly premeditated form; the director then must be a sort of "referee," mediating between the various actors' ideas of how to play their roles. Remember that rehearsal is a time for *mutual* exploration through trial and error.

Depending on the demands of the play, your preparation may take various forms. You might need to develop certain technical skills related to the manner of the production, such as fencing, dancing, tumbling, the use of canes, fans, large skirts, or robes, and so on.

There may be technical demands on your voice or body related to the specific character; we have mentioned, for example, the year devoted by Laurence Olivier to his vocal preparation for *Othello*; Robert DeNiro did extensive physical preparation for his role as a prizefighter in *Raging Bull*. Many of the physical and vocal skills demanded by your role will have to be practiced almost daily throughout the rehearsal period, and it is never too early to start.

In order to understand the character's world, you will want to have some sense of the fashion of the time, the ideas of grace, beauty, and social behavior. Experiencing the music, painting, and architecture of the time is valuable; documents such as diaries, letters, and newspapers can also be helpful.

Besides technical preparations of vocal and physical skills related to the external behavior of the character, you will also want to prepare yourself to enter their mind as well. For this purpose you may need to do research into the intellectual world from which the character comes; you will be most interested in those things which established the character's psychological and moral qualities, such as the religious and philosophical beliefs of the time, the educational experiences of the character, the quality of home life, the work environment, the system of governance and justice, and so on.

The social background of a play as recent as *The Glass Menagerie* or *Death of a Salesman*, is different enough from our own to require you to learn about life in the Great Depression and World War II, and about the popularity of "The American Dream" through such self-help methods as the Dale Carnegie books. Our credit-card culture, for example, cannot fully relate to the importance for Willy Loman of "weathering a twenty-year mortgage," or the humiliation for Amanda Wingfield of having to ask Garfinkle's Delicatessen for credit.

Two good ways to focus your research into the character's inner world is by writing an autobiography and a diary entry for them.

### Exercise 90:
### Autobiography and Diary

A. Imagine that as your character, you have been asked to write a short autobiographical sketch of yourself; limit yourself to two pages and include only those things which were most influential in your life; title your essay, "The Things Which Made Me Who I Am."

B. Imagine also that you keep a diary; select an important day within the time frame of the play and write the diary entry for that day.

As valuable as it is to do this sort of personal and psychological research on your character, you must also remember that your character is a creature of the theatre; it will be useful for you to understand the theatrical world in which they were created. Reading other plays by your author and their contemporaries can help; so can study of the physical and social environment of the theatre of the time. For instance, the open-air, thrust quality of the Elizabethan playhouse with its pit in which the "groundlings" stood throughout the performance is important to an understanding of Shakespeare's early plays. Just so, it is revealing to learn that the Moscow Art Theatre in which Chekhov's plays were first presented sat 1,200 persons, so that the scale of the performances must have been somewhat larger than we usually think.

Likewise, coming to understand the literary conventions which influenced the playwright may help you to understand your character. It is revealing to learn of Chekhov's passion for the writing of the French Naturalists and their "scientific" approach to personality and behavior; this is even more illuminating when we consider his training as a doctor and the fact that he wrote his four great plays knowing that he was dying of tuberculosis. In the same way, understanding the playwright's psychological and moral values can be revealing; it is helpful to know that Bertolt Brecht was an ambulance driver in World War I and was permanently affected by the carnage and misery he experienced then.

In all, remember that good plays are written out of a deep need to communicate some important insight into the human condition, and that you must approach your work with the same sense of purpose. This requires commitment, preparation, and homework beyond the confines of the rehearsal hall.

### Exercise 91:
### The World of the Play

    A. Imagine that you are someone attending the very first performance of the play in which your character appears. Write an account of that performance, or simply relive it in your mind. Start from the approach to the theatre before the performance begins.

    B. Pretend you are the author of your play, and that you have just begun to write it. Write a letter to a friend and try to explain how you feel about this new play, why you are writing it, and what you hope to achieve with it.

## EARLY READ-THROUGHS

You are meeting for the first time with your fellow cast members. Your director may greet you in a variety of ways: some will outline their interpretation and approach to the play; some will lead a discussion about it; some may do exercises to "break the ice" and to establish a working rapport in the ensemble; many will dispense with any such preliminaries and begin at once to read the play.

These first readings are your first forays into the heart of the material as it will come to live within your ensemble. Begin to work at once on the play as a whole; listen to it in the living voices of your fellow actors and begin to discover how it will live within this particular group of people.

Above all, read *in relationship*, with a spirit of give and take, reaction and action; get your awareness and your eyes out of your book as much as you can and contact the other characters in your scenes. Begin at once to search for the action which lives only in the specific transactions between the characters.

Read also with deep muscle involvement, so that you involve your whole self; you will find that a wealth of associations and ideas well up.

These early rehearsals are exploration, but never indiscriminate exploration. Any meaningful exploration has a sense of goal, which directs the out-flow of energy and prevents it from degenerating into blind groping. Even though goals are rarely clear at the outset, and a good bit of the rehearsal process consists of clarifying them, there is usually in the vision of a play as communicated by the director some sense of the direction in which our exploration must go.

Not all of your rehearsal discoveries will result from conscious experimentation, of course; you must have the courage to invite the *happy accident*. Such spontaneous discovery grows only from the receptiveness and responsiveness of each cast member to each other and to the moment; do not let your work on your own role make you oblivious to the work of others.

In these very early stages of rehearsal, before rapport has been established within the company, it is especially important that each actor make an act of faith to work together toward the defining of goals with respect, trust, good humor, and a generous heart.

## GETTING UP AND OFF BOOK

As soon as possible, you will begin to put your book aside so that you can explore the action on your feet. This, of course, requires learning the lines. You will have to find your own best method for line memorization. Some actors like to have a friend read the other parts (cue them); some make a tape recording of their lines to listen to at night; some even write out their lines. Many find it useful to begin working in paraphrase, finding the ideas behind the lines in their own words first.

However you work, learn the *action* as well as the lines; that is, learn the words in the context of the give and take of the scene, paying considerable attention to what the other character is saying in addition to your own responses. This is not only an easier way of learning lines, it also makes learning them a useful first step in your exploration of the action.

The transitional rehearsal period during which you are putting the book down can be a frustrating one. During the earlier phase of rehearsal, when you were still reading your lines, the information which your eyes received from the text passed directly the short distance to the brain; now you are beginning to recreate the whole process of action which motivates the text, the chain of perception/reaction/action which you experienced in Lesson Nine. This requires the formation of a longer, deeper neurological pathway of response within your total organism; you are literally translating the play from the "literary" form into the complete psychophysical form of the live performance.

During this period you must not waste rehearsals by stopping the flow of the emerging action, even if you must call for lines; it is expected that you will call for lines, so don't waste time apologizing, and above all *keep the action going* while you *call for lines in character.*

You must also be sure that your rehearsal clothing and props are acquired early and used regularly. Pay special attention to the effect of the character's clothing on the body, and be sure to wear the correct type of shoes to rehearsal so as to establish the correct relationship to gravity.

## EXPLORING THE ACTION

Now that you are off book, the blocking is being done, or is beginning to emerge from the action. You and your partners are beginning to shape and specify the transactions of action/reaction which will form, link by link, the chain of the scenes and of the play, and making choices about each connection.

The many choices that must be made during rehearsal cannot be prejudged: you must actually do a thing in order to know whether it is right. Hopefully, one of the most common expressions you will hear during rehearsal is "Let's try it." Each choice you make will reveal more about the whole play, and in turn each of these revelations of the larger pattern will help you to find the rightness of each detail.

The rightness of any action will be determined by the way it fits into the cause-effect chain of interactions between characters, and which in turn moves the play. There is a great difference between *making* something happen on stage and *letting* it happen; you can let a thing happen when the energies you receive and your response to them are in perfect accord with your desired results. When this has been accomplished, you *feel* the connectedness of every moment with every other moment.

The main business of these first weeks of rehearsal is to establish the connections through which the energy of the play may flow naturally to its ultimate destination.

### Exercise 92:
### Making Connections

Work through your scene with your partner; either of you may stop the rehearsal at any point when you do not feel connected to the flow of the action, when you are not being "made" to do what you do.

At each point of difficulty, examine the moments which lead up to it; what can the others supply that will correct the problem? What do you need to be getting from your partner in order to be *made* to do what you do next? Work it out between you.

Note: you do *not* tell your partner what to do, you only tell them what you need from them; you might say something like "I need to be more threatened by that," but you leave it entirely to your partner to determine how best to threaten you.

This exercise will help you to realize that the problems we encounter in playing a scene are often symptoms of mistakes that were actually made earlier. Don't always try to fix a problem by making an immediate adjustment; trace back and see if you can clear it up by approaching the moment differently, or establishing some other value or relationship earlier. Remember that the through-line carries you along, and this is the phase of rehearsal in which you are beginning to find and establish it.

Your through-line is part of the action/reaction chain of cause and effect that moves the entire play. This fact binds the actors inseparably to each other, and each has the right to receive, and the obligation to give, what will best serve the common purpose. By serving one another, we serve the play and our own creativity!

## ESTABLISHING THE SCORE

As you discover the specific connections of stimulus/choice/objective which form the links in the chain of action and reaction, the action of the scene will begin to flow "under its own power." You and your partners will naturally begin to set each of these connections as they develop. These connections are not so much an external form as they are an understanding of the *scenario* of the scene, *the underlying sequence of actions which will generate the form of the scene "anew" each time you play it.* It is the "map" of the scene's energy which you will follow each time you take the journey.

Take a moment to recall what we learned about a scenario when we examined the prison scene from Shakespeare's *Measure for Measure*. First, of course, we considered the Given Circumstances: Isabella, who is about to become a nun, has been informed that her brother has been arrested for making his fiance pregnant; the temporary Duke, Angelo, has offered to spare his life if she will sleep with him; outraged, she has refused. She then visits her brother in his cell to tell him that he must die the next morning in order to save her honor and eternal soul.

If you were playing Isabella, your scenario for this scene might sound like this: "I find you in your awful prison cell, and I must tell you that you will die tomorrow because I have refused to sleep with Angelo. I see your desperation and I fear that you won't be strong enough to accept the rightness of my choice, and that you might choose the ignoble path that will condemn your eternal soul, so I first try to prepare you to receive this news; it takes a bit of prodding, but finally I see that you are ready; I then actually tell you what happened and share my pain over it with you, and thank God you are strong like father was. I try to help you prepare for death, but then you start to become terrified; I try to help you regain your manly courage, but when you actually suggest that I commit this crime to save you, I can't bear to see you throwing your soul away, and I renounce you for being a coward."

Notice again that the score is not expressed as external behavior but rather as the inner process of the action which will generate that form each time it is enacted. This sequence of actions has the logical momentum of your character's through-line. It forms what Stanislavski called the *score* of the scene.

You come to understand the score partly through analysis, but mostly through trial and error in rehearsal. As the score emerges from the actual experience of action and reaction, stimulus and response between you and your partner, you will begin naturally to assimilate it until it becomes part of you, an "inner model" which will guide you through the scene.

The score eventually becomes habitual; you absorb it so totally that you can begin to experience the scene fully, moment by moment, without thinking about anything except what your character is thinking about. This is the point at which your actor's awareness begins to give way to the character's awareness; when the score is completely automatic, then you can give yourself fully to each moment with complete attention to "the here and now," confident in the knowledge that the scene will move toward its proper conclusion. In a way, you must be able to do the scene "in your sleep" in order to be able to do it fully awake!

In *Creating a Role*, Stanislavski describes the operation of the score like this:

> With time and frequent repetition, in rehearsal and performance, this score becomes habitual. An actor becomes so accustomed to all his objectives and their sequence that he cannot conceive of approaching his role otherwise than along the line of the steps fixed in the score. Habit plays a great part in creativeness: it establishes in a firm way the accomplishments of creativeness. In the familiar words of Volkonski it makes what is difficult habitual, what is habitual easy, and what is easy beautiful. Habit creates second nature, which is second reality. The score automatically stirs the actor to physical action.[1]

In *Stanislavski Directs*, he is reported as saying:

> The law of theatrical art decrees: discover the correct conception in the scenic action, in your role, and in the beats of the play; and then make the correct habitual and the habitual beautiful.[2]

At what point do you commit to a choice and allow a particular element of the score to become habitual? Some actors wait a long time before making their final choices and approach their roles warily in early rehearsals, gradually filling in the full performance. Others work at performance levels right off, though they maintain enough flexibility to avoid making final choices too soon.

You will have to determine your own best approach, in terms of the disposition of the director, your fellow actors, the nature of the play, the length of the rehearsal period, and so on. To lie back and play the waiting game is usually unfair to your coworkers since they depend upon you for their reactions, but neither should you make final choices too soon, committing yourself to insufficiently tested actions.

## MAKING PERFORMANCE ADJUSTMENTS

We make adjustments constantly in the course of rehearsal, and even in the course of performance. We make them for the sake of our audience, for the sake of the play, and also for the sake of our fellow actors.

It is in the inner phase of the action that adjustments must be made. If we alter only the external form of our activity without adjusting the process of thought from which it springs, the results will seem forced, unnatural, and incomplete. For instance, if the director yells, "Louder!" you do not merely say the line more loudly: You instantaneously review the process of inner action from which the line springs and adjust that choice so that the line *must* be said more loudly for a reason within the world of the play.

This is called *justifying* your stage behavior; you must take your *actor needs* and turn them into *character realities*. You can make such adjustments at any point within the inner phase of action—at the stimulus, attitude, alternatives considered, or strategic choice, or by adjusting your feelings about the other character.

You can also make adjustments by redefining the given circumstances; if the pace of the scene is poor you might find a source of urgency by providing a deadline or other condition that will drive your character's action within the scene.

Further, since your stimulus is almost always the action of another character, you can even make adjustments by asking your fellow actor to provide you with a stimulus that will move you more readily toward the desired goal, as you did in the previous exercise.

### Exercise 93:
### Justifying Adjustments

Select a section from your scene and use it to experiment with the making of performance adjustments: justify each of the following by adjusting some phase of your inner action, the given circumstances, or the stimulus you are getting from your partner.

1. Explore adjustments that might be demanded by style:
   a. do the scene as if it were a Classical tragedy;
   b. as if it were a romantic comedy;
   c. as if it were a farce;
   d. as if it were modern realism.
2. Explore adjustments that might be demanded by the theatre:
   a. do the scene for a huge auditorium;
   b. for an arena stage;
   c. for a film.
3. If possible, work with someone as director, and practice justifying changes in blocking, tempo, volume, etc., as requested by the director.

## TECHNICAL AND DRESS REHEARSALS

The final phase of the rehearsal period is devoted to incorporating the full production elements: make-up, props, costumes, set, lights, and sound. Ideally, this is a time of completion and crystallization; many actors do not feel that their work comes fully to life until all the physical production elements are in place. Stanislavski spoke of completing a characterization only when, in full make-up and costume, he would rehearse before a mirror to be sure that his external appearance was correct.

In most American theatres, only the final week of rehearsal is devoted to the assimilation of all the completed technical elements. This can be a period of tremendous frustration and distraction for you if you have not prepared yourself for it in the earlier stages of rehearsal.

There are two main ways in which you must be prepared: first, to have a solid score—your "energy map" or "sequence of actions"—which helps you to keep your focus on the action without being distracted by all the new elements; second, to have rehearsed "mentally" by visualizing the completed costume and environment.

Be sure to study the set drawing or model and be clear about how the tape marks in the rehearsal hall represent the final set; select rehearsal props and costumes with care as accurate substitutes for the real things; take full advantage of costume fittings to get the feel of your clothes, making all the movements your part may require (and to alert the costumer to any problems of motion); once the set is in place, make it part of your homework to spend some time in it, walking your part or simply getting the feel of the environment.

Once you have a good idea of what the finished product is going to look like, you can begin to *visualize* it. Visualization is an excellent form of private rehearsal in this later phase of the working process. It is most effective when used during periods of deep muscle relaxation, after a relaxation exercise, meditation, or as you are about to fall asleep. Not only will your visualization be most vivid at these times, but your deep muscles will actually participate and the motor skills demanded by the role will be enhanced as well.

Following is an exercise in the technique called Visuo-Motor Behavior Rehearsal. It was first developed for the 1980 Winter Olympics, and has been used by athletes like Jean-Claude Killy with great effectiveness.

### Exercise 94:
### Visuo-Motor Behavior
### Rehearsal

Using the Phasic Relaxation, put yourself into deep muscle relaxation and mental restful alertness.

Now visualize the following: you are about to open in the play from which your scene comes; the theatre is ready, you hear the buzz of the audience in the house, you are standing in your costume with your fellow actors ready to take your places.

Go into the set and take your opening positions; feel the stage lights shining on you, smell the makeup, feel your clothing, see your fellow actors and the set.

The scene begins; live through it totally; let your deep muscles respond to the experience; feel the props and all the business.

Such visualization can be an effective preparation for performance conditions, and tests have shown that this form of rehearsal can be just as effective as ordinary rehearsal, and sometimes more so!

Above all, avoid the temptation to "freeze" your work during this final phase of rehearsal. Many fine performances wither on the vine before opening because the outer form becomes the focus of the actor's attention and the inner phase of action ceases to live and grow. Use the addition of the technical elements as an opportunity to extend and specify the score of your role, and to explore further the life of the character within a more complete environment.

## GROWTH AFTER OPENING

The opening of the show is never the completion of your work, but only the start of a new phase of the growth process. The audience contributes in many ways, perhaps most by providing the responses that complete the rhythmic shaping of the work. These responses take many forms, from the overt (such as laughter or sobs) to the covert (such as rapt stillness or restlessness, or just the "feeling" inside the auditorium). Whatever their form, the audience's responses are an important element in the rhythm of the scene; so far, you have been guessing what those responses will be, and your director has been substituting for them as "an ideal audience of one," but now you have the real thing and can get to work fine-tuning the shape and flow of your action accordingly. This is the business of "previews," if you are lucky enough to have them.

The audience's presence will also probably cause a shift in context, a change in the way you will experience your own work; there will likely be many discoveries for you to make from this altered point of view. Some things you thought would work well may turn out to be too personal or obscure, while other things that you hadn't really noticed turn out to be powerful or worth developing further. At last you have a sure basis for judgment.

This sure basis for judgment will naturally cause you to begin economizing. You will find after a time that you expended more energy during rehearsals than you do in performance, and that you will generally expend less and less energy as the run continues. This is not because you begin doing your part mechanically, without thought or feeling, but because you will penetrate deeper and deeper to its essence; as this happens, unessential detail begins to fall away. Your performance is made more effective by distilling it to its essentials in this way; you are doing more with less!

# Lesson
# Twenty-Three

# The Profession of Acting

We use the word "professional" to describe a high level of skill, reliability, and commitment in many fields, but it means something special among actors. When actors want to pay someone a real compliment, they say they're "a real pro." But what is it that defines a professional?

In athletics, we distinguish between professional and amateur on the basis of money: the professional is paid, while the amateur (from the root *amat*, to love) participates only for the love of the sport itself. But in acting, "professional" seems to mean much more than the fact that someone receives money; the term carries an implication of integrity, reliability, high standards, and most of all *commitment*.

The root of the word comes from the idea of "professing," which means *making a public vow*. Professionals, as a result of their special knowledge or skill, have power over other people: doctors, lawyers, clergymen, and others of the "professional class" are responsible for the wellbeing of their clients. Society has placed a special trust in them, and in return they are expected to use their special powers only for the benefit of those they serve. Thus a professional is *someone who publicly professes an ethical standard* and takes personal responsibility for work which will effect the lives of others.

As an actor, you *will* have special power over others. We don't usually take acting that seriously, but it is true. With this power comes a public responsibility for the wellbeing of those whose lives you will effect, and this demands an enormous commitment.

This commitment operates on three levels simultaneously: first, you must be committed to *your own development as an artist*. Without this commitment to yourself, you cannot offer to others all of which you are capable.

Second, you must be committed to *your work*; if you are merely using your work to advance yourself, you will obscure its value to others.

Third, you must be committed *to the world you serve through your work*. Acceptance of this social responsibility gives you a sense of purpose to something greater than yourself which can lead you to extraordinary accomplishments. As the director Eugenio Barba said in a letter to one of his actors:

> Whatever hidden, personal motives led you to the theatre, now that you have entered that profession you must find there a sense which goes beyond your proper person and fixes you socially in the sight of others. . . . If the fact of being an actor means all that to you, then a new theatre will be born.[1]

## YOUR SERVICE TO THE WORLD
## THROUGH ACTING

The philosopher Descartes said that reading good books was like conversing with the greatest minds of history, minds that had distilled their experience and wisdom in their art. We who perform good plays go a step further: we actively participate in the experience of peoples, places, and times which have been shaped and condensed by the artistic consciousness of great playwrights. Theatre is the most human of all the arts, and we can preserve and expand our humanity through our art in ways denied us by everyday life. As the American playwright David Mamet says,

> What can be preserved? What can be communicated from one generation to the next?
>
> Philosophy. Morality. Aesthetics.
>
> These can be expressed in technique, in those skills which enable the artist to respond truthfully, fully, lovingly to whatever he or she wishes to express.
>
> This is what can and must be passed from one generation to the next. Technique—a knowledge of how to translate inchoate desire into clean action—into action capable of communicating itself to the audience.
>
> This technique, this care, this love of precision, of cleanliness, this love of the theatre, is the best way, for it is love of the *audience*—of that which *unites* the actor and the house; a desire to share something which they know to be true.[2]

Besides the desire for personal growth discussed earlier, there are many other personal motivations for those who want to be actors: desire for fame, for respect and love, for wealth, or simply to be paid attention to, none of which is wrong or unimportant. But the desire of which Mamet speaks, this *need* to express the truth within the techniques of art, is not merely personal. It involves a sense of service to something greater than ourselves, and as such it is the deepest and most lasting motivation of the actor. As he says,

> Our workers in the theatre—actors, writers, directors, teachers—are drawn to it not out of intellectual predilection, but from *necessity*. We are driven into the theatre by our need to express—our need to answer the question of our lives—the questions of the time in which we live. Of this moment.[3]

This need "to answer the question of our lives" demands both the highest artistry and the deepest humanity. Again, Mamet:

> Who is going to speak up? Who is going to speak for the American spirit? For the human spirit?
>     Who is capable of being heard? Of being accepted? Of being believed? Only that person who speaks without ulterior motives, without hope of gain, without even the desire to *change*, with only the desire to *create*: The artist. The actor. The strong, trained actor dedicated to the idea that the theatre is the place we go to hear the truth, and equipped with the technical capacity to speak simply and clearly.[4]

This sentiment, expressed recently by one of our leading playwrights, harkens back to the original impulses of the founders of our modern school of acting when, more than eighty years ago, Stanislavski and Nemirovich-Danchenko debated the requirements for actors to be taken into the company of the Moscow Art Theatre:

> "Take actor A," we would test each other. "Do you consider him talented?"
>     "To a high degree."
>     "Will you take him into the troupe?"
>     "No."
>     "Why?"
>     "Because he has adapted himself to his career, his talents to the demands of the public, his character to the caprices of the manager, and all of himself to theatrical cheapness. A man who is so poisoned cannot be cured.
>     "And what do you say about Actress B?"
>     "She is a good actress, but not for us."
>     "Why?"
>     "She does not love art, but herself in art."
>     "And actress C?"
>     "She won't do. She is incurably given to hokum."

"What about actor D?"

"We should bear him in mind."

"Why?"

"He has ideals for which he is fighting. He is not at peace with present conditions. He is a man of ideas."

"I am of the same opinion. With your permission I shall enter his name in the list of candidates."[5]

It is important, then, to consider how you may serve through acting. Though I have given some examples of the ethical commitment of others, there are many ways to serve: you must find the spirit of service for yourself and in your own terms.

Traditionally, artists have announced their specific commitment through the publication of a *manifesto*; this was their way of taking the same kind of public vow that lawyers and doctors take when they are licensed. A manifesto is a brief, passionate, and personal statement of belief and purpose. It requires considerable thought, and should be as simple and direct as possible.

### Exercise 95:
### Your Manifesto

Write your own manifesto for the art of acting. Make yours just two paragraphs long:
  A.  What you want to do for the world through your acting: how do you want to make a difference?
  B.  What techniques and process are necessary to achieve your purpose? What skills and capabilities must *you* develop to empower yourself to achieve your purpose?
  C.  When you are satisfied with it, publish it in some public forum; read it in class, or put it up on the wall.

## YOUR FUTURE GROWTH
## AS AN ACTOR

Your commitment to serve your world through your art drives you to become the best actor that you can be. As you grow older, you are constantly having new experiences and gaining new insights which will be valuable to you in your acting; you must also continue to develop and refine your techniques and basic skills.

Actors face several special difficulties in continuing their artistic development during the course of their careers. First, unlike a dancer or musician who can practice individually, an actor can achieve only limited solo practice of physical and vocal skills; the art of acting itself requires a collaborative situation. For this reason, many working actors continue to take professional classes long after their formal training has ended; some have even banded together to create collective studios to assist one another in continuing their growth.

Second, since actors rarely have the opportunity to select the material they perform, and since they are usually cast according to their proven abilities, they cannot count on their paid work to offer meaningful challenges which will expand their range of skills; they must provide that ongoing sense of challenge for themselves. They must, in short, take charge of their own growth through personal discipline.

Your future growth depends entirely on your ability to define your own needs, to set priorities, and then to establish the mechanisms necessary to meet those needs. Basically, you must ask yourself two questions: "What do I want from acting?" and "What do I need in order to get it?"

## WHY YOU ACT

You were probably initially attracted to acting because it seemed to offer the possibility of satisfying some deep personal needs, even if you were unconscious of those needs at the time. Many great actors have spoken of their inescapable need to act in spite of many misgivings about it. As Sir Laurence Olivier once told some reporters, "It does seem sometimes that acting is hardly the occupation for an adult. . . I can't stand it any more. . . But without it I would die, I suppose."[6]

For those who, like Olivier, have made acting not just a career but a way of life (and this includes all of our greatest actors) it is clear that acting addresses needs far deeper than the desire for attention or material success. These actors often speak of the release which playing a role gives them from what Alec Guinness called "my dreary old life," and for many acting seems to provide a compensation for some sense of unworthiness. Whatever the motive may be, most agree that acting is a fairly dreadful way to earn a living, and only very deep needs can provide sufficient motivation to sustain a career.

Whatever the needs that are urging you to act may be, they are the source of your personal satisfaction as an actor, as well as a source of tremendous power on stage. Acting turns you on, so let yourself go for it!

### Exercise 96:
### Your Motives for Acting

A.  Below are a number of phrases; working with a partner, take turns repeating and completing each spontaneously. Answer from your feelings; tell the truth.

1. The first theatre I remember seeing was. . .
2. The theatre experience I remember most vividly is. . .
3. Some of the theatre artists I admire most are. . .
4. The thing I like most about working in theatre is. . .
5. The most recent time that I was really happy working in theatre was. . .
6. The thing I hate most about working in theatre is. . .
7. My work in the theatre really hurt when. . .
8. The kind of theatre I most want to do in the future is. . .
9. The thing I want most out of theatre is. . .
10. Some of the things I would rather do than theatre are. . .
11. I would give up a career in theatre if. . .
12. What I would need for a career in the theatre would be. . .

B. Relax and recall your earliest memory of theatre.
   1. How did it make your body feel?
   2. What did it make you think about?
   3. Did it remind you of any early personal experiences?
   4. Did you make any decisions, conscious or unconscious, that have effected you since?

It will be useful to review your motives and needs periodically throughout your acting life: your needs change, and you may outgrow early motives; as you work, you may also discover new reasons for acting that are even stronger than those with which you began.

## DEFINING GROWTH OBJECTIVES

As you grow and develop as an actor, you will continually be making greater and greater demands upon yourself. Throughout your career, you will discover new needs which demand to be satisfied; these needs can become *growth objectives*, opportunities for personal expansion.

The most fruitful growth objectives are not merely idealized capabilities which you think you "ought" to have, but specific and deeply felt needs which you have encountered in the natural course of your work. So far, you have been a student and have had to trust me and your teachers that the things we have been studying are indeed important; now you must begin to define your own needs and learn to solve particular problems that are important to you in what you are actually trying to do; these are the things you will learn best and most rapidly because they are the most real to you. Learn to keep in touch with your own work and to identify real problems as they arise.

A growth objective may take many forms: it may be *technical*, relating to some physical or vocal skill; it may be *conceptual*, relating to your understanding of your work; it may be *methodological*, relating to your "way of working"; or, as we discussed in Lesson 21, it may be *attitudinal*, relating to your feelings about your own work.

### Exercise 97:
### Defining Growth Objectives

Review your most recent working experiences; what were the needs you felt? Think over each of these categories and jot items down as they occur to you.

    A.   Technique: Did any physical or vocal needs arise? Was your psychological technique (concentration, imagination, etc.) adequate?

    B.   Conception: Did you understand the work? Was there information you needed?

    C.   Methodology: Were you able to define your actions and objectives? Develop your score? Was your rehearsal and homework effective? Are you finding a way of going about your work that suits you, your partners, and your material?

    D.   Attitude: Is your attitude toward your work, toward your fellow workers, and toward yourself a productive one?

Just as you must define an acting objective in playable terms, so you must learn to define your own growth objectives in ways that enable you to address them. The idea of "SIP" applies: your growth of objective must be *singular, immediate,* and *personally important.*

To make your objectives singular, learn to boil your problems down into a simple description, the more specific the better; don't think merely about "relaxation," but be specific about what kind of relaxation you need, and when. One way to do this is to identify the *symptoms* of the problem; ask yourself, "how do I know I have this problem?" In the case of relaxation, you would ask yourself where in your body you feel the tension, and in what situations you feel it; are there times when you *are* relaxed in your acting? If so, what enables you to relax at these times and not at others?

Another good way to proceed is to prepare yourself for success by imagining yourself *without* the problem. How would you be different if you didn't have this problem? How would your body be different? How would your thinking and feeling be different?

By identifying the specific symptoms of the problem, you can begin to see how to work on those symptoms; don't worry about discovering causes; improving the symptoms often clears up the cause!

To make your growth objectives *immediate* and *personally important,* you must learn to take inventory of your needs on a regular basis and recognize your own priorities amongst those needs.

## SETTING GROWTH PRIORITIES

When we stop to consider all the things we need to work on, we sometimes become depressed or terrified at the enormity and complexity of the task: what a mountain of work! But a mountain can be climbed, one step at a time: you must bring that mountain down to manageable size by setting attainable interim goals. This requires that you set personal priorities and decide which needs should be addressed first.

This sense of priority is an essential aspect of personal discipline. Just as you select the most productive objectives on stage, having personal priorities enables you to focus your energy in a more effective way. No one else, and no "ideal," can set your priorities for you; in this, you are totally responsible for yourself. Your personal priorities are a direct expression of your evolving artistic vision.

### Exercise 98:
### Setting Growth Priorities

Prepare a sheet of paper with three columns headed SURVIVAL, COMPETENCE and MASTERY. Using the list of growth objectives which you made in the previous exercise, place each in one of these columns using the following criteria:

SURVIVAL: needs which, if they were to remain unmet, would cause you to give up acting as a hopeless career choice;

COMPETENCE: needs which you would consider necessary to be a good, capable actor, though not a great one;

MASTERY: those skills and abilities which would set you apart as a great actor.

Notice that different levels of the same skill may be placed in different columns: for instance, a minimum level of concentration is necessary for survival, still more disciplined concentration is needed for competence, but the master would be able to achieve total concentration at will.

Throughout your acting life, your efforts will probably be directed at column one, SURVIVAL. As the level of your work goes up, so will your standards of acceptable performance, so that items which are today in your MASTERY column will someday appear under SURVIVAL. The master, you see, is unaware of their own mastery; they are simply doing the job according to their own standards.

## OPPORTUNITIES FOR GROWTH

Once you have identified those needs most vital to your own survival as an actor, you will be able to seize or create opportunities to address them. Most fundamental needs can be worked on in almost any situation. If you have identified "relaxation" as an important problem, for example, you will find ways to further define, specify, and explore it in everything else you do. For more specific needs, you may have to wait for an opportunity; learn to *match need to opportunity*.

When an opportunity fails to arise, it is also possible for you to create opportunities to work on specific growth objectives. In order to do this, you must learn to recognize the difference between *wants* and *needs:* what you *want* is a specific result, but what you *need* is the means whereby you can get those results.

The means does not always feel like the desired goal; those hours of vocal exercise, for instance, don't feel much like that inspired moment in performance when the voice wells up from some mysterious emotional depth and soars into the hearts of the audience. But once you understand the difference between what you want and what you need to get it, then you are ready for the real test of personal discipline: daily regularity and tenacity in pursuit of your goal.

Here is an exercise that can help you to design a plan of action to pursue a specific growth objective.

**Exercise 99:**
**Writing a Contract**
**for Growth**

Select one of your survival needs, and give yourself a relatively short period of time in which you will work on some aspect of this need, say one or two weeks.

A.  Close your eyes, relax, and imagine yourself at the end of that time having fulfilled your need.

How do you feel? What are you doing differently now that you no longer have this need? How do you know that you have fulfilled the need?

Experience yourself as not having this need; prepare yourself for success.

B.  Now select some behavior based upon this fantasy which will move you toward not having this need; pick something which you will do (or not do) and specify when, how often, and in what circumstances you will do (or not do) it.

C.  Write yourself a simple contract specifying this behavior; having a witness can be useful, especially if it is someone who once had this problem themselves.

Be sure you have specified exactly what you will do and when you will do it. If your growth objective relates to *attitudinal* problems, your first step is to develop a specific awareness of your own feelings. If, let's say, you tend to make timid choices in your acting, or find yourself censoring your stronger impulses, you might examine those moments when the censorship occurs. Your contract for doing this might look like this:

> In my next two scenes I will watch those times when I censor my impulses
> and see what messages I may be sending myself at those moments.

You might find that at such moments of self-censorship you are telling
yourself, "Watch out! You'll make a fool of yourself!" You might even
recognize this "little voice" as an echo of some early authority figure, or the
residue of some earlier experience. Your next step will be to replace this
self-defeating message with a more useful one, such as, "Oh boy, here's a
chance to experience something new!" Eventually this replacement message
will become a new habit of thought, and a new attitude will have been
formed.

If your growth objective is *technical* and requires a regimen of regular,
spaced drill, your contract will establish the time and place for it; you will
"make an appointment" with yourself. For example, if you have identified
the need to improve your articulation as a growth objective, you might
have a contract like this:

> For the next two weeks I will get up 15 minutes earlier every weekday, and
> do the articulation exercises in Lesson 6 of *The Actor at Work.*

In these cases, it may be useful to tie your work sessions to activities that
are already part of your regular schedule, so you won't have to remind
yourself to find time each day; in this example, you might decide to do
your articulation exercises every time you take a shower.

At the end of your contract period, review your work; do you need to
extend the contract or change the plan of attack? Don't waste time either
celebrating or berating yourself for success or failure; get on with your
work.

Eventually actual written contracts will be unnecessary; you will have
learned the crucial element of personal discipline: to change the underlying
structure of your behavior in response to identifiable needs arising from
your work.

However you proceed, your aim is to take responsibility for your
own future development. You want to be in a better position to turn
your working opportunities to personal advantage, recognizing how each
can serve your artistic growth at the same time that you are fulfilling the
demands of the job at hand. This contributes not only to your growth, but
to the quality of your immediate work as well: it has been my experience
that actors tend to do better work when there is something of genuine
personal significance at stake.

This sense of ongoing development can be of value to your audiences
as well: One of the things we enjoy in the theatre is the sense that the
actors are growing through their work, for when they are, we are reminded
by example that we can be in charge of our own lives too.

You have embarked on an exciting and unending journey!

# Afterword

# Transformation

We return at last to the concern with which we began; the mastery of the self as the central discipline of the actor. We have learned that the self is mastered, paradoxically, by the ability to forget the self through a transcendent commitment to a significant purpose, be it a playable objective for your character or a sense of purpose for you as an actor.

Your sense of purpose grows from your respect for your own talent, your love for the specific material you are performing, and your desire to use both to serve your audience. It is this drive to be *at service* through your art that will finally overcome the self-consciousness of your ego and carry you beyond yourself, giving you a transcendent purpose from which comes dignity, fulfillment, and ongoing artistic vitality.

Stanislavski called this ongoing artistic vitality "theatrical youthfulness." Near the end of his life he addressed a group of young actors who were entering the Moscow Art Theatre with these words:

> The first essential to retain a youthful performance is to keep the idea of the play alive. That is why the dramatist wrote it and that is why you decided to produce it. One should not be on the stage, one should not put on a play for the sake of acting or producing only. Yes, you must be excited about your profession. You must love it devotedly and passionately, but not for itself, not for its laurels, not for the pleasure and delight it brings to you as artists.

You must love your chosen profession because it gives you the opportunity to communicate ideas that are important and necessary to your audience. Because it gives you the opportunity, through the ideas that you dramatize on the stage and through your characterizations, to educate your audience and to make them better, finer, wiser, and more useful members of society. . . .

You must keep the idea alive and be inspired by it at each performance. This is the only way to retain youthfulness in performance and your own youthfulness as actors. The true recreation of the play's idea—I emphasize the word true—demands from the artist wide and varied knowledge, constant self-discipline, the subordination of his personal tastes and habits to the demands of the idea, and sometimes even definite sacrifices.[1]

The art of acting has always had a very special service to render, one which has become increasingly important today: it is rooted in the actor's ability to transform, to become "someone else." At a time when mass culture, big business, and bigger government make us, as individuals, feel more and more insignificant and impotent, the actor's ability to be "in charge" of personal reality can be a source of hope and inspiration to others.

The deepest, most ancient root of the actor is this exemplification of our need and ability to define our own existence. The actor's ability to undergo transformation with consummate skill is itself a kind of potency, a kind of power over the future. While a play may teach us something about who we are, it is the actor's ability to be transformed that teaches us something about whom we may *become*. The actor's ability to redefine personal reality before our very eyes reminds us of our own spiritual capacity for self-definition, and thus the theatre becomes a celebration of our vitality and of the ongoing flow of life.

Sensing the capacity of the theatre to help enrich our spiritual lives at a time when we have a great need of spiritual revivification, we have begun to explore more than ever before the full richness of the experience that may pass between actor and spectator, and the way in which the theatrical moment can resonate in the totality of our being, affecting our lives long after the curtain has fallen.

The actor's horizons are thus being continually broadened, and the art of acting has begun to encompass not only an expanding range of performance techniques and possibilities, but a renewed sense of ethical and spiritual purpose as well.

It is a wonderful time to be an actor.

# Appendix One

# Sample Speeches

**FROM *KING LEAR*, ACT III,**
**SCENE 4, BY WILLIAM SHAKESPEARE:**

1. Poor naked wretches, wheresoe'er you are,
2. That bide the pelting of this pitiless storm,
3. How shall your houseless heads and unfed sides,
4. Your loop'd and window'd raggedness, defend you
5. From seasons such as these? O! I have ta'en
6. Too little care of this. Take physic, pomp;
7. Expose thyself to feel what wretches feel,
8. That thou mayst shake the superflux to them,
9. And show the heavens more just.

**FROM *THE ZOO STORY***
**BY EDWARD ALBEE**

It's just. . . it's just that. . . (JERRY is abnormally tense, now). . . it's just that if you can't deal with people, you have to make a start somewhere. WITH ANIMALS! (Much faster now, and like a conspirator) Don't you see? A person has to have some way of dealing with SOMETHING. If not with people. . . if not with people. . . SOMETHING. With a bed, with a cockroach, with a mirror . . . no, that's too hard, that's one of the last steps. With a cockroach, with a. . . with a. . . with a carpet, a roll of toilet paper. . . no, not that, either. . . that's a mirror, too; always check bleeding. You see how hard it is to find things? With a street corner, and too many lights, all colors reflecting on the oily-wet streets. . . with a wisp of smoke, a wisp. . . of smoke. . . with. . . with pornographic playing cards, with a strongbox. . . WITHOUT A LOCK. . . with love, with vomiting, with crying, with fury because the pretty little ladies aren't pretty little ladies, with making money with your body which is an act of love and I could prove it, with howling because you're alive; with God. How about that? WITH GOD WHO IS A COLORED QUEEN WHO WEARS A KIMONO AND PLUCKS HIS EYEBROWS, WHO IS A WOMAN WHO CRIES WITH DETERMINATION BEHIND HER CLOSED DOOR. . . with God who, I'm told, turned his back on the whole thing some time ago. . . with. . . some day, with people. (JERRY sighs the next word heavily) People.*

*Reprinted by permission of Coward-McCann, Inc., and Jonathan Cape Ltd., from *The Zoo Story* by Edward Albee. Copyright © 1960 by Edward Albee.

# Appendix Two

# Shakespeare Twosome Scenes

**WOMAN-MAN**

| | | |
|---|---|---|
| *Anthony & Cleopatra* | Cleopatra–Anthony | I, i, 14; I, iii, 13; IV, xv, 9 |
| | Cleopatra–Messenger | II, v, 23 |
| | Cleopatra–Clown | V, ii, 236 |
| *Hamlet* | Ophelia–Polonius | I, iii, 86; II, i, 74 |
| | Ophelia–Hamlet | III, i, 88 |
| | Gertrude–Hamlet | III, iv, 7 |
| *King Lear* | Goneril–Albany | IV, ii, 26 |
| *Macbeth* | Lady–Macbeth | I, vii; II, ii; III, ii |
| *Othello* | Desdemona–Othello | III, iii, 41; III, iv, 32; IV, ii, 20; V, ii |
| *Romeo & Juliet* | Juliet–Romeo | II, ii; III, v |
| | Juliet–Friar | IV, i, 44 |
| *All's Well* | Helena–Parolles | I, i, 94 |
| | Helena–King | II, i, 99 |
| | Countess–Lavatch | II, ii |
| | Diana–Bertram | IV, ii |
| *As You Like It* | Rosalind–Orlando | III, ii, 282; IV, i, 27 |
| | Touchstone–Audrey | III, iii |

| | | |
|---|---|---|
| *Measure for Measure* | Isabella–Lucio | I, iv, 16 |
| | Isabella–Angelo | II, ii, 26; II, iv, 30 |
| | Juliet–Duke | II, iii, 19 |
| | Isabella–Claudio | III, i, 54 |
| *Merry Wives* | Anne–Slender | I, i, 239 |
| | Quickly–Falstaff | II, ii, 31 |
| *Midsummer Night's Dream* | Helena–Demetrius | II, i, 188 |
| | Hermia–Demetrius | III, ii, 43 |
| *Much Ado* | Beatrice–Benedick | IV, i, 253; V, ii, 24 |
| *Taming of the Shrew* | Kate–Petruchio | II, i, 181; IV, v |
| *Troilus & Cressida* | Cressida–Pandarus | I, ii, 35 |
| | Cressida–Troilus | III, ii, 60 |
| *Twelfth Night* | Viola–Captain | I, ii |
| | Viola–Orsino | II, iv, 14 |
| | Viola–Feste | III, i |
| *Henry IV, Part 1* | Lady–Hotspur | II, iii |
| *Henry VI, Part 1* | Countess–Talbot | II, iii, 13 |
| | Margaret–Suffolk | V, iii, 45 |
| *Henry VI, Part 2* | Eleanor–Gloucester | I, ii |
| | Queen–Suffolk | I, iii, 40; III, ii, 300 |
| *Henry VI, Part 3* | Widow–Edward | III, ii, 18 |
| *Richard III* | Anne–Richard | I, ii |
| | Elizabeth–Richard | IV, iv, 199 |
| *Henry VIII* | Katherine–Griffith | IV, ii |
| *Cymbeline* | Imogen–Iachimo | I, vi, 56 |
| | Imogen–Cloten | II, iii, 91 |
| | Imogen–Pisanio | III, iv |
| *Pericles* | Dionyza–Cleon | IV, iii |
| | Marina–Lysimachus | IV, vi, 60 |
| | Marina–Boult | IV, vi, 144 |
| | Marina–Pericles | V, i, 83 |
| *The Tempest* | Ariel–Prospero | I, ii, 88 |
| | Miranda–Ferdinand | III, i |
| *Winter's Tale* | Hermione–Leontes | II, i, 36 |
| | Perdite–Florizel | IV, iv |

## MAN–MAN

| | | |
|---|---|---|
| *Antony & Cleopatra* | Antony–Eros | IV, xiv |
| *Hamlet* | Hamlet–Horatio | I, ii, 160 |
| | Hamlet–Polonius | II, ii, 171 |
| | Hamlet–Claudius | IV, iii |
| | Laertes–Claudius | IV, vii |
| | Two Clowns | V, i |
| | Hamlet–Clown | V, i, 109 |
| | Hamlet–Osric | V, ii, 80 |

| | | |
|---|---|---|
| *Julius Caesar* | Cassius–Brutis | I, ii, 25, IV, ii, 37 |
| *King Lear* | Gloucester–Edmund | I, ii, 23 |
| | Lear–Fool | I, iv, 97; I, v, 6 |
| | Gloucester–Edgar | IV, vi |
| *Macbeth* | Lennox–Lord | III, vi |
| | Malcolm–Macduff | IV, iii |
| *Othello* | Iago–Roderigo | I, iii, 296; IV, ii, 170 |
| | Iago–Cassio | II, iii, 258 |
| | Iago–Othello | III, iii, 93; III, iii, 327 |
| *Timon of Athens* | Timon–Steward | II, ii, 121; IV, iii, 454 |
| | Timon–Apemantus | IV, iii, 197 |
| *All's Well* | Lafew–Parolles | II, iii, 183 |
| *As You Like It* | Orlando–Adam | II, iii |
| | Touchstone–Corin | III, ii, 11 |
| | Jaques–Orlando | III, ii, 241 |
| *Comedy of Errors* | Antipholus–Dromio | I, ii, 33 |
| | Antipholus–Dromio | II, ii; III, ii, 71 |
| *Love's Labor's Lost* | Don Armado–Moth | I, ii; III, i |
| | Berowne–Costard | III, i, 127 |
| *Measure for Measure* | Duke–Lucio | III, ii, 81 |
| | Duke–Provost | IV, ii, 64 |
| *Merchant of Venice* | Antonio–Bassanio | I, i, 113 |
| | Launcelot–Gobbo | II, ii |
| | Salerio–Solanio | II, iii |
| *Merry Wives* | Ford–Falstaff | II, ii, 140; III, v, 51 |
| *Taming of the Shrew* | Pedant–Tranio | IV, ii, 72 |
| *Troilus & Cressida* | Troilus–Pandarus | I, i |
| | Ajax–Thersites | II, i |
| | Pandarus–Servant | III, i |
| *Twelfth Night* | Sebastian–Antonio | III, iii |
| | Malvolio–Feste | IV, ii, 20 |
| *Two Gents of Verona* | Speed–Proteus | I, i, 62 |
| | Speed–Valentine | II, i |
| | Speed–Launce | II, v; III, i, 284 |
| *King John* | Arthur–Hubert | IV, i |
| *Richard II* | Gaunt–Bolingbroke | I, iii, 253 |
| *Henry IV, Part 1* | Falstaff–Hal | I, ii; II, iv, 310 |
| | Hotspur–Glendower | III, i, 3 |
| *Henry IV, Part 2* | Falstaff–Justice | I, ii, 87 |
| | Silence–Shallow | III, ii |
| *Henry V* | Pistol–Fluellen | V, i |
| *Henry VI, Part 1* | Talbot–John | IV, v |
| *Henry VI, Part 2* | Iden–Cade | IV, x |
| *Henry VI, Part 3* | Richard–Henry | V, vi |
| *Richard III* | Catesby–Hastings | III, ii, 35 |
| | Richard–Buckingham | IV, ii (beginning & end) |
| | Richard–Derby | IV, iv, 456 |

| | | |
|---|---|---|
| *Henry VIII* | Norfolk–Buckingham | I, i, 118 |
| | Porter–Man | V, iv |
| *Cymbeline* | Iachimo–Posthumus | II, iv, 27 |
| | Cloten–Pisanio | III, v, 70 |
| *Winter's Tale* | Leontes–Camillo | I, ii, 211 |
| | Camillo–Polixenes | I, ii, 362 |
| | Shepherd–Clown | III, iii, 58 |
| | Autolycus–Clown | IV, iii |
| | Florizel–Camillo | IV, iv, 455 |

## WOMAN–WOMAN

| | | |
|---|---|---|
| *Othello* | Desdemona–Emilia | IV, iii, 11 |
| *Romeo & Juliet* | Juliet–Nurse | II, v; III, ii |
| | Juliet–Mother | III, v, 65 |
| *All's Well* | Helena–Countess | I, iii, 121 |
| | Helena–Widow | III, vii |
| *As You Like It* | Rosalind–Celia | I, iii, 86; III, ii, 157 |
| *Merchant of Venice* | Portia–Nerissa | I, ii |
| *Merry Wives* | Mrs. Page–Ford | II, i |
| *Much Ado* | Ursula–Hero | III, i, 15 |
| *Twelfth Night* | Viola–Olivia | I, v, 160; III, i, 90 |
| *Two Gents of Verona* | Julia–Lucetta | I, ii |
| | Julia–Silvia | IV, iv, 113 |
| *Henry V* | Katherine–Alice | III, iv (in French) |
| *Henry VIII* | Anne–Old Lady | II, iii |

# Bibliography

APPEL, LIBBY, *Mask Characterization*. Carbondale, Illinois: Southern Illinois University Press, 1982.

ARISTOTLE. *The Poetics*, trans. KENNETH A. TELFORD. Chicago: Gateway, 1961.

ARTAUD, ANTONIN. *The Theatre and Its Double*, New York: Grove Press, 1958.

BACH, GEORGE. *Aggression Lab*. Dubuque, Iowa: Kendall/Hunt, 1971.

BACON, WALLACE A. and ROBERT S. BREEN. *Literature as Experience*. New York: McGraw-Hill, 1959.

BALL, DAVID. *Backwards & Forwards: A Technical Manual for Reading Plays*. Carbondale, Illinois: Southern Illinois University Press, 1983.

BARTON, JOHN. *Playing Shakespeare*. London and New York: Metheun, 1984.

BATES, BRIAN. *The Way of the Actor*. Boston: Shambhala Publications, 1987.

BECK, JULIAN. *The Life of the Theatre*. San Francisco: City Lights Books, 1972.

BECKERMAN, BERNARD. *Dynamics of Drama*. New York: Drama Book Publishers, 1979.

BENEDETTI, ROBERT. *Seeming, Being, and Becoming*. New York: Drama Book Specialists, 1975.

—— *The Director at Work*. Englewood Cliffs, New Jersey: Prentice Hall, 1984.

—— "Zen in the Art of Actor Training," in *Master Teachers of Theatre*, ed. Burnet Hobgood. Carbondale: Southern Illinois University Press, 1988.

BERNE, ERIC. *Games People Play*. New York: Grove Press, 1964.

BIRDWHISTLE, RAYMOND. *Introduction to Kinesics*. Louisville: University of Louisville Pamphlet, 1957.

BOLESLAVSKY, RICHARD. *Acting: The First Six Lessons*. New York: Theatre Arts Books, 1933.

BRANDEN, NATHANIEL. *The Disowned Self*. New York: Bantam, 1973.

—— *The Psychology of Self-Esteem*. New York: Bantam, 1971.

BRAUN, EDWARD. trans. and ed. *Meyerhold on Theatre*. New York: Hill and Wang, 1969.

BROCKETT, OSCAR G. *The Theatre: An Introduction* (4th ed). New York: Holt, Rinehart & Winston, 1979.
BROOK, PETER. *The Empty Space.* New York: Atheneum, 1968.
BULLOUGH, EDWARD. *Aesthetics.* Stanford, California: Stanford University Press, 1957.
CAMPBELL, JOSEPH. *The Masks of God.* New York: Viking, 1959.
CASSIRER, ERNST. *The Philosophy of Symbolic Forms* (Ralph Manheim trans.). New Haven: Yale University Press, 1953.
CHAIKIN, JOSEPH. *The Presence of the Actor.* New York: Atheneum, 1972.
CHEKHOV, MICHAEL. *To the Actor.* New York: Harper & Row, Pub., 1953.
COHEN, ROBERT. *Acting Power.* Palo Alto, California: Mayfield Publishing Co., 1978.
COLE, TOBY, ed. *Acting: A Handbook of the Stanislavski Method.* New York: Crown Publishers, 1971.
COLE, TOBY and HELEN CHINOY, eds. *Actors on Acting.* New York: Crown Publishers, 1970.
CRAWFORD, JERRY. *Acting in Person and in Style* (3rd ed.). Dubuque, Iowa: Wm. C. Brown Company, 1983.
DEWEY, JOHN. *Experience and Nature.* La Salle, Ill.: Open Court Publishing Co., 1925.
ERNST, EARLE. *The Kabuki Theatre.* New York: Grove Press, 1956.
ESSLIN, MARTIN. *Brecht: The Man and His Work.* New York: Doubleday, 1960.
—— *The Theatre of the Absurd.* New York: Doubleday, 1961.
FELDENKRAIS, MOSHE. *Awareness through Movement.* New York: Harper & Row, Pub., 1972.
GIELGUD, JOHN. *An Actor and His Time.* New York: Penguin, 1981.
GOFFMAN, ERVING. *The Presentation of Self in Everyday Life.* New York: Doubleday, 1959.
GORCHAKOV, NIKOLAI. *Stanislavski Directs.* New York: Funk and Wagnalls, 1954.
GREEN, MICHAEL. *Downwind of Upstage.* New York: Hawthorn, 1964.
GROTOWSKI, JERZY. *Towards a Poor Theatre.* New York: Simon and Schuster, 1968.
GUTHRIE, TYRONE. *Tyrone Guthrie on Acting.* New York: Viking, 1971.
HAGEN, UTA. *Respect for Acting.* New York: Macmillan, 1973.
HALL, EDWARD. *The Silent Language.* New York: Doubleday, 1959.
HALPRIN, LAWRENCE. *The RSVP Cycles.* New York: George Braziller, Inc., 1969.
HARROP, JOHN and SABIN EPSTEIN. *Acting with Style.* Englewood Cliffs, New Jersey: Prentice Hall, 1982.
HERRIGEL, EUGEN. *Zen in the Art of Archery.* New York: Vintage, 1971.
JACOBSON, EDMUND. *Progressive Relaxation.* Chicago: University of Chicago Press, 1938.
JOHNSTONE, KEITH. *Impro: Improvisation and the Theatre.* New York: Theatre Arts Books, 1983.
JONES, FRANK PIERCE. *Body Awareness in Action.* New York: Schocken Books, 1976.
JOSEPH, BERTRAM. *Acting Shakespeare.* New York: Theatre Arts Books, 1960.
KALTER, JOANMARIE. *Actors on Acting.* New York: Sterling Publishing Company, 1978.
KIRBY, E.T., ed. *Total Theatre.* New York: Dutton, 1969.
KURITZ, PAUL. *Playing.* Englewood Cliffs, New Jersey: Prentice Hall, 1982.
LAING, R.D. *The Politics of Experience.* New York: Ballantine, 1967.
LAO TSU. *Tao Te Ching.* (Gia Fu Feng and Jane English trans.). New York: Vintage, 1972.
LESSAC, ARTHUR. *Body Wisdom: The Use and Training of the Human Body.* New York: Drama Book Specialists, 1978.
LEWIS, ROBERT. *Advice to Players.* New York: Harper & Row, Pub., 1980.
—— *Method or Madness?.* London: Heinemann, 1960.
LINKLATER, KRISTIN. *Freeing the Natural Voice.* New York: Drama Book Specialists Publishers, 1976.
LOWEN, ALEXANDER. *The Language of the Body.* New York: Collier, 1971.
MASLOV, ABRAHAM. *Motivation and Personality.* New York: Harper & Row, Pub., 1954.
MAY, ROLLO. *The Courage to Create.* New York: W. W. Norton & Co., Inc., 1975.
O'CONNOR, GARY. *Ralph Richardson: An Actor's Life.* New York: Atheneum, 1982.
OLIVIER, LAURENCE. *Confessions of an Actor.* New York: Simon & Schuster, 1982.
OTTO, WALTER. *Dionysus.* Bloomington, Ind.: Indiana University Press, 1965.
PERLS, FREDERICK, RALPH HEFFERLINE, and PAUL GOODMAN. *Gestalt Therapy.* New York: Julian Press, 1951.
RAM, DASS. *Be Here Now.* New Mexico: Lama Foundation, 1971.

—— *The Only Dance There Is.* New York: Doubleday/Anchor, 1974.

REDGRAVE, MICHAEL. *In My Mind's I.* New York: Viking, 1983.

RICHARDS, MARY CAROLINE. *Centering.* Wesleyan: Wesleyan University Press, 1964.

SAINER, ARTHUR. *The Radical Theatre Notebook.* New York: Discus/Avon, 1975.

ST. DENIS, MICHEL. *Theatre: The Rediscovery of Style.* New York: Theatre Arts Books, 1960.

SAPIR, EDWARD. *Language.* New York: Harcourt, Brace & World, 1949.

SCHECHNER, RICHARD. *Environmental Theatre.* New York: Hawthorn, 1973.

SCHLAUCH, MARGARET. *The Gift of Language.* New York: Dover, 1955.

SHURTLEFF, MICHAEL. *Audition.* New York: Walker and Co., 1978.

SPOLIN, VIOLA. *Improvisation for the Theatre.* Evanston, Ill.: Northwestern University Press, 1963.

STANISLAVSKI, CONSTANTIN. *An Actor Prepares* (Elizabeth Reynolds Hapgood trans.). New York: Theatre Arts Books, 1936.

—— *Building a Character* (Elizabeth Reynolds Hapgood trans.). New York: Theatre Arts Books, 1949.

—— *My Life in Art.* (J.J. Robbins trans.). New York: Theatre Arts Books, 1952.

—— *Creating a Role.* (Elizabeth Reynolds Hapgood trans.). New York: Theatre Arts Books, 1961.

SUZUKI, D. T. *Zen Buddhism.* New York: Doubleday/Anchor, 1956.

SUZUKI, SHUNRYA. *Zen Mind, Beginner's Mind.* New York: Weatherhill, 1970.

TRUNGPA, CHOGYAM. *Cutting through Spiritual Materialism.* Berkeley: Shambala Publications, 1973.

WATTS, ALAN. *The Book.* New York: Random House, 1972.

WELLEK, RENE and AUSTIN WARREN. *Theory of Literature.* New York: Harvest/Harcourt, Brace & Co., 1942.

WILLET, JOHN, ed. *Brecht on Theatre.* New York: Hill and Wang, 1964.

# Notes

## INTRODUCTION

1. Brian Bates, *The Way of the Actor* (Boston: Shambhala Publications, 1987), p. 7.
2. Ibid., p. 9.


## LESSON ONE

1. Frederick S. Perls, Ralph F. Hefferline, and Paul Goodman, *Gestalt Therapy* (New York: The Julien Press, 1951), p. 134. Dell Paperback, 1964.
2. Ibid., p. 33.
3. Ibid., p. 41.


## LESSON THREE

1. Mary Caroline Richards, *Centering* (Wesleyan: Wesleyan University Press, 1964), p. 38-39. Copyright by Mary Caroline Richards, by permission of Wesleyan University Press.

## LESSON FOUR

1. Raymond Birdwhistle, *Introduction to Kinesics* (Louisville: University of Louisville Pamphlet, 1957), pp. 29-30.

2. Edward T. Hall, *The Silent Language* (New York: Doubleday, 1959), p. 43. Copyright 1959 by Edward T. Hall. Reprinted by permission of Doubleday & Company, Inc.

3. Ibid., p. 42.

4. Bates, *The Way of the Actor*, p. 114.

5. Bacon and Breen, *Literature as Experience*, p. 32.

## LESSON FIVE

1. Bacon and Breen, *Literature as Experience*, p. 298.

2. Margaret Schlauch, *The Gift of Language* (New York: Dover Inc., 1955), p. 3. Reprinted by permission of the publisher.

3. Edward Sapir, *Language* (New York: Harcourt, Brace & World, Inc., 1949), pp. 8-9.

4. Ibid., p. 5.

5. Bacon and Breen, *Literature as Experience*, p. 286.

## LESSON SIX

1. Ernst Cassirer, *The Philosophy of Symbolic Forms*, trans. Ralph Manheim (New Haven: Yale University Press, 1953), p. 148.

2. Quoted by Martin Esslin in *The Theatre of the Absurd* (New York: Doubleday & Co., 1961), p. 206.

## LESSON SEVEN

1. Richards, *Centering*, p. 25.

2. August Strindberg, "Notes to the Members of the Intimate Theatre," trans. Everett Sprinchorn, *The Tulane Drama Review*, 6, no. 2 (Nov. 1961), p. 157. This material is also copyrighted by The Drama Review, 1967.

## LESSON EIGHT

1. Alan Watts, *The Book: On the Taboo Against Knowing Who You Are* (New York: Random House, 1972), p. 6.

## SUMMARY TO PART ONE

1. From *Writing in Restaurants* by David Mamet. Copyright (c) 1986 by David Mamet. All rights reserved. Reprinted by permission of Viking Penguin Inc. pp. 20-21.

2. From an unpublished letter.

3. Constantin Stanislavski, *My Life in Art*, trans. J. J. Robbins (New York: Theatre Arts Books, 1952). Copyright 1924 by Little, Brown & Co. and 1952 by Elizabeth Reynolds Hapgood. Used with the permission of the publishers, Theatre Arts Books, 153 Waverly Place, New York, N.Y. 10014, and Geoffrey Bless Ltd., London.

4. Mamet, *Writing in Restaurants*, p. 116.

## INTRODUCTION TO PART TWO

1. Constantin Stanislavski, *An Actor's Handbook*, trans. and ed. Elizabeth Reynolds Hapgood (New York: Theatre Arts Books), p. 8. Copyright 1936, 1961, 1963 by Elizabeth Reynolds Hapgood. Used with the permission of the publishers, Theatre Arts Books, 153 Waverly Place, New York, N.Y. 10014.

## LESSON NINE

1. Mamet, *Writing in Restaurants*, pp. 26-27.

2. Constantin Stanislavski, *Creating a Role* (New York: Theatre Arts Books, 1961), p. 62. Used by permission of the publisher, Theatre Arts Books, 153 Waverly Place, New York, N.Y. 10014.

3. Stanislavski, *An Actor's Handbook*, p. 9.

4. Ibid.

5. Erving Goffman, *The Presentation of Self in Everyday Life* (New York: Doubleday & Company, 1959), pp. 71-74. Copyright by Erving Goffman. Reprinted by Permission of Doubleday & Company, Inc.

## LESSON ELEVEN

1. Mamet, *Writing in Restaurants*, p. 76.

2. Jan Kott, "King Lear or Endgame," *The Evergreen Review* (August-September, 1964), p. 55.

3. Moshe Feldenkrais, *Awareness Through Movement* (New York: Harper & Row, 1972), pp. 45-46.

## LESSON THIRTEEN

1. Stanislavski, *An Actor's Handbook*, pp. 137-38.

2. Arthur Miller, *Death of a Salesman* (New York: Viking Press, 1958), p. 81.

3. Stanislavski, *An Actor's Handook*, p. 138.

## LESSON FOURTEEN

1. David D. Burns, M.D., *Feeling Good* (New York: Signet, 1980), pp. 11-12.

2. Stanislavski, *An Actor's Handbook*, p. 56.

3. Mamet, *Writing in Restaurants*, p. 127.

4. Stanislavski, *Building a Character*, p. 70.
5. Ibid.

## LESSON FIFTEEN

1. Alexander Lowen, *The Language of the Body* (New York: Collier, 1971), p. 32.
2. This list is adapted from Nathaniel Branden, *The Disowned Self* (New York: Bantam, 1973), pp. 111-14.

## LESSON SIXTEEN

1. Sapir, *Language*, p. 221.
2. This is not technically a sentence: it is an "appositive," a statement of equality, as in "officer: a policeman." The analysis given, however, will produce an intelligible reading.

## LESSON SEVENTEEN

1. Stanislavski, *Building a Character*, pp. 218-36.

## LESSON EIGHTEEN

1. Stanislavski, *Building a Character*, pp. 218-36.
2. Ibid.
3. Ibid.
4. Ibid.

## LESSON NINETEEN

1. Peter Barnes, *Red Noses* (London: Faber and Faber, 1985). Used by permission.
2. Bertram Joseph, *Acting Shakespeare* (New York: Theatre Arts Books, 1960), pp. 46-47. Used by permission of the publisher, Theatre Arts Books, 153 Waverly Place, New York, N.Y. 10014. Copyright (c) 1969 by Bertram Joseph.
3. Ibid., pp. 163-64.
4. Michel Saint-Denis, *Theatre: The Rediscovery of Style* (New York: Theatre Arts Books, 1960), pp. 76-77. Used by permission of the publisher, Theatre Arts Books, 153 Waverly Place, New York, N.Y. 10014. Copyright 1960 by Michel Saint-Denis.

## SUMMARY TO PART THREE

1. Joseph, *Acting Shakespeare*, pp. xvii, 2.

## LESSON TWENTY

1. Quoted in an interview.

2. Constantin Stanislavski, *Building a Character* (New York: Theatre Arts Books, 1949), pp. 218-36. Used with the permission of the publisher, Theatre Arts Books, 153 Waverly Place, New York, N.Y. 10014.

## LESSON TWENTY-ONE

1. This exercise adapted from the work of Dr. George Bach.

2. Oscar G. Brockett, *The Theatre, Third Edition* (New York: Holt, Rinehart and Winston, 1974), p. 39-40. Reprinted by permission of Holt, Rinehart and Winston, Inc.

3. Ibid.

## LESSON TWENTY-TWO

1. Stanislavski, *Creating a Role* (New York: Theatre Arts Books, 1961), p. 62. Used by permission of the publisher, Theatre Arts Books, 153 Waverly Place, New York, N. Y. 10014.

2. Nikolai Gorchakov, *Stanislavski Directs* (New York: Funk & Wagnalls, 1954), p. 77.

## LESSON TWENTY-THREE

1. From an unpublished letter.

2. Mamet, *Writing in Restaurants*, pp. 20-21.

3. Ibid., p. 19.

4. Ibid., p. 21.

5. Stanislavski, *My Life in Art*, pp. 217-218.

6. Quoted in Bates, *The Way of the Actor*, p. 16.

## AFTERWORD

1. Gorchakov, *Stanislavski Directs*, pp. 40-41.

# INDEX

*Note: This index does not duplicate items listed in the Table of Contents.*